Revolutionary War Soldiers

of

Western North Carolina

Vol. 2

(Burke County)

Southern Historical Press, Inc.
Greenville, South Carolina
1998

Copyright 1998 by:
Southern Historical Press, Inc.

All rights reserved. No part of this publication may be reproduced, stored in a retrieval system, transmitted in any form, posted on to the web in any form or by any means without the prior written permission of the publisher.

Please direct all correspondence and orders to:

www.southernhistoricalpress.com
or
SOUTHERN HISTORICAL PRESS, Inc.
PO BOX 1267
375 West Broad Street
Greenville, SC 29601
southernhistoricalpress@gmail.com

ISBN #0-89308-520-0

Printed in the United States of America

TABLE of CONTENTS

Allen, Daniel..........1	Coffey, Benjamin.....81
Arwood, John..........3	Coffey, Reuben.......83
Ashenbrunner, Henry...5	Conrad, Rudolph......85
Baker, Dimion.........6	Cook, Issac..........87
Baker, James..........7	Cresson, Andrew......89
Baker, Jehu...........9	Culberson, David.....91
Baker, John..........10	Curtis, Thomas.......92
Baldwin, Elisha......11	Dalton, William......95
Baldwin, Jacob.......12	Davidson, James......96
Baldwin, John........14	Davidson, Samuel.....98
Baldwin, William.....16	Davis, Clement......100
Ballew, Stephen......18	Davis, Snead........102
Banning, Benoni......20	Davis, Samuel.......104
Barkley, Robert......21	Dawsey, William.....106
Barr, Caleb..........22	Deal, Michael.......107
Barr, Silas..........24	Dement, John........108
Bates, Humphrey......25	Eberhart, David.....109
Beck, Jacob..........27	Fears, Edmund.......110
Beekman, Christopher.29	Fleming, Abraham....112
Berry, Enoch.........33	Floyd, Abraham......114
Biffle, Jacob........35	Ford, Peter.........116
Blair, Colbert.......37	Franklin, John......118
Blair, James.........39	Fullwood, William...120
Boyd, John...........41	Gasperson, John.....122
Brank, Peter.........43	Ginger, Henry.......123
Brevard, Hugh........44	Gray, William.......125
Bridget, Walter......47	Green, John.........126
Brittain, James......48	Haney, Charles......128
Brittian, Philip.....52	Harshaw, Abraham....130
Brown, Richard.......54	Hawkins, John.......132
Brown, Robert........55	Hawkins, Joseph.....134
Brown, Samuel........57	Hayes, George.......136
Brown, Thomas........59	Helderman, Nicholas.138
Biggerstaff, John....60	Hice, Conrad........140
Burchfield, John.....62	Hice, George........141
Burchfield, Meshack..64	Higdon, Leonard.....143
Burchfield, Nathan...66	Highland, Henry.....145
Burchfield, Robert...67	Hildebrand, Conrad..147
Capps, William.......70	Hood, John..........150
Cathey, William......72	Huffman, Samuel.....152
Chapman, Nicholas....73	Hughes, Francis.....154
Clarke, Alexander....75	Husbands, Veazey....156
Clarke, Jeremiah.....76	Inman, Shadrack.....158
Clarke, Samuel.......77	Jackson, James......160
Cline, Christopher...79	James, Joseph.......162

TABLE of CONTENTS

James, Rollings.....164
Jenkins, Charles....165
Jewell, William.....166
Johnson, John.......168
Johnston, Robert....169
Johnston, Lewis.....171
Killian, Daniel.....173
Kuykendall, Matthew.175
Leatherwood, Edward.177
Ledford, Peter......179
Lewis, William......181
Lock, James.........183
McCall, Robert......184
McDaniels, James....186
McDowell, John......188
McDowell, Joseph....190
McKissock, Daniel...194
McPeters, Jonathan..196
McPeters, Joseph....199
Mackey, James.......201
Marshall, Jesse.....203
Martin, Henry.......204
Miller, Robert......205
Montgomery, David...207
Moore, William......209
Morris, William.....212
Morrison, James.....214
Mull, Peter.........216
Murphy, James.......219
Murray, John........222
Murray, Joshua......224
Muscanook, George...227
Neill, John.........229
Neill, William......231
Neill, William......233
Northern, Soloman...236
Painter, Joseph.....237
Painter, John.......239
Parks, George.......241
Parks, Samuel.......244
Patton, Thomas......246
Penland, George.....248
Penland, John.......250
Penland, Robert.....252
Penland, William....255

Pepper, Robert......257
Piercy, Blake.......258
Poteat, Edward......260
Powell, Elias.......262
Queen, Thomas.......263
Reed, Richard.......265
Reed, Robert........267
Richardson, Amos....269
Scott, Thomas.......271
Scott, Thomas.......272
Sharpe, Horatio.....274
Sherrill, Ute.......276
Sherrill, George....278
Prichard, James.....280
Sharpe, Hoartio.....282
Sigmon, George......284
Sorrels, John.......286
Steele, Samuel......287
Sullivan, Daniel....289
Sumter, William.....290
Swanson, William....291
Tate, John..........293
Thompson, Alexander.295
Trosper, Nicholas...297
Turner, Robert......299
Wakefield, Thomas...302
West, Alexander.....303
White, James........305
White, William......307
Whitener, Abram.....309
Whitener, Daniel....310
Whitener, Henry.....311
Whitson, Benjamin...313
Wilson, Greenberry..314
Wiseman, William....316
Woods, Henry........318
Woods, Samuel.......320

FOREWORD

This volume represents the second of three planned volumes from the Revolutionary War soldiers of Old Burke County, embracing all or part of present day Burke, Catawba, Caldwell, and McDowell Counties.

The listings contain biographical sketches of both Patriots and Loyalists. The purpose of doing it in this manner is to include as much of the soldiery of the area as possible, and for the matter of pure convenience. As one studies the lives of these brave men, it becomes apparent that many fought on both sides. Many were impressed into service merely because of their sentiments or the sentiments of their family. Often they fought firmly and resolutely for the American Cause. Much of this occurred in the latter phases of the war. The Revolutionary War was no different than other subsequent long, drawn-out affairs -- enthusiasm and patriotism waned as the war dragged on, similar to the Vietnam experience of recent years.

There are several excellent source references for Tories from this area who participated in the Revolutionary War. The so called "Tory list" of late 1782 contains the names of over 150 Loyalists from Burke County. Witnesses are also listed. There is no disposition of the cases on record, excepting a few subsequent Court actions. (Peace was declared only 6 months later.)

It is noteworthy that several of those on the Tory list were already in the American Army at the time of the docket. Another valuable reference are the still extant minutes of the Court Martial proceedings of Col. Charles McDowell of Burke County. Dozens of active Tories are listed in this document. This serves as a valuable contemporaneous cross reference for those listed in the Tory Docket. The excellent multi-volume publication by Murtie June Clark contains several Burke County Loyalists. Other source references include the diary of Anthony Allaire, Morgan District Court records relating to the Confiscation Acts, etc. The pension records provide a valuable source of where these men fought and the circumstances under which they served. They also provide a composite reference for officers, most of whom died prior to enactment of the major pension legislation.

I have thoroughly enjoyed the research and labors that it has taken to put these volumes together. Words cannot express how much I appreciated those chroniclers and genealogists concerned with Burke County. I have drawn heavily from them. Some deserve special credit such as Dan Swink, Betsy Pittman and others in the Burke County Genealogical Society and the Burke County data assimilated by the late Edith Huggins and Ned Phifer, both of whom I shared information with on numerous occasions. The work on South Carolina Revolutionay War Patriots by Professor Bobby

Moss is invaluable because of the multiple listings of Burke County soldiers who were placed into South Carolina units.

I would like to give special thanks to Mrs. Agnes Burns of Valdese, NC who did my typing and secretarial work relating to this publication.

Emmett R. White, M. D.,
Rutherford College, NC 28671

ALLEN, DANIEL

SUMMARY OF EARLY LIFE

Daniel Allen was born in Burke County (then Rowan County) NC in 1762 or 1763. His family appeared to be residing in the Muddy Creek area of Burke County, now McDowell County. Allen was living in Burke County at the beginning of the American Revolution.

SUMMARY OF PARTISAN ACTIVITY

Daniel Allen first entered military service in Capt. Joseph McDowell's (P.G.) Company of light horse. Field officers were Col. Charles McDowell and Major Joseph McDowell of Quaker Meadows. He was also associated with Capts. William and Robert Patton. Their company was stationed on the Catawba frontier, guarding against the incursions of the hostile Cherokee Indians. Allen was a draftee and served for a period of three months.

Following this tour of duty, Allen moved to Washington County Georgia and enlisted in the militia company of Capt. Jonathon Beard. Field officers were General Fish and Col. (John?) Milton, both of Greene County, GA. His Company, like the one in North Carolina, was mainly occupied in protecting the frontier against hostile Indians and Tories.

Later Allen served another tour of duty in Oglethorpe County, GA. under Capt. Finazer (or Frazer). They were in Col. Milton's Regiment.

The above service was probably in 1780-82, in view of his age.

SUMMARY OF LATER LIFE

Daniel Allen, in his Federal pension declarations, mentions a wife and family, but no names.

Allen lived in Burke County, NC, Washington and Oglethorpe Counties, GA during the war. After the war he moved to Lincoln County, TN and remained there until after the turn of the century, when he moved to Greene County, IL. He applied for Federal pension in Greene County, IL in 1832, age 70 years. He was awarded a pension of $30.00 per annum.

LAND HOLDINGS AND TRANSACTIONS

A Daniel Allen received Tennessee land grants in Giles Co., adjacent to Lincoln Co., as follows:

1. Gen. TN Grant # 15353 Giles Co. 160 ac. May 9, 1821 Bk.R/114.
2. Gen. TN Grant # 15783 Giles Co. 10 ac. Sep 21, 1821 Bk.S/297.
3. Gen. TN Grant # 23168 Giles Co. 12 ac Feb 7, 1825 Bk.Z/430

REFERENCES

US National Archives Pension Data # S32093
Tennessee State Archives and Library; Nashville; Land Grant Records.

ARWOOD, JOHN (ARROWOOD, ERWOOD)

SUMMARY OF EARLY LIFE

John Arwood was living in Rowan County, NC during the first part of the American Revolution. Later he moved to Lincoln County, NC, and still later to Burke County, NC.

SUMMARY OF PARTISAN ACTIVITY

John Arwood first entered military service in the summer of 1776. He served in the Rowan County, NC militia, Col. Matthew Locke commanding his regiment. Arwood participated in the Cherokee Expedition of 1776 under Gen. Griffith Rutherford. His Company Commander was Capt. Elijah Lyons. He served three months, was discharged, and returned to Rowan County.

In his Federal pension declarations, Arwood was somewhat confused as to dates, services, etc., undoubtedly due to his old age. He stated that he was "a minute man" for about eighteen months duration.

During this time, he was either acting against local Tories or being stationed on the Catawba frontier. His commanding officers included Col. John Harden, Capt. Benjamin Harden and Capt. Chronicle. Arwood relates service in which he was marched to Wilmington and back, again under Col. Cocke and Capt. Douglas Hayden. This was probably the Wilmington Expedition of 1781, headed up by Gen. Griffith Rutherford. Arwood very vividly describes the time of year of the Wilmington Expedition. He stated that the weather was cool when they started. On their return, the fishermen were catching shad fish in the Yadkin River. They usually "ran" on or about the last of February or the first of March.

SUMMERY OF LATER LIFE

Arwood applied for Revolutionary War Pension on October 25, 1832 in Burke County, NC. He was awarded a pension of $50.00 per annum. John Arwood's brother, Zachariah Arwood, testified in his behalf relating to this pension application.

LAND HOLDINGS AND TRANSACTIONS

1. NC Land Grant, Burke County, NC for 250 acres on waters of Second Broad River. The parcel included 50 acres previously granted to John Forsythe. Entered September 15, 1828, No. 8387 Grant No. 2754, Book 136, p. 180, Iss. Dec 17, 1825.

2. NC Land Grant, Burke County, NC for 100 acres of land on waters of Second Broad River, adjacent to land belonging to Joseph Neil and Nichols. Ent. Feb 15, 1828, No. 9472, Grant No. 5356, Book 128, p. 147, Iss. Sep 16, 1829.

3. 1815 Burke County NC Tax Lists show 50 acres on Broad River.

CENSUS LOCATIONS

```
1790 Lincoln County, NC  10th Co. "Arrowood"
1800 Lincoln County, NC  "Earwood"
1810 Burke County, NC    "Arrwood"
1820 Burke County, NC    "Arriwood"
1830 Burke County, NC    "Attawood"
1840 Burke County, NC    "Arrowood"
```

REFERENCES

US National Archives, Pension No. S 6535
Burke Co., NC Land Grant Data, Morganton-Burke Library, Morganton, NC.
Pittman, Betsy Dodd, "Burke Co., NC 1815 Tax Lists" (1990) p.13
AIS Census Indices

ASHENBRUNNER, HENRY

SUMMARY OF EARLY LIFE

Henry Ashenbrunner, son of pioneer Urban Ashenbrunner, was born c. 1747, probably in Pennsylvania. His father settled early in what is now Catawba County. Henry Ashenbrunner was a brother of Philip Ashenbrunner.

SUMMARY OF PARTISAN ACTIVITY

Henry Ashenbrunner was cited to Burke County Court in 1782 to show cause as to why his property should not be confiscated, for being disloyal to the American Cause. His brother, Philip was also a Loyalist and served in Nicholas Welch's Company of the North Carolina Royal Regiment.

SUMMARY OF LATER LIFE

Henry Ashenbrunner married Barbara _____.
Another source gives his wife's name as Sarah Khyzer.

Children included: Abraham,, Mary (Kistler), Catherine (Speagle), Barbara (Seagle), Esther.

Henry Ashenbrunner died May 29, 1800 and is buried in the Mosteller graveyard, Catawba County, NC.

LAND HOLDINGS AND TRANSACTIONS

1. Burke County, NC 120 acres both sides of Jacobs fork on Wolf Branch, adjacent to land of Jacob Yorty (c.c. Jacob Yorty, Philip Whitener). Ent. 19 June 1779, Ent. No. 1750 Grant No. 1062 Iss. August 7, 1787. Book 65, p. 403.

2. Lincoln County land records show (A) grant of 25 acres on Potts Creek, adjacent to Samuel Seigel and Daniel Shuford (Ent. 3/6 1811) and (B) grant of 50 acres on Jacob,s River adjacent to his own land, above. (Ent. October 2, 1798).

CENSUS LOCATIONS

1790 Lincoln Co., NC
1800 Lincoln Co., NC

REFERENCES

Articles by Gracie Cook, Violet Barkley and Helen L. Bradshaw in' Heritage Book of Catawba County; 1986 pp 32-33. (Winston Salem) Burke Land Misc. Records as given in Huggins Vol. I & II
Clark, Murtie, Loyalists in the Southern Campaign of the Revolutionary War 1981 Vol.I pp. 376, 403,404.

BAKER, DIMION DEMION

SUMMARY OF EARLY LIFE

The exact relationship of Dimion Baker to the several Baker families of Burke County unknown. There were Bakers on Lower Creek (John Baker), on middle Little River (Henry Baker), and in the mountain Area, now Mitchell Co. (David Baker). A witness in his Burke County Court appearances in 1782 lived in Turkey Cove (now McDowell Co., NC).

SUMMARY OF PARTISAN ACTIVITY

Dimion Baker was shown by Moss as having served in S.C. troops under Col. (Charles S.) Myddleton, Capt. Francis Moore - all under the command of Gen. Thomas Sumter. He was listed as being a dragoon.

This regiment was active in middle S. C. During the siege of Ninety-Six (June 1781). Later they fought in the important battle of Eutaw Springs, SC (Sept. 1781).

In November 1782, Baker was cited to Burke County Court, on charges of being disloyal to the American Cause (see foreword this Vol.). Witnesses included William McCullen and wife, John Armstrong, and Micheal Edington.

SUMMARY OF LATER LIFE

Not known to author.

LAND HOLDINGS AND TRANSACTIONS

None known.

CENSUS LOCATIONS

None

REFERENCES

Moss, Bobby G. <u>Roster of South Carolina Patriots in the American Revolution</u> GPC 1983 p. 38
Huggins, Edith <u>Burke County Records</u> Vol. II 1977 p. 154

BAKER, JAMES

SUMMARY OF EARLY LIFE

James Baker was born November 9, 1755. He was living in Hertford County, NC at the commencement of Revolutionary activities.

SUMMARY OF PARTISAN ACTIVITY

James Baker entered Revolutionary service in Hertford County, NC as a private in the NC Continental Line and served under Capt. Ward and Col. Benjamin Wynn. During the war, he moved to Burke County, NC and served an additional twelve months as a private in Capt. (Edward) Yarborough's Company of Abraham Shepherd's 10th NC Regiment. He enlisted on May 12, 1781 and was discharged April 22, 1782.

SUMMARY OF LATER LIFE

After the war James Baker moved from NC to Madison County, KY. He died in Madison County, KY on September 7, 1831. Baker married on August 20, 1781 in Burke County, NC, Elizabeth Montgomery (b. Nov. 27, 1766). Their children were as follows:

Rebecca b. Nov. 20, 1782
Charles b. Jan. 4, 1784
Margaret m. Wallis, b. Feb,8, 1787
Sary (Sarah) b. Feb. 2, 1789
Elizabeth b. MY 31, 1791
Jane b. Sept, 20, 1793
James b. Dec. 5, 1795

Mary b. April 1797
Elias b. April 2, 1799
John b. April 1801
Nancy b. Jun. 30, 1804
Rachel b. June 30, 1804

The Widow applied for Federal pension in 1851 and was awarded a pension of $40.00 per annum retroactive to 1848. She also received a bounty warrant for 160 acres of land by the Act of 1855.

LAND HOLDINGS AND TRANSACTIONS

1. 400 acres in Burke County, NC on Johns River, granted jointly to James, David, John and Charles Baker. The land lay adjacent to that of William Knox (later Andrew Rudolph) and John Lawrance. James Baker was chain carrier.
Ent. 13 July 1778, # 227, Grant No. 27, Iss. Dec 10, 1778, Book 29, p.27.

CENSUS LOCATIONS

1790 Burke Co., NC (One each in 3rd and 12th Cos.)
1800 Madison Co., KY
1810 Madison Co., KY
1820 Madison Co., KY
1830 Madison Co., KY Census list a Charles, Elias, and John Baker

but no James Baker.

REFERENCES

US National Archives, Pension Statements No. W9338
<u>Roster of N.C. Soldiers in the American Revolution</u>
NCDAR GPC, Reprint ed 1967 p. 110

BAKER, JEHU

SUMMARY OF EARLY LIFE

Probably related to Moses and John Baker (Lower Creek, Burke Co.), as they are grouped together on Court Docket in 1782.

SUMMARY OF PARTISAN ACTIVITY

Moss lists Jehu Baker as being a dragoon in Capt. Francis Moore's Company of Myddleton's 2nd SC Regiment. (Col. Charles Starke Myddleton). This regiment, under Gen Thomas Sumter's command, took part in middle SC actions during and after the siege of Ninety-Six. Later in Sept. 1781 they participated in the battle of Eutaw Springs, SC, under Gen. Nathaniel Greene.

In November of 1782 Jehu Baker, along with John and Moses Baker, was cited to Burke County Court on charges of being disloyal to the American Cause. Witnesses include Wm. Patton, John Poke (Polk?), Joseph White.

LAND HOLDING AND TRANSACTIONS

** A "Jehue Baker" received a middle Tennessee Land Grant in Perry County 1855. 5000 acres # 23699. Relation to subject not known.

CENSUS LOCATIONS

None known.

REFERENCES

Moss, Bobby G. Roster of S.C. Patriots in The American Revolution GPC 1983 p. 39.
Huggins, Edith Burke County Records Vol. II p. 151
Tennessee State Archives and Library. Land Records.

BAKER, JOHN

SUMMARY OF EARLY LIFE

John Baker was probably related to Moses and Jehu Baker, as they were grouped together in the 1782 Burke Co. Court Docket. A John Baker lived on Lower Creek, another in Western Burke, now McDowell County.

SUMMARY OF PARTISAN ACTIVITY

Moss records a John Baker serving as a dragoon in Capt. Francis Moore's company, Col. Charles S. Myddleton's SC Regiment. This was probably the Burke County Baker since Jehu and Dimion Baker (also of Burke Co.) Served in the same unit.

This regiment participated in the mid SC actions following the siege of Ninety-Six, SC (June 1781). Later the regiment fought in the battle of Eutaw Springs, SC on Sept. 8, 1781. In November of 1782, John Baker was cited to Burke Co. Court on charges of being a Tory. Witnesses included William Patton, John Poke (Polk?), and Joseph White.

CENSUS LOCATIONS

1790 Burke Co., NC (one John Baker in 12th Co., and another in 3rd Co.).

REFERENCES

Moss, Bobby G. Roster of SC Patriots in the American Revolution GPC 1983 p. 39.
Huggins, Edith, Burke County Records Vol. II p. 151 1977

BALDWIN, ELISHA

SUMMARY OF EARLY LIFE

Elisha Baldwin was a member of the active Baldwin family who lived on Lower Creek, Burke Co., now Caldwell Co., NC. Other members of the family included John Sr., John, Jr., Isaac, William, Jacob and Joshua. His birth date by DAR is given ca. . 1755.

SUMMARY OF PARTISAN ACTIVITY

Elisha Baldwin (along with four other Baldwins) was cited to appear in Burke Co. Court to answer to charges as to why this property should not be confiscated, for being disloyal to the American Cause. Witnesses against the Baldwins included James Davenport, Phileman Franklin, Wm. & Thos. White, Charles & Thos. Wakefield and Charles Adams.

Being neighbors of Veazy Husbands, it is likely that the Baldwins served under his command.

SUMMARY OF LATER LIFE

After the Rev. War, several members of the Baldwin family migrated to the New River Valley of Wilkes Co., NC, later Ashe County. Elisha Baldwin seems to have located in Ashe Co. As indicated by Land and Census Records, and later returning to Burke Co. (?). DAR lists Baldwin's death date as c. 1820.

LAND HOLDINGS AND TRANSACTIONS

1. 12 Acres Burke Co. NC on south side Lower Creek adj. To his own land, Abraham Sudderth and Albert Corpening. (cc A. Sudderth, Elisha Hayes).
Ent. 27 Jan 1814 Ent, 6171 Grant # 3702 Iss, 5 Dec 1815, Book 129 p. 351.

2. 26 acres Burke Co., NC on east side Lower Creek adj. To his own land and to that of Benjamin Coffey,
Ent. 22 Dec 1814 Ent, 6388, Grant No. 3740 Iss, 23 Nov 1816 Book 130, p.215.

3. Wilkes Co. Records show a land grant of 400 acres of east side of W. Fork Potato Creek, a tributary of the New River. (6 Dec 1794), now Ashe Co., NC. Smaller tracts were also obtained in the same general area, near Potato Creek.

CENSUS LOCATIONS

1790 Wilkes Co., NC 10th Co.
1800 Ashe Co., NC

BALDWIN, JACOB

SUMMARY OF EARLY LIFE

Jacob Baldwin was a member of the well known Loyalist family of Lower Creek, Burke Co., now Caldwell Co., NC. See biography of Elisha Baldwin for further details. The family may have been related to the pioneer William Baldwin of Deep Creek, now Yadkin Co., NC.

SUMMARY OF PARTISAN ACTIVITY

Jacob Baldwin was on the Court Docket Nov. 1782 of persons suspected of being Loyalists. Witnesses against him included James Davenport, Phileman Franklin, William White, Thomas White Charles Adams and Charles and Thomas Wakefield. See further comments concerning Court Docket in forward, this volume.

SUMMARY OF LATER LIFE

Land records indicate that Jacob Baldwin remained in Burke County following the close of the Revolutionary War. Court records show that he served on Jury Duty in 1797 and also acquired 15 acres of land in the same year. The 1790 and 1800 censuses list him. He acquired land in 1800 and 1807, Burke County. (See following).

LAND HOLDINGS AND TRANSACTIONS

1. 300 acres Burke County, NC on west side Lower Creek, adjacent to land of William Sumter, David Jackson, Isaac Baldwin (c.c. John Hayes, Joshua Baldwin) and adjacent to William Isbell's land. Also crosses Brumley's Fork of Lower Creek.
Ent. 10 Dec 1778 Grant No. 830 , Iss. 9 Nov 1784 Book 57, p.29.

2. 145 Acres Burke County, NC on waters of Jumping Branch, a tributary of Lower Creek and adjacent to land belonging to William James, John Clarke, Albert Corpening, John Tarter and to Baldwin's old survey. Ent. 5 Sept 1801 #4219, Grant # 3137 Iss, 27 Nov 1802 Book 110, p. 53. (C.c. Wm Wiseman, John Tarter).

3. 350 acres Burke Co., NC in 3 contiguous tracts of 150, 100 and 100 acres each. The land lay adjacent to his own survey and to land belonging the Albert Corpening, Willian Ursury, Daniel Poll and John Bolen. The land lay on Smokey Creek, but included part of Pack's Branch and Reedy Branch. Ent. 25 Oct 1799 #3735, 36,3677. Grant No. 2886 Iss. 18 Dec 1800 Book 112, p. 161.

4. 150 acres Burke Co. NC on waters of Meadow Branch of Lower Creek and of Smokey Creek adjacent to land belonging to Albert Corpening, his own land, and adjacent to where "one Snow lives". Ent. 30 Jul 1800 #3904, Grant No. 2986, Iss. 4 Dec 1801, Book 1 p. 324.

CENSUS LOCATIONS

1790 Burke County, NC 7th Co.
1800 Burke County, NC

REFERENCES

Huggins, Edith, Vol II op.cit. P. 149
AIS Census Indices
Burke County, N.C. Land Grant Records, Morganton Burke Library, Morganton, NC

BALDWIN, JOHN

SUMMARY OF EARLY LIFE

John Baldwin came to Burke County "during his infancy" and continued to live there until the end of the Revolutionary War. He was age 72 when applying for Federal Pension in August 1832. Many members of the Burke County Baldwin family were Loyalist in sympathies.

SUMMARY OF PARTISAN ACTIVITY

John Baldwin entered militia service in Burke County, NC in 177 and again in 1778. He served in Capt. (Daniel) Smith's Company of Col. Charles McDowell's Burke Regiment. He was stationed on the western Catawba frontier at Davidson's and Edmisten's Forts. He served for about eighteen months, guarding against the Cherokee Indian incursions. He was on a large raid into the Cowee area directed by Col. McDowell.

In late 1780 - early 1781, he volunteered again and was placed Maj. Joseph McDowell's mounted Battalion of Riflemen. He served in a Company commanded by Capt. Alexander Erwin. Under McDowel and Erwin, he took part in the great American victory at Cowpens SC, on January 17, 1781. Their overall Commander was Gen. Dani Morgan. Baldwin, in his pension declaration, tells how McDowell instructed them to act at the beginning of the conflict "... to take aim when they fired ..."and as they retreated to bear to the right and combine with the backup troops. Baldwin also stated that "... a great many of the Tories were taken...". Under Erwin they retreated with Morgan to Cowans Ford on the Catawba. He took part in the skirmish at that place on Februar 2, 1781. Baldwin states that he "... saw Gen Davidson when he was shot off from his horse...". Baldwin, along with fellow patriots, faced the British at Torrence's Tavern, but were quickly dispersed by the Dragoons. He then returned home and w discharged.

* In November 1782, a John Baldwin was placed on the subpoena docket of Burke County Court on charges of being disloyal to the American Cause, (along with several other family members). This could possibly have been his uncle by the same name (mentioned Baldwin's pension statements). Of course, it could have been th soldier himself. (Wilkes, Ashe) County records show a John Baldwin's estate settlement, 1794.

SUMMARY OF LATER LIFE

John Baldwin applied for Revolutionary War pension on August 28 1832. He was awarded an annual pension of $80.00.

LAND HOLDINGS AND TRANSACTIONS

John Baldwin entered 150 acres of land in Wilkes County, NC, later Ashe County. The land lay on waters of New River and next to Zachariah Wells' Big Ridge. The property was adjacent to that belonging to William Ballard Lenoir. Ent. No. 708, August 5, 1799. Surveyed October 22, 1800. Jacob Baldwin and James Baldwin were chain carriers.

CENSUS LOCATIONS

1790 Burke County, NC 7th Co. ("Jno Baldwin, Sr.,")
1800 Ashe County, NC
1810 Ashe County, NC

REFERENCES

U. S. National Archives Pension Statements # S 6565
AIS Census Indices
Absher, Mrs. W. O., Wilkes Co. Deed Abstracts SHP 1989

BALDWIN, WILLIAM

SUMMARY OF EARLY LIFE

William Baldwin was a member of the well known Loyalist family who resided in Burke County, now Caldwell County, NC. For further information, see biography of Elisha Baldwin in this volume. Family probably related to pioneer settler, William Baldwin of Deep Creek, Yadkin Co., NC.

SUMMARY OF PARTISAN ACTIVITY

William Baldwin was cited to Burke County Court in Nov. 1782 to show cause as to why his property should not be confiscated, for being disloyal to the American cause i.e. a suspected Tory. Witnesses included James Davenport, Philemon Franklin, William & Thomas White, Charles & Thomas Wakefield, Charles Adams.

Murtie Clark, in her Vol. I of Loyalists of the Southern Campagin, lists a William Baldwin in Charleston as a refugee in 1782, exact relationship to above, if any, unknown.

SUMMARY OF LATER LIFE

William Baldwin is on the 1790 census of Burke County. In Burke County, after the Revolutionary War, Baldwin acquired land on Catawba River near present day Castle Bridge. Later records have him listed in Ashe Co., perhaps going there with his kinsmen, John Baldwin (2 John Baldwins...John Baldwin, the pensioner and Revolutionary War soldier, and his Uncle John Baldwin - maybe the one who died in Wilkes Co. (Ashe Co.) Ca. 1794.

LAND HOLDINGS AND TRANSACTIONS

1. 10 acres Burke Co., NC On the Catawba River and partly covered with water and including land on both North and South sides, adjacent to land belonging to Edward Bowman and William Ballew. Land used as a fishery. (C.c. Robert Allew, Adam Smith). On south side, land extended to mouth of Cold Ass Creek (now Mountain Creek).

2. 200 acres Burke County, NC on north side Catawba River adjacent to land of Benjamin Bush and extending toward the Horse Ford. Included two islands and a fishery. (c.c. Michael Grindstaff, Michael Hart).
Ent. 3 may 1791 #13 Grant No. 1619 Iss. Nov. 27, 1792 Book 80 p.62

CENSUS LOCATIONS

1790 Burke Co., NC 2nd Co.
1800 Ashe Co., NC
1810 Ashe Co., NC

REFERENCES

Huggins, Edith, Burke Co. Records op.cit. Vol. II p. 149 SHP
Burke County NC Land Grant Records, Morganton-Burke Library Morganton, NC.
Clark, Murtie June, Loyalists in the Southern Campaign of the Revolutionary War, Vol. I p. 550 (Genealogical Publishing Co., Baltimore 1981).
Absher, Mrs. W. O., Wilkes Co., NC Will Abstracts 1778-1811 SHP 1989 p. 39

BALLEW, STEPHEN (BALLOU)

SUMMARY OF EARLY LIFE

Stephen Ballew was born in Amherst County, VA. He was age 77 years in 1832 when applying for federal pension. He was the son of Robert Ballew. He had a younger brother, Thomas Ballew and a sister, Jane, who was married to Capt. John Connelly. Robert Ballew lived on the south side of the Catawba near present day Rutherford College, NC.

SUMMARY OF PARTISAN ACTIVITY;

Stephen Ballew first entered military service in June 1779 in Capt. William Johnson's Company, Burke County militia. His regimental commander was Col. William Wofford. He was marched to the western frontier and served on duty at Wofford's Fort in the North Cove of the Catawba River. On this tour he served as a substitute for his father, who had been drafted.

In October of 1781 he served in a company commanded by Capt. Mordecai Clarke. They marched to the vicinity of Charlotte joining with Gen. Smallwood of Virginia. They, in turn, joined with Gen. Nathaniel Greene's Army and Staff. They marched through Anson County, NC To the vicinity of Cheraw, SC Ballew was then ordered back to Salisbury where he assisted in building a stockaded fort. Becoming ill a short while later, he was discharged home in February 1782.

Ballew's final tour of duty was in Lt. William Jones' Company of Col. Charles McDowell's Burke Regiment. The tour beginning July 1782 and completed in September of 1782. He was stationed at Davidson's Fort on the Catawba frontier.

SUMMARY OF LATER LIFE

Stephen Ballew applied for Revolutionary War pension in Burke County, NC On October 23, 1832. He was awarded an annual pension of $26.66.

LAND HOLDINGS AND TRANSACTIONS

1. 100 acres Burke County, NC on south side of Catawba River adjacent to land belonging to George Houck and John Phelps. Ent. September 2, 1796 No. 2720, Grant No. 2231, Iss. December 18, 1797, Book 94, p. 209. c.c. George Houck, John Houck.

2. 1815 Burke Co., N. C. Tax lists show 284 acres Martin Kibler's Co. On Mull's Branch

CENSUS LOCATIONS

1790 Burke County, NC 2nd, Co.
1800 Burke County, NC (Blew)

1810 Burke County, NC (Bolew)
1820 Burke County, NC
1830 Burke County, NC
1840 Burke County, NC

REFERENCES

US National Archives and Pension Statements, # S16835
Pittman, Betsy Dodd; "1815 Burke County NC Tax Lists"; 1990

BANNING, BENONI

SUMMARY OF EARLY LIFE

Benoni Banning was living in Washington County VA during the Revolutionary War.

SUMMARY OF PARTISAN ACTIVITY

Benoni Banning (sometimes spelled "Benning") first entered military service while a resident of Washington County VA. He served in Col. William Campbell's regiment and took part in the epic Kings Mountain Compaign and battle of Sept. And Oct. 1780. During the short but intense battle of Oct. 7, 1780, many of his regiment were killed or wounded. Banning was one of those wounded.

SUMMARY OF LATER LIFE

Having become familiar with the upper Catawba valley during his Kings Mountain days, Banning, toward the end of the war settled in Western Burke Co., now McDowell Co., on Crooked Creek.

Benoni Banning died prior to April 1827, date of will probate. Exec Henry Banning.

LAND HOLDINGS AND TRANSACTIONS

1. 100 acres Burke Co., NC on Little Crooked Creek adj. to land of Benjamin Cockran and also adj. to his own land.
Ent. Oct. 16, 1799 #3726 Grant No. 2889 Iss. Dec. 18, 1800
Book 112 p. 163. (C.c. carriers James and Frazier Banning).
(1815 tax lists show 275 acres on Crooked Creek in four tracts). Frazier Banning, Henry Banning and Alex Banning also listed.

CENSUS LOCATIONS

1800 Burke Co., NC
1815 Tax Lists, Burke Co., NC
1820 Burke Co., NC

REFERENCES

History of Southwest Virginia 1746-1786 by Summers, Lewis Preste Reprint GPC 1966. P. 327 (Orig. Pub. 1903)
Land Grant Data
Morganton Burke Library, Morganton, NC
Pittman, Betsy Dodd, "Burke County, NC 1815 Tax Lists 1990".

BARKLEY, ROBERT

SUMMARY OF EARLY LIFE

Robert Barkley was raised in Rowan County, NC, the son of Henry and Mary Barkley. Henry Barkley had acquired land on Mountain Creek in Rowan County in 1767, later Burke, and then Catawba County. They were probably related to Robert Barkley of Buffalo Creek, Rowan County.

SUMMARY OF PARTISAN ACTIVITY

Robert Barkley first entered military service in 1776, serving in a company commanded by Capt. William Knox of Rowan County. He participated in the Cross Creek Expedition. This was the latter phase of the Moores Creek campaign of Feb. and March 1776.

In 1780 Barkley served under Col. William Graham and was in the battle of Ramsour's Mill on June 20, 1780.

In September and October 1780, he participated in the Kings Mountain campaign and battle.

Robert Barkley served on the Catawba frontier, guarding against the incursions of the hostile Cherokee Indians. His last tour of duty was in the Wilmington expedition of late 1781.

SUMMARY OF LATER LIFE

Robert Barkley was married to Ellenar (Nellie) Cathey, the daughter of John Cathey of Mecklenburg County, in 1776. There were children. (1790 census lists 2 males and 3 females). One son, Henry, appears on pension records. Robert Barkley died in Lincoln Co. NC on Jan. 13 or 14, 1813. His widow later applied for federal pension and was awarded $34.76 per annum (she was age 87 in 1841).

CENSUS LOCATION

1790 Lincoln Co., NC
1800 Lincoln Co., NC
1810 Lincoln Co., NC

REFERENCES

US National Archives Pension Data # W17252
AIS Census Indices
Linn, Jo White "Abstracts of The Deeds of Rowan Co., N.C.1753-1785" Salisbury N.C. 1983 ed. P. 88

BARR, CALEB

SUMMARY OF EARLY LIFE

At the time of entry into Revolutionary service, Caleb Barr was living on Muddy Creek, Burke County, NC. He was a brother of Silas Barr. Burke County court records show him as being "over 50 years " of age in 1804.

SUMMARY OF PARTISAN ACTIVITY

Caleb Barr entered military service in Burke County, NC. In 1778 He entered the North Carolina Continental Line for a nine month tour of duty. In late 1778 troops were recruited in Salisbury District and marched to South Carolina, joining the army of General Benjamin Lincoln, then opposing the British invasion of Florida, Georgia and lower South Carolina. Salisbury District soldiers were headed initially by Gen. Griffith Rutherford and later by Col. Charles McDowell. Their Continental Line Commander was Lt. Col. Archibald Lytle.

Caleb Barr and his brother Silas Barr took part in the battle of Stono Ferry on June 20, 1779. Silas Barr was killed in this action.

SUMMARY OF LATER LIFE

In 1792, Barr acted as administrator of his brother's estate (the Silas Barr, above, who died in the battle of Stono Ferry, SC, 1799) From 1792 through 1799, Barr appeared in several court functions and duties. In 1799, he assigned land to John Hood, possibly indicating his impending departure from Burke County. His name in not on 1800 census schedules, nor is it on 1815 tax lists, Burke Co. In 1804 Barr was declared insolbent by Burke County Court and exempted from poll tax. After the beginning of the Century, Barr appears to have moved to Tennessee, Franklin County. He received land grants there in 1818, and is on the 1820 TN census, Franklin County.

Caleb Barr died c. 1823 as indicated by will and probate records of March 3, 1823, Franklin County, TN. Mentioned are sons William McCrary Barr, Selox Barr, Joseph Barr, deceased son Samuel Barr, and daughters Jenny Barr, Margaret Barr, Betsy Barr Also son-in-law William Nobles.

LAND HOLDINGS AND TRANSACTIONS

1. 300 acres on South Muddy Creek adjacent to land belonging to Andrew Woods and including improvements made earlier by John McAdams.
Ent. December 18, 1778, Grant No. 502, Iss. 28 October 1782, Book 44, p. 228.

2. 150 acres South Muddy Creek adjacent to above.

Ent. January 29, 1779, Grant No. 349, Iss. October 28, 1782 Book 44, p. 131.

3. 100 acres South Muddy Creek. Ent. December 18, 1778, Grant No. 701, Iss. October 11, 1783, Book 50, p. 260.

4. 100 acres main Muddy Creek adjacent to land belonging to John Griffeth. Ent. December 18, 1778, Grant No. 357, Iss. October 28, 1782, Book 44, p. 135,

5. Tennessee Land Grants, Franklin Co., 30 acres, August 15, 1818 # 12368, 20 acres August 15, 1818 # 12365. Book 8, pp. 170-171.

CENSUS LOCATIONS

1790 Burke County, NC 6th Co.
1800
1810
1820 Franklin County, TN

REFERENCES

Roster of NC Soldiers in the American Revolution NCDAR Reprint edition 1967, pp. 197,210,225.
Comptroller's papers, NC Department of Archives and History, A-Z Boxes 14-20.
Revolutionary Army Accounts: Vouchers for service in the NC Continental Line.
Tennessee State Archives and Library; Land Records.
Swink, Dan D. "Minutes of the Court of Pleas and Quarter Sessions", Burke Co. NC 1791-1795 and 1795-1798. 2 Vol. 1986, 1987, Lawndale, NC Multiple listings.
Partlow, Wm. E. "Franklin Co. Wills and Deeds, 1800-1876" pp 55-56, Lebanon, TN 1989. Copy in TN St. Arch. & Library, Nashville.
Huggins, Edith, Burke Co. NC Records SHP Vol I-IV.

BARR, SILAS

SUMMARY OF EARLY LIFE

Silas Barr was living in Burke County, N. C. at the beginning of the Revolutionary War. He was a brother of Caleb Barr, also a Revolutionary War soldier. Silas Barr lived in the Muddy Creek section of Burke County.

SUMMARY OF PARTISAN ACTIVITY

Silas Barr entered Revolutionary military service in late 1778 a soldier in the NC Continental Line (nine months enlistment) under Lt. Archibald Lytle. He was marched southward, joining the army of Gen. Benjamin Lincoln in South Carolina.

While taking part in the battle of Stono Ferry on June 20, 1779 Silas Barr was killed in action.

SUMMARY OF LATER EVENTS

The estate of Silas Barr was probated in July of 1792. His brother Caleb Barr acted as administrator. Caleb Barr selected Brice Collins as attorney to receive pay benefits due his late brother for military service. Supporting statements concerning the military service rendered by Silas Barr were given by Col. Charles McDowell and Capt. James Mackey.

REFERENCES

Revolutionary War final settlements 1777-1792 as quoted in Huggins, Edith, p. 158.

BATES, HUMPHREY

SUMMARY OF EARLY LIFE

Humphrey Bates was born Jan. 13, 1765 in Lincoln County, NC but moved when very young to Burke Co. He was living in Burke Co. during his Revolutionary War service.

SUMMARY OF PARTISAN ACTIVITY

Humphrey Bates first entered military service in 1781, serving in a company of frontier militia commanded by Capt. James McFarland, Lt. George Walker and Ens. Peter Rust. He was stationed at Davidson's Fort at the head of the Catawba River and served a tour of three months.

In late 1781 he volunteered for another tour under Capt. McFarland. Under McFarland he participated in the Wilmington Expedition, headed up by Gen. Griffith Rutherford and Col. Charles Mcdowell.

They joined the main brigade between Salisbury and Charlotte and then progressed southeasterdly through the Uwharrie area to the Cape Fear River and Raft Swamp. There were skirmishes with the Tories under David Fanning and Elrod. Later they were stationed on the outskirts of Wilmington on the Northeast Cape Fear River and remained there until the surrender of Cornwallis in Virginia in October 1781. Wilmington in the meantime was evacuated by Major Craig.

Bates' Company assisted in guarding the supply wagons on the return home.

In the late summer of 1782 he served in a company commanded by Capt. John Watson of Col. Charles McDowell's Regiment. They conducted a raid on the Middle Towns of the Cherokee nation.

SUMMARY OF LATER LIFE

Shortly after the American Revolution, Humphrey Bates moved to Rutherford Co., NC and was married to Rachel Mitchell in 1788. By 1790, census records list him as living in Union Co., SC but back in Rutherford Co. by 1800.

In the early 1800's he moved to Garrard, KY and lived there for about 30 years, in the Paint Lick area (home also to Gen. Thomas Kennedy and Robert Brank, both formerly of Burke Co. And both of whom saw service with the McDowells).

By the time he applied for federal pension in 1832, he was living in Rockcastle Co., KY. He received a pension in the amount of $20.00 per annum. He later moved back to Garrard Co. And died there on March 23, 1853. His wife survived him and received bounty land by the Congressional Act of 1855.

CENSUS LOCATIONS

1790 Union County, SC (See Buncombe listings below)
1800 Rutherford Co., NC
1820 Garrard Co., KY
1830 Garrard Co., KY
(Another Humphrey Bates in Buncombe Co., NC 1820-1830)

LAND HOLDINGS AND TRANSACTIONS

The following Kentucky Land Warrants were issued to Humphrey Bates.

1. Garrard Co., KY, Paint Lick Cr. 50 ac 24 Nov. 1824 Bk. Q p. ?
2. Garrard Co., KY Fall Lock Cr. 100 ac 14 April 1825 Bk R p. 29
3. Garrard Co., KY Fall Lick Cr. 50 ac 3 April 1826 Bk T p.292
4. Garrard Co., KY Fall Lick Cr. 50 ac 29 March 1830 Bk X p.307
5. Garrard Co., Cooper Cr. 50 ac 29 March 1830 BkX p. 308

REFERENCES

US National Archives; Pension Data # W25204
AIS Census Indices
1820 Census Index, Kentucky, Volkel, Lowell 1975 2 Vol.
1830 Census Index, Kentucky, Smith, Dora W. 1973 2 Vol.
Jillson, Willard R., The Kentucky Land Grants Part I
Reprint GPC Baltimore 1971. Pp. 464-465.

BECK, JACOB

SUMMARY OF EARLY LIFE

Jacob Beck appears in Burke County as early as 1773, when he was issued a Crown grant of 150 acres on Henry River. When entering 500 acres of land in 1778, the entry stated "an old improvement Beck now lives on". This land was on Henry River but entry was transferred to Peter Mull.

Later records place Beck on Upper Creek, Burke County. Rowan land records list a Jacob Beck adjacent to Squire Boone (father of Daniel Boone) in what is now Davie County, exact relationship to Burke County Jacob Beck, unknown. A Nicholas Beck, possibly his father or brother, received a Crown grant on Henry River in 1769.

SUMMARY OF PARTISAN ACTIVITY

In 1782 Jacob Beck was cited to Burke County Court to show cause as to why his property should not be confiscated, for being disloyal to the American Cause. Witnesses cited to appear included Jessie Rogers, Joseph Dobson and George Penland. In 1783 Beck was indicted by Morganton District Court for assault on Capt. John Dellinger, in Dec. 1782 "with force and arms in Burke Co."

SUMMARY OF LATER LIFE

Miscellaneous Burke County records show that Jacob Beck was a "planter" but that he also ran a mill on Upper Creek.

Family names, possibly his sons, included Jacob Beck, Jr., Nicholas Beck, John Beck, Joseph Beck, and Daniel Beck.

Jacob Beck died ca 1810. His will was probated in July 1810. Elizabeth Beck and John Beck executors.

LAND HOLDINGS AND TRANSACTIONS

1. 100 acres Burke County, NC on Stephen Piercy's Branch and adjacent to his own land and that of Stephen Piercy and Phillip Shuffler. Ent. 11 Feb 1801 #4084 Grant No. 3057 Iss. 17 Dec 1807 Book 114 p. 355.

2. 400 acres Burke County NC on waters of Johns River entered 5 January and 14 January 1799 #'s 3526 and 3497 Grant No. 3630 Iss. 16 Dec 1816 (Jacob Beck, Jr.?)

3. Tax lists of 1797 Burke County NC showed Jacob Beck with 540 acres in Capt. John Fox's Company adjacent to Bartlett Henson.

4. Crown Grant (Josiah Martin, Royal Governor) to Jacob Beck 30 January 1773 150 acres in Tryon on both sides of Henry's River adjoining a rock on the side of Henry's River. (Now Burke County NC).

5. Deed from David Beck to Jacob Beck 275 acres Upper Creek, Burke County, NC 26 Nov 1791.

CENSUS LOCATIONS

1790   Burke Co. NC 3rd Co.
1800   Burke Co. NC
1810   Eliza Beck, Burke Co. NC

REFERENCES

1. Huggins, Edith W., Burke Co. Records Vols I-IV
2. Hofmann, Margaret Colony of North Carolina abstracts of Land Patents Vol II p. 696, Weldon NC 1984.
3. AIS Census indices.
4. Minutes of the Court of Pleas and Quarter Sessions Burke Co. NC 1791-1795 abstracted by David D. Swink 1986 p. 14.
5. McAllister, Anne W. and Sullivan, Kathy G., "Civil Action Papers 1771-1806 of the Court of Pleas and Quarter Sessions Lincoln Co. NC". p. 73.
6. Beck Papers by Harris, John, Boca Raton, Fl., Morganton Burke Library, North Carolina Room.

BEEKMAN, CHRISTOPHER W.

SUMMARY OF EARLY LIFE

Christopher Beekman was born in New Jersey, the son of Christopher and Mary Cox Beekman, (sometimes given as Sarah). They resided on the Millinstone at Lanington, N J. He was a brother of William and James Beekman. Christopher Beekman was a grandson of Christopher Beekman of New York and a great grandson of Gerard Beekman.

Prior to the Revolutionary War Beekman had moved to the western part of North Carolina ca. 1769 or 1770. He was listed a being a merchant but was also a trained surveyor. He resided initially in Salisbury.

SUMMARY OF PARTISAN ACTIVITY

While residing in Salisbury (or while he was in the process of relocating) Christopher Beekman became an active member of the Rowan Committee of Safety. In the meantime he was making active plans to move to the western part of the county . Beekman served on the Committee of Safety from Sept. 1774 to early 1776. He became one of the more active members and was frequently called upon to carry out military duties including raising a company of men.

As a Captain of militia, he participated in the "Snow Campaign" of late 1775 in South Carolina and then the Cross Creek Expedition of February and March of 1776 (the later part of the Moore's Creek Bridge campaign, which suppressed Tory activity in eastern and middle North Carolina).

In April 1776, after the assembly at Halifax, the military structuring of Revolutionary North Carolina was carried out. Rowan County, being one of the largest in population, was drawn up as having two regiments, instead of the usual one. Christopher Beekman, being at that time the most influential partisan west of the Catawba, was given the rank of Colonel, commanding the Western or 2nd Rowan Regiment (Francis Locke commanded the 1st Regiment; Griffith Rutherford, promoted to Brigadier General, commanded the Brigade, made up of the counties in the Salisbury military-judicial district).

Charles McDowell of Quaker Meadows, who was also a Captain of militia and served with Beekman on the Committee of Safety, was the ranking field officer behind Beekman, with the grade of Lt. Colonel. Hugh Brevard and George Wilfong were appointed Majors.

One of the first actions of the newly created Rowan Regiment was to take part in the Cherokee Expedition in the late summer and early autumn of 1776. The 2nd ranking officer of the 2nd Regiment, Lt. Col. McDowell, had been surrounded by hostile

Indians, then on the warpath. At least thirty to forty settlers had been slain. Gen. Rutherford quickly assembled his Brigade and began a punitive march through the Cherokee Country of western North Carolina. The campaign was in concert with similar actions in Virginia and South Carolina. Col. Beekman, along with his Regiment, took an active role in this campaign. By October 1776 most of the units had returned home. Col. McDowell, along with settlers huddled around him at Cathey's Fort, was rescued.

In February of 1777 plans were made for the establishment of a new county, to be carved from western Rowan. The new county, Burke, was to come in existence on June 1, 1777. At the time of the creation of the new County there was a change in the command structure. Beekman was chosen as one of the nine commissioners to select the site for the new courthouse. One can only speculate that the change in command involved Griffith Rutherford and his old Scotch-Irish compatriot, Charles McDowell. At any rate, McDowell became the commanding officer of the Burke Regiment as well as the chief entry officer of lands. Col. Beekman stepped down altogether from the military structure and was selected as chief Surveyor (the land offices were opened in January 1778). Throughout 1778 and 1779 the signatures of McDowell and Beekman appear on hundreds of land documents. Beekman had resided first in Salisbury then moved to what is now Catawba County. He deeded this property over to his brother William Beekman and Galbraith Falls and purchased property in the Lower Creek section of Burke County, now Caldwell County. Beekman continued to operate as chief surveyor into 1780. A later note in Burke documents stated that Beekman had left the county. Another document stated that he returned to New Jersey, becoming Surveyor General of the state.

SUMMARY OF LATER LIFE

Holgate states that Christopher Beekman returned to Princton, N. J. from North Carolina and that he died in New York City. Beekman was married to Margaret Veghte.

LAND HOLDINGS AND TRANSACTIONS

1. Rowan County NC 16 Feb 1770 Lewis Coffer to Christopher Beekman Lot #24 East Square of Salisbury proved Feb. Ct. 1770. Sold to George Owens 1 July 1771.

2. Rowan County NC Sheriff's sale of William Harrison's property to Christopher Beekman, merchant. Lot #5 Salisbury proved in Aug court 1770. Sold a portion to George Patton 5 Nov 71.

3. Rowan County NC. Two entries 16 Dec 1777 John Kelly of Orange Co, NC to Christopher Beekman of Burke Co. Lot #4 Salisbury
for 10 lots S. Square of Salisbury proved May Court 1774.

4. Rowan Co. NC 7 July 1779. Sale of portions of Lot #4 Salisbury and Lots 3 & 12 W. Square proved Nov. Court 1781.

5. Rowan Co. NC 3 July 1779. Purchased by Christopher Beekman from William Slaven and wife Lot #3 Salisbury. Proved May Court 1782.

6. Burke Co. NC 320 acres head of McLin's Creek "including improvements that he now lives on". Ent 27 Feb 1778. Transferred to Galbraith Falls (would have to be transferred prior to June 1780, date of Falls death at Ramsour's).

7. Burke Co. NC 320 acres Anthony Mill Creek, the "clear swamp" between his improvements and Albert Corpening's. Transferred to Galbraith Falls. Ent 27 Feb 1778.

8. Crown Grant State of N C 25 Jan 1773 359 acres in Tryon County on branch of McLin's Creek.

9. Burke Co. NC 320 acres Lower Creek previously Granville Grant to Philip Curr. Ent 24 June 1778. Warrant ordered.

10. Burke Co. NC 100 acres west side Lower Creek joining William Cragg. Ent. 25 June 1778. Warrant ordered.

Note: The entering of this property in June of 1778, instead of earlier, may indicate the approximate time Beekman moved to Lower Creek from McLin's Creek.

In summary: His moves were from New Jersey to Salisbury c late 1769.
From Salisbury to McLin's Creek c 1773
From McLin's Creek to Lower Creek c 1778
From Lower Creek to New Jersey 1780 or 1781.

REFERENCES

Holgate, Jerome B., American Genealogy 1848 Albany NY p. 79
AIS Census Indices
DAR Patriot Index Washington D.C., 1966 Nat. Soc. DAR p.49
Huggins, Edith W. Burke County Records Vols. I&II 1977.
Wheeler, John H., Historical Sketches of North Carolina Regional Publishing Co., Baltimore 1964 (from original 1851 edition).pp 356-399.
History of North Carolina   Ashe Vol. I
Burke Co. Land Grant data Morganton Burke Library, Morganton, N.C.
Linn, Jo White; Abstracts of the Deeds of Rowan Co. 1753-1785. Salisbury 1983. Multiple entries.
Hofman, Margaret M., Colony of North Carolina, Abstract of Land Patents 1765-1775 Vol. II Weldon, N.C. 1984 p. 326.
Revolutionary Army Accounts Book 1-6 p.9-10. N.C. Dept. of Archives and History.
Revolutionary Army Accounts Vol VIII NC Dept. of Archives and

History (Cherokee expedition).
U.S. National Archives Revolutionary War Pension declarations of Philip Anthony, William Beekman, Casper Bolick, Robert Brank, John Carson, Benjamin Coffey, Richard Crabtree, Jonathan Curtis, William Davidson, Joseph Dobson, Jr., John Dysart, William Hamb, Thomas Kennedy, Thomas Lytle, Arthur McFalls, Patrick O'Neal, Andrew Shook, Jacob Shook ,Leroy Taylor, Isaac Thompson, Conrad Tipps, Jacob Tipps, George Walker, James Reuben Walker, Belfiel Wood. All of the above pension data included in Vol. I&II, this work.

→

BERRY, ENOCH

Enoch Berry was born December 11, 1763. He lived with his father and brothers in Burke County, NC during the Revolutionary period. His father and one of his brothers was killed at Kings Mountain in October 1780.

SUMMARY OF PARTISAN ACTIVITY

Enoch Berry first entered Revolutionary service as a drafted militiaman in April 1780, at age 16. He served in Samuel Woods Company of Charles McDowell's Burke Regiment. In the summer of 1780 he served in McDowell's South Carolina actions against Ferguson (July and August 1780). His tour expired in August, but he volunteered his services on McDowell's retrograde movement through Burke County in 1780. They marched to the Watauga Settlements, joining the troops of Shelby and Sevier. Berry stated that the Burke troops were grouped as a Battalion, under the command of Joseph McDowell of Quaker Meadows, then a Major. Under Joseph McDowell, Berry, his father and brother, took part in the Kings Mountain campaign ending in the epic battle of October 7, 1780. During the Kings Mountain battle, Berry's father was killed. His brother was badly wounded. Berry carried his brother home to Burke County where his brother died of wounds. Berry was discharged at Burke Courthouse.

In the summer of 1781 he once again volunteered and served against the Tories of South Carolina, soon after the seige of Ninety Six. He served in a company commanded by Capt. Samuel Moore for about a month.

In early 1782, in Capt. Samuel Wood's company, he participated in McDowell's (Joseph) spring campaign against the Cherokees. They marched to the Cowee towns, killed several Indians and took about "30 prisoners".

Berry also took part in the Fall 1782 campaign against the Cherokees, this time in Capt. John Russell's Company of Joseph McDowell's Regiment.

Berry's last duty was under Capt. Samuel Woods. He was assigned as a guard at a frontier outpost, Templeton's Station.

SUMMARY OF LATER LIFE

Shortly after the close of the Revolution Berry moved from Burke County, NC to Pendleton District, SC, living there for about twenty years. Later he lived for about ten years in Madison County, AL. His final home was in Warren County (later Cannon County) TN. Berry applied for Revolutionary War pension in Warren County, TN in October 1832. He was awarded a pension of $23.10 per annum.

On November 13, 1823 at about age 60 Berry married Barbara

Thomson, then about age 47. Pension records state that she was his second wife. The records also mention his son (by a previous marriage), Auguston Berry.

Enoch Berry died in Cannon County, TN on September 21, 1848. His home was at Mountain Spring, TN. Will probate Cannon Co., Nov. 17, 1848. Wife Barbara listed.

His widow was still living in 1855 at which time she applied for a warrant for 160 acres of Bounty land as specified by the Congressional Act of 1855. She was allowed a pension of $23.10 per annum.

LAND HOLDINGS AND TRANSACTIONS

Burke Co., NC 10 Dec. 1794.
Transfer of 381 acres of land from Enoch Berry to Robert Montgomery.

CENSUS LOCATIONS

1790 Pendleton District, SC
1800 Pendleton District, SC
1810 ? Bedford County (1812 tax list)
1820 Bedford County, TN
1830 Warren County, TN
1840 Cannon County, TN

REFERENCES

U.S. National Archives Pension Data # W 8128
Cannon Co. TN Will Book A p. 63 TN St. Archives & Library records.
AIS Census Indices
Swink, Dan D., "Minutes of the Court of Pleas and Quarter Sessions Burke Co., NC 1791-1795 Vol. 1986 p. 42 Abstr.
Sistler, Byron and Barbara: Early Tennessee Tax Lists 1977 Evanston IL p. 14.

BIFFLE, JACOB

SUMMARY OF EARLY LIFE

Jacob Biffle was born in Rowan County, N.C. March 2, 1763. As a boy he moved with his father and family from Rowan County, NC to that area of North Carolina which later became Sullivan County, TN. He was living in this area when he first enlisted. After the war, he moved to Burke County (later Buncombe County, NC).

SUMMARY OF PARTISAN ACTIVITY

Jacob Biffle first entered military service in 1780 under Col. Isaac Shelby. Under Col. Shelby he participated in the Kings Mountain Campaign, culminating in the battle of October 7, 1780, Biffle described, in his pension application, the Kings Mountain battle and its aftermath. He specifically mentions the hanging of the nine Tories at Bickerstaff's. He stated that they were hanged "...upon a pine and post oak...". He also mentions the march to the Moravian Towns and the hanging of a Tory escapee.

His second tour of duty was again under Col. Shelby and Capt. Lopp. They marched (in 1781) to South Carolina, serving in the Charleston area under Gen. Nathaniel Greene. Biffle notes the capture of a hospital housing about eighty prisoners. Biffle was discharged after returning to their Santee River base. On his return home, they were harassed by Indians in the Blue Ridge area.

Biffle's final military tour was for three months in 1782, under Col. Shelby and Capt. King. This tour was directed against the hostile Cherokees of East Tennessee and Holston Valley. He specifically described how they killed two Indians during this action.

SUMMARY OF LATER LIFE

Jacob Biffle married Mary Deaver. One child, Millie, b. 6/1/1795 m. Samuel Aiken.

Jacob Biffle, after the war, moved to Burke County, NC, later Buncombe County, N. C. And in 1810 to Maury County, TN. Jacob Biffle applied for Revolutionary War pension in Maury County, TN in December, 1832, age about 70 years. He was awarded a pension of $30.00 per annum.

Jacob Biffle died in Maury County, TN February 16, 1844. He is buried in Pisgah Cemetery, Pisgah Hill, west of Mt. Pleasant, Maury County, TN.

LAND HOLDINGS AND TRANSACTIONS

1. Jacob Biffle received a NC Land Grant in Buncombe County for 100 acres on the east side of the south west fork of Pigeon

River, adjacent to land belonging to James Greenlee.
Ent. July 18,1797, No. 7296, Grant. No. 792, Book 109. P. 288
Iss. September 1, 1800.

2. State of Tennessee Land Grant (with Sam Akins) Maury County
640 acres July 4, 1821. # 15486.

CENSUS LOCATIONS

1790 Burke Co., NC 11th Co.
1800 Buncombe Co., N. C.
1816 Maury County, TN (tax lists)
1820
1830 Maury County, TN
1840 Maury County, TN

REFERENCES

U. S. National Archives Pension Declaration No. S 3003
DAR Patriot Index 1966 p. 58
Roster of Soldiers and Patriots of the American Revolution buri
in Tennessee
Tennessee Society DAR 1979 (edited by Bates and March)
AIS Census Indices
Sistler, Byron & Barbara. Early Tennessee Tax List, Evanston, I
1977.
Tennessee State Archives & Library Nashville Land Records.

BLAIR, COLBERT

SUMMARY OF EARLY LIFE

Colbert Blair was born in Bucks Co. Pa. in 1730, the son of James and Mary Colbert Blair. Colbert Blair arrived in Burke County (now Caldwell County) in 1770. His home was on Muddy Fork of Lower Creek.

SUMMARY OF PARTISAN ACTIVITY

Colbert Blair was recognized as one of the better known Loyalists of Burke County, though his family was divided in their sentiments.

The best documentation of Blair's loyalty came in the diary of Lt. Anthony Allaire (as given in Draper's <u>Kings Mountain and Its Heroes</u>). Allaire was a Provincial British officer who served under Ferguso at Kings Mountain. Captured at Kings Mountain, he was conveyed, along with several hundred loyalists, from the battleground in South Carolina through Rutherford, Burke and Wilkes Counties to Salem in Stokes County (now Forsyth).
At Salem Allaire escaped and made a retrograde secret march through Wilkes and Burke Counties and eventually to safety at the British held garrison at Ninety-Six, S. C.

While in Burke County (now Caldwell), he was secreted by Colbert Blair. He states thusly:"Friday (November) 10th. Suffered very much from the cold. At six o'clock in the evening set out again ...we marched about thirty miles and arrived at Colbert Blair's just at daybreak.

Saturday 11th. It began to rain just as we got to Mr. Blair's. This good man secreted us in his fodder-house and gave us the best his house afforded.

...Monday 13th. Set out from this good man's fodder-house. He conducted us about three miles to a Mr. F. Rider...".

SUMMARY OF LATER LIFE

Colbert Blair was married to Sarah Morgan Blair. Their children were:

1. Enos 1760-1814 m. Hannah Milliken.
2. James 1753-1839 m. (1) Elizabeth Powell (2) Elizabeth Cleveland.
3. John 1764-1846 m. Frances Hill.
4. Colbert 1770-1846 m. Jane Murrey.
5. Mary m. Moses Guest.

Colbert Blair died 1805; Estate proceedings Burke County Court 1806. Colbert Blair buried Cedar Valley Methodist Church.

The exact burial site not definitely known otherwise.

LAND HOLDINGS AND TRANSACTIONS

1. 323 acres Burke Co. NC on Muddy Fork of Lower Creek, adjacent to land belonging to Elias Powell, Ambrose Powell, Edward Wilson, and Alexander Douglass. Entry data states land "where he now lives".
Ent. 23 Dec. 1778 #787 Grant No. 788 Iss. Nov. 9, 1784.
Book 57 p. 8.

2. 125 acres Burke Co., NC on N. E. Side of Lower Creek adjacent to land belonging to himself, Elias Powell, and Alexander Douglass. (cc. James Blair, Alexander Douglass).
Ent. 23 Sept. 1778 # 787 Grant No. 1469 Iss. 4 Jan. 1792.
Book 75 p.439.

CENSUS LOCATIONS

1790   Burke Co., NC 9th Co.
1800   Burke Co., NC

REFERENCES

Blair, Robert Eoae, in Caldwell County Heritage, Winston Salem, N.C. 1983 p.256.

Burke County Land Grant records, Morganton Burke Library Morganton, N. C.

AIS Census Indices

Draper, Lyman C. Kings Mountain and Its Heroes;

GPC Reprint issue 1967, originally 1881. pp. 513-514.

BLAIR, JAMES

SUMMARY OF EARLY LIFE

James Blair was born in Augusta Co. Va. on March 6, 1761 (other records say 1763). He was the son of the well known Loyalist Colbert Blair. (1730-1805) and Sarah Morgan Blair. He was a brother to Enos, John, Colbert Jr., and Mary Blair. During the Revolution he lived on Blair's Fork, a tributary of Lower Creek.

SUMMARY OF PARTISAN ACTIVITY

During the Revolution, beginning in the summer of 1778, Blair served as a scout or "spy", orderly Sergeant and later on as an Ensign. Blair served with Burke Militia under Charles McDowell, with the Wilkes Militia under Col. Benjamin Cleveland and with the Rutherford Militia under Col. Hampton. The Captains under whom he served included Captains Richardson, Ford, Bowman, and Joseph McDowell of Burke County, Captains Sharpe, Gray, Barton of the Wilkes Militia and Captains Hampton and Hambright of Rutherford Militia. In his pension statements Blair states that he was in the battle of Ramsours Mill (June 20, 1780) Cane Creek (Sept. 12, 1780) Kings Mountain (Oct. 7, 1780), Sumpter's Surprise (Fishing Creek), Blackstocks and the siege of Augusta.

During the Kings Mountain Campaign, Blair was sent as an express rider by Col. Charles McDowell to the Wilkes and Surry Militia, alerting them to the British presence and ordering them to rendezvous at Quaker Meadows. During this duty assignment Blair was wounded in the shoulder.

SUMMARY OF LATER LIFE

After the Revolutionary War Blair moved to Rhea Co., TN, Pendleton Co., SC, Franklin and Habersham Cos.' GA. He was married to (1) Elizabeth Powell and (2) Elizabeth Cleveland. Children by his second wife; Anne d. 1854, Joseph Terrell, Oliver Elston, James Blair, Jr.

James Blair served in the Georgia Legislature from Franklin, Co. (1810-1818). Blairsville, the County set of Rabun Co., is named for him. James Blair applied for and received a Federal pension in 1834. He died in Habersham, Co. Ga. In 1839.

LAND HOLDINGS AND TRANSACTIONS

James Blair received an N. C. Grant for 388 acres, Burke Co. NC on Blair's Fork. The land lay adjacent to that of Benjamin Coffey and Thomas Stepp.
Ent. 5 June 1778. Surveyed 1 Feb. 1779. cc. Abner Stepp and Benjamin Coffee.

CENSUS LOCATIONS

1790 Pendleton Co., (Ninety Six Dist.) SC.
1800 Blount Co. TN. Tax list--Parent County of Roane and Rhea Counties.
1810
1820
1830 Habersham Co., GA.

REFERENCES

U.S. National Archives and Pension Data #S22125
Blair, Robert E. in Caldwell Co., N.C. Heritage Winston Salem 1983 p. 256.
AIS Census Indices.
Land Grant Data Morganton Burke Library, Morganton, NC.
McCall, Mrs. Howard H." Roster of Revolutionary Soldiers in Georgia and other States" GPC Baltimore 1968 p. 13.
Draper, L.C. An Kings Mountain and Its Heroes GPC Reprint 1967 (original 1881) pp. 180-181.
DAR Patriot Index Nat. Soc. DAR; Washington, DC 1966 p.63

BOYD, JOHN

SUMMARY OF EARLY LIFE

John Boyd was born in North Carolina in the year 1761. At the time of the American Revolution, John Boyd was living with his family in Burke Co.

SUMMARY OF PARTISAN ACTIVITY

John Boyd first entered military service at about age 18 Or 19 in 1780, enlisting in Capt. Joseph White's Company of Col. Charles McDowell's Burke Regiment. This would be in the summer of 1780 shortly after the battle of Ramsour's Mill. Boyd participated in McDowell's South Carolina actions and was engaged in the skirmishes at head of Pacalet River and in upper South Carolina. He describes the action in which the British Dragoons had staged a surprise attack but were chased back to Prince's Fort in South Carolina.

After returning home to Burke County, Boyd once again volunteered and was mustered in with the Wilkes militia. He was placed in Capt. James Sheppard's company. Other officers were Major Joseph Winston and Major Jesse Franklin of Surry County. In September he joined the march from Surry and Wilks County to Quaker Meadows and then headed down the so-called Victory Trail toward Kings Mountain. Boyd stated that he was with the foot soldiers initally but later procured a horse and eventually took part in the epic battle of October 7, 1780 (only the mounted troops fought in the battle).

He volunteered again with the Surry County troops in early 1781 and was placed in a company commanded by Major John Armstrong and Lt. David Umphrey. They took park in the skirmishes which preceded the battle of Guilford Courthouse.

He was discharged at Guilford Courthouse but did not state that he had actually participated in the battle itself which was fought on March 15, 1781. This was his final tour of duty.

SUMMARY OF LATER LIFE

John Boyd was married to Mary Roberts in Surry Co., N.C. in 1784 or 85. By this union were born the following children:

Alexander Smith died young
John Jr. b.1788
James
Martha
Elizabeth b.1794
Spencer b.1796
Joshua b. 1797
Jane b. 1799

Susan (Suey) b.1801
Elisha   b. 1804
Hugh   b. 1806
Matilda
Matthew   b.1792
William   b.1787
One boy not named

John Boyd appeared to have moved from Burke County, NC, to Surry County during the war. After living for a while in Surry County and being married in 1785 he moved to Greene County, TN, back to Surry County and then to Grayson County, VA and Hawkins County TN. From Hawkins County, TN, they moved back to Surry County. His final move from Surry Co., NC to Hendricks County Indiana.

John Boyd applied for federal pension in Hendricks County India in November 1833, age 72 years. He was awarded a pension in the amount of $30.00 per annum. He died in Hendricks Co., IN on January 6, 1840. Buried, Clayton Cemetery.

CENSUS LOCATIONS

1800 Surry Co., NC

REFERENCES

US National Archives Pension Date # R1089
AIS Census Index 1800 NC
Hatcher, Patricia L. Graves of Revolutionary War Patriots Vol I p. 101 Dallas 1987.

BRANK, PETER

SUMMARY OF EARLY LIFE

Peter Brank, the son of Robert Brank, Sr. and Jean Brank, was born in 1742. During the early part of the Revolutionary War he was living on his father's property, now Morganton, NC, Burke County.

Peter Brank was married to Rebecca Alexander (1745-1825). He was a brother of Robert Brank, Jr., also a Revolutionary War veteran who later moved to Kentucky. He was a brother to Elizabeth Brank who married Robert Penland, of Pricilla Brank who married David Vance, Rachel Brank who married William Brittain and Jane Brank who married Robert Henry.

SUMMARY OF PARTISAN ACTIVITY

Peter Brank was member of Charles McDowell's Burke regiment of militia. During the early phases of the Kings Mountain campaign in September 1780, he was a member of a small force that opposed the northward advances of the British under Maj. Patrick Ferguson. At a skirmish at the head of Cane Creek in lower Burke County on September 12, 1780, Peter Brank was mortally wounded.

LAND HOLDINGS AND TRANSACTIONS

Peter Brank was living with his father during the early part of the war and acted as a chain carrier for the survey of his father's two grants. One was on the south side of the Catawba River and the other was on the main wagon road and a meadow branch. These tracts currently are in the city of Morganton. The entry data on the larger tracts states "... including said Brank's improvement and his son Peter's for complement ...". Ent. 13 Feb. 1778 Granted 1779.
Peter Brank entered 73 acres on 16 Feb. 1778 which stated "... including land Brank now lives on for complement...." not processed, most likely due to Brank's demise in 1780. The land was on the south side of the Catawba River and adjacent to that of Robert Brank, Sr.

REFERENCES

Land Grant Data, Morganton-Burke Library, Morganton, NC
White, Emmett R., Vol I of this work on Robert Brank, Jr. p.29 (1984).
Morganton-Burke Library Vertical files on Brank family.
US National Archives Pension Declaration of James Withrow.
Huggins, Edith, Burke County, NC Land Records. Vol.I pp. 22,72 (1977).
Draper, L. C. Kings Mountain and its Heroes Reprinted (details of Cane Creek Skirmish).

BREVARD, HUGH

SUMMARY OF EARLY LIFE

Hugh Brevard was born c. 1747 or 1748, possibly earlier. As he was one of the older siblings, he was perhaps born in PA. or Maryland (Elk River section). His father, John Brevard, was one of Rowan County's pioneer settlers, now South Iredell Co. near Centre Church. All of his seven brothers were active during the Revolutionary War and were officers. His brothers were Ephraim, Adam, Robert, Joseph, John, Benjamin, and Abraham Brevard. Their mother was Jane McWhorter. After marriage, Hugh Brevard lived in eastern Catawba Co. (earlier Rowan, Burke and Lincoln Counties).

SUMMARY OF PARTISAN ACTIVITY

Early in the Revolutionary period, Hugh Brevard was chosen a member of the Rowan Co. Committee of Safety. In Nov. 1775, he, along with several others, was asked to recruit a military company. The action against the Scovellite Tories of South Carolina occurred about this time. Rowan Co. soldiers did participate, but Brevard's inclusion is not definitely documented. He was on the Cross Creek expedition of March 1776 (this was the latter action of the Moore's Creek Bridge Campaign). During this expedition, he was a ranking field officer with a grade of Major. He served for about a month.

Responding to the call of Col. Charles McDowell in July of 1776 (who was being besieged by hostile indians), Rowan troops took part in Gen. Griffith Rutherford's Cherokee Expedition in August and September of 1776. Brevard served in this campaign, again as a field officer. Brevard was a member of the western Rowan 2nd Regiment under Col. Christopher Beekman and Lt. Col. Charles McDowell. Rutherford was Brigade Commander. In 1777, on the creation of Burke Co., the western Rowan Militia Regiment became the Burke Co. Regiment. As Brevard lived in Burke Co. (later Catawba Co.) he became associated with this Regiment. Lt. Col. Charles McDowell became the new Regimental Commander and promoted to Col. Col. Beekman stepped down and became County Surveyor. Brevard was second in command with the rank of Lt. Col. Joseph McDowell Q.M. and Joseph White were Majors. At the same time McDowell became the new entry taker and Brevard the Register (Deeds).

In late 1778 and early 1779, soldiers of the Salisbury district were ordered to serve in the SC area. The British had launched their Southern Campaign with the capture of Charleston and Savannah as chief objectives. The Rowan and Burke troops did little to affect the capture of Savannah on New Years Day of 1779 but did take part in the actions above Savannah and toward Augusta and later Charleston. Brevard served in the disastrous Brier Creek Campagign of April 1779. The McDowells served at Stono Ferry, near Charleston, in June and probably Brevard also. The action by the Americans at Stono Ferry delayed the British attempts to take Charleston. In the 1780 push against Charleston the Salisbury militia had been split by Rutherford into three distinct units. McDowell was on the outskirts of Charleston with Salisbury militia, mainly mounted troops attempting to break the Brittish cordon. The main body of Salisbury militia under Rutherford was in the Mallard Creek section of Mecklenburg County, ready to head south to counter any British moves. The rear guard in Rowan was left in command of Col. Francis Locke. The Burke troops were commanded by Lt. Col. Brevard. With little advanced warning Major Joseph McDowell's reconnaissance had discovered major Loyalist activity in the vicinity of Clark's Creek now present day Lincolnton, NC.

A quick, lightning like thrust was planned by Locke and Brevard. Advancing quickly via Anderson's Mountain (after having joined forces) the combined Rowan and Burke militia struck the larger Loyalist units at Ramsour's Mill June 20, 1780. After a protracted, bloody, hard fought battle, the Loyalists were turned by a flank attack by Col. John Hardin's Burke men. The initial onslaught was by the mounted men under Capt. Falls and McDowell. Capt. Falls was mortally wounded. The Loyalists were routed and many prisoners taken. Rutherford, having been joined by Charles McDowell, arrived on the battle site shortly after its successful conclusion. Much credit was due to Lt. Col. Brevard and to Col. Locke for their well earned victory. After Ramsour's, Brevard participated in the great Kings Mountain campaign of September and October 1780. There is some evidence that he may have missed the main action of October 7th by commanding foot men rather than mounted troops. This would account for the belief that Joseph McDowell, (either Quaker Meadows or Pleasant Gardens) commanded the Burke troops during the battle, since Brevard obviously outranked both of them. Brevard's experience would be similar to that of Major Herndon of Wilkes County, as described by Draper.

In late 1780 the Burke militia was split, the mounted men under Col. Joseph McDowell joined with Morgan and fought at Cowpens in January 1781. Brevard led his foot men to join with Gen. Davidson at Cowan's Ford in the belated attempt to oppose Cornwallis' 2nd North Carolina invasion. The last action of Brevard was in February of 1781. It should be mentioned that Brevard served in the N. C. House of Commons in 1780 and 1781.

Sometime between February and June 1781 Hugh Brevard died prematurely. He left his widow, Jane Young Brevard, and two daughters. There is little doubt that Hugh Brevard was one of the front runners of early Burke County history.

LAND HOLDINGS AND TRANSACTIONS

1. 640 acres Burke Co. NC (now Catawba Co.) on south side of (west) Catawba river. The property lay near the mouth of Tan Vat Creek.
Ent. Sept. 10, 1778 #283 Grant No. 296 Iss. Mar. 14, 1780 Book 28 p. 295.
2. 300 acres Burke Co., NC on south (W) side of Catawba river. The land lay adjacent to the property of Jacob Sherrill and to his upper survey.
Ent. Sept. 10, 1778 #284 Grant No. 314 Iss. Mar. 14, 1780 Book 28 p. 313..
3. 150 acres Burke Co., NC lying on a branch that empties into Ball's Creek. The land formerly belonged to John Fish, Jr. and contained improvements of Robert Erwood. The property was adjacent to that of John Bridges and William Coles.
Ent. Nov. 28, 1778 #502 Grant No. 117 Iss. Mar. 15, 1780 Book 28 p. 117.

REFERENCES

1. Committee of Safety Minutes, Rowan Co. NC, as given in Wheeler, John Hill p. 360-377.
2. N.C. Treasurer & Comptroller Accounts, as listed by Haun 1989, pp. 4-5 (Cross Creek Expedition).
3. Pension statements Benjamin Brevard, James Graham (Ramsour's).
4. Pension statment Joseph Knox (Cherokee Expedition).
5. Rev. Army Accounts Vol VIII p. 6 folio 1 (Aug-Nov 1776). Verification of Service, Cherokee Expedition.

BRIDGET, WALTER

SUMMARY OF EARLY LIFE

A William Bridget was living on Second Broad River, near the Rutherford County line. A James Bridget lived in Rutherford County -- relationship to Walter Bridget not known.

SUMMARY OF PARTISAN ACTIVITY

In the Court Martial of Col. Charles McDowell of 1782, Col. Joseph McDowell (of Pleasant Gardens) gave testimony that Walter Bridget was Loyalist and fought on the side of the British in the battle of Kings Mountain on October 7, 1780.

REFERENCES

Court Martial records, Col. Charles McDowell, facsimile presented to author by Miss Eunice Ervin, Morganton, NC, undated.
Huggins, Edith W., Burke County records Vol II SHP 1987 p. 154.

BRITTAIN, JAMES

SUMMARY OF EARLY LIFE

James Brittain was born c. 1750-55 in Virginia (DAR records give 1740).

He was the oldest son of Joseph and Jemima Brittain. The Brittain family migrated from Virginia to North Carolina and were in Orange County in 1764. His father died c. 1774 and at that time was living in Rowan County, the part that later became Burke County. In the early 1770's James Brittain was living in the vicinity of Hunting Creek in Burke County. Other siblings included Mary (m. Elrod), Phoebe (m. Poteat), Philip, William, Rachel (m. Brank), Benjamin, Aaron and Samuel.

SUMMARY OF PARTISAN ACTIVITY

During the first part of the Revolution, while living on Huntin Creek, James Brittain served in the Rowan militia with the rank of Lieutenant. He, along with his company, took part in the Cherokee Expedition of August and September 1776. In December of the same year, Brittain joined the North Carolina Continental Line for a three year tour of duty. He served in Capt. Richard Cook's Company of Col. John Williams' 9th Regimen Later he was transferred to Lt. Col. Robert Mebane's Company of the First North Carolina Battalion, under Col. Thomas Clark. Brittain's tour of duty expired in February of 1780. He thus missed capture at Charleston in May 1780. Most of his officers and fellow soldiers, however, were captured and imprisoned, including Col. Clark and Lt. Col. Mebane.

SUMMARY OF LATER LIFE

James Brittain was married to Delilah Stringfield, the daughter of James Stringfield of Burke and Buncombe Counties. Their children were as follows:

Mary b. c. 1782 m. Thomas Edwards
Joseph b.c. 1783-4
Amelia b. 1785 m. Ellis Edwards
Phillip b. 1787 m. Sophia Lewis
Keziah b. 1789 m. Jeremiah Pace
Benjamin b. 1793 m. Celia Vance
Nancy b. 1794 m. Jacob Stuart
Comfort b. 1796 m. Montgomery Bell
William b. 1798 m. Rachel Clayton
Susannah b. 1800 m. Asaph Wilson
James Jr. b. 1803 m. Rachel Smith
Lorenzo Dow b. 1805 m. Arminta Russell
Horatio Nelson b. 1815 m. Elizabeth Morrow
Delilah b. c. 1816

James Brittain and his family lived in Burke County throughout the period of the American Revolution and continuing into the late 1780's. In 1786 and 1787 he was a Justice of the Peace and appeared in several court cases. In about 1790 it appears that Brittain and his family along with his father in law James Stringfield and family moved to the Mills River section of Rutherford County.(later Buncombe, and eventually Henderson County.) In Buncombe County James Brittain became a distinguished public servant and land holder. He served as a Magistrate. He also became a militia officer with the rank of Major. During the border dispute between North Carolina and Georgia in 1804, he commanded a company of militia ("Walton's War").

Brittain acquired large land holdings in the newly formed Buncombe County. Some of his land lay on French Broad River, Boylston's Creek, Richland Creek, Reems Creek, Hominy Creek, Mills River, Mud Creek and others. Brittain donated land for the Mills River Presbyterian Church and for Mills River Academy He also acquired property in Morristown, later Asheville. Brittain became an important political figure in western North Carolina and represented Buncombe County on six occasions in the North Carolina Senate from 1796-1807.

The name of James Brittain begins to appear less often on records of the 1820's. One source says he died in 1823, but a land transfer of 1826 states "James Brittain, Sr., et.al." By this time James Brittain, Jr. was of age (born 1803) and probably accounts for at least some of the later transactions. Most give James Brittain's date of death as 1832. He was buried at his old home place on Mills River, now Henderson County, NC. A DAR marker is in place at Mills River Presbyterian Church. James Brittain, along with other Brittain family members, contributed much to the history of western North Carolina as well as to the early pioneer expansion areas in the Mississippi valley.

LAND HOLDINGS AND TRANSACTIONS

Burke County, North Carolina: During Brittain's three year duty in the North Carolina Continental Line, land was entered on his behalf by George Killian. It was in the proximity of land belonging to his father in law, James Stringfield. A cabin had been built.

Buncombe County, North Carolina: Brittain received land in Buncombe County as follows. (include dates of instrument).

1. 100 acres NC Grant #1064, 1802
2. 50 acres NC Grant #1968, 1811
3. 150 acres Soloman Israel's branch, 1811 NC Grant #1963

4. Morristown (from John Benton et.al.) 1795
5. 640 acres Richland Creek, 1800 NC Grant #640
6. 100 acres Boidston's Creek, 1799 from James Boidston
7. 100 acres NC Grant #454, 1798
8. 100 acres Mills River, 1812, from James Stringfield,Jr.
9. 490 acres, Mud Creek, 1826, from James Justice
10. 170 acres Little Mud Creek, 1828, from Elizabeth Thomas
11. 100 acres Sulars Creek, 1809, from David McCarson
12. 200 acres Little River, 1810, NC Grant #1886
13. 80 acres French Broad River,1798, from James Davidson
14. 600 acres McLoud Creek, 1804 NC Grant #1304
15. 82 acres Boidston's Creek, 1807 from George L. Davidson
16. 640 acres Richland Creek, 1806 from William Whitson
17. 640 acres Richland Creek, 1806 from Thomas Whitson et.al.
18. 274 acres Sumner Co. TN State of NC Mil.Grant # 1803
    BKE-5, p. 198

CENSUS LOCATIONS

1790 Rutherford County, NC 14th Co.
1800 Buncombe County, NC
1810 Buncombe County, NC
1820 Buncombe County, NC

REFERENCES

N.C. Revolutionary Army Accounts, various pay vouchers.
Roster of Soldiers from North Carolina in the American Revoluti
   GPC reprint 1932 ed. N.C. DAR. pp. 253, 506, 403, 619.
DAR Patriot Index National Society DAR, Washington, DC 1966
   p. 87.
U.S. National Archives Revolutionary War Pension declarations.
   Joseph Dobson, Jr. # W19187.
Cawyer, Shirley Brittain, Stephenville, Texas. Data and letter
   to author 1986 including detailed information on Brittain
   and Stringfield families. Data also included copies of
   Revolutionary War vouchers, land information, etc.
Wooley, James E., Buncombe County,NC Index to Deeds SHP 1983
   pp.53-55.
Huggins, Edith W., Burke County Records Vols. I-IV.
Burke County "Minutes of Court of Pleas and Quarter Sessions"
   1791-1795. Abstracts of. Published and edited by Swink, Danie
   D. 1986. Multiple listings.
AIS Census Indices 1790-1820
Land Records, Morganton-Burke Library, Morganton, NC
Old Buncombe County Heritage (old Buncombe Co. Genealogical
   Society) Vol II 1987. Articles on Brittain family by Shirley
   Cawyer (above) and Beth Lolley.
Wheeler, John H. Historical Sketches of N.C. Regional Publishin
   Co., Baltimore, Reprint 1964. (Original 1851) pp. 53-54.
McCrary, Mary Jane; "Transylvania Beginnings: A History"; SHP
   1984. P. 105.
White, William R. And McCrary, Mary Jane, Brevard, NC
   Conversation with author, c. 1984.

Tennessee State Archives and Library. Land Grant Records. Nashville.

BRITTAIN, PHILIP

Philip Brittain was the son of Joseph and Jemima Brittain of Orange County, NC, later of Burke County, NC. He was a brother of Revolutionary War soldier James Brittain. He was age 58 in 1818, when applying for federal pension.

SUMMARY OF PARTISAN ACTIVITY

Philip Brittain first entered military service in Orange County, NC as a volunteer in the N.C. Continental Line, He was placed in a company commanded by Capt. John Rochel of the 9th Regiment, Col. John Williams commanding. He enlisted for a term of four years beginning in December 1776. Under Col. Williams, they were trained and prepared. In late 1777, they marched northward joining the army of Gen. George Washington. After wintering at Valley Forge in 1777-78, they were later marched out in pursuit of the British army that had evacuated Philadelphia. In July of 1778 he participated in the battle of Monmouth, N.J. Brittain first served in Col. William's 9th Regiment but was later transferred to the 6th Regiment, Col. Clark commanding. Brittain was discharged in December 1780.

SUMMARY OF LATER LIFE

Philip Brittain and his family had already moved to Burke County near the middle of the Revolutionary War. After his discharge Brittain himself came to Burke County remaining here until his move to the west. Phillip Brittain served as a juror in 1793-94 Burke County Court sessions. He served as a Constable of Burke County in 1794 and 1795.

Brittain applied for federal pension in Bedford County, TN on June 15, 1818. He was awarded an annual pension of $96.00. Philip Brittain married _____ . Children:
Nancy b. 1807
Mary b. 1808
Samuel b. 1809
Philip b. 1811

LAND HOLDINGS AND TRANSACTIONS

Philip Brittain was deeded 273 acres of land by Jesse Walker, dated January 4, 1792. Recorded January 1793, session Burke Count Court.

CENSUS LOCATIONS

1790 Burke County, NC 13th Co.
1800 Burke County, NC
1810 Burke County, NC
1820 Bedford County, TN
1830 Bedford County, TN

REFERENCES

U.S. National Archives Pension Statements No. 539243
Soldiers and Patriots of the American Revolution Buried in
Tennessee (edited by Bates and Marsh) 1979, p. 22
Minutes of the Burke County Court of Pleas and Quarter Session
1791-1795 (prepared by D.D. Swink) 1986.

BROWN, RICHARD

SUMMARY OF EARLY LIFE

Richard Brown was living in the Middle Little River area of old Burke County during the Revolutionary period.

SUMMARY OF PARTISAN ACTIVITY

Richard Brown was a Loyalist soldier of Burke Co. In October 1780, he was in the troops under Major Freguson and fought in the battle of Kings Mountain, SC. The information was brought to light in the sworn testimony given in the Court Martial trial of Col. Charles McDowell in early 1782.

In 1781 he was in the service of South Carolina troops in Lt. Col. C.S. Myddleton's S. C. Regiment, 2nd Dragoons of Capt. Francis Moore. Brown served as a saddler. Myddleton's Regiment saw action at Ninety-Six, SC and at Eutaw Springs (September 8, 1781).

SUMMARY OF LATER LIFE

In 1787, Richard Brown was one of the founding members of the New Meeting House Baptist Church begun by Edward Teague, its first minister.

LAND HOLDINGS AND TRANSACTIONS

1. 200 acres Burke Co., NC on both sides of Middle Little River, adj. to land belonging to Andrew Steele, George Brown and his own land (c.c. Nicholas Jones, Robert Moore).
Ent. 17 Oct 1778 #890 Grant No. 1279 Iss. Nov 16, 1790
Book 77 p. 123.
@. 100 acres Burke Co., NC on east side Middle Little River, adj. to his own land (c.c. Nicholas Jones, Robert Moore)
Ent. 15 Oct 1779 #894 Grant No. 1377 Iss. 16 Nov 1790
Book 77 p. 148.
3. Sale of land Richard Brown to Robert Carrethers 173 acres October session Burke County Court 1797.

CENSUS LOCATIONS

1790 Burke Co., NC 8th Co.
1800 Wilkes Co., NC ??

REFERENCES

Col. Charles McDowell Court Martial data, facsimile donated to author by Miss Eunice Ervin of Morganton, NC, undated.
AIS Census Indices
Burke County Land Grant data, Morganton, NC, public Library
Moss, Bobby, G., Roster of South Carolina Patriots in the American Revolution. 1983 p. 110.

BROWN, ROBERT

SUMMARY OF EARLY LIFE

Robert Brown was born in Rowan County, NC in 1758. He was living in Burke County at the time of the Revolutionary War.

SUMMARY OF PARTISAN ACTIVITY

Robert Brown entered Revolutionary service as a militiaman for two or three months in 1779. He was stationed at the upper Fort on the Catawba and saw no significant action (Davidson Fort). Later he served another tour of duty at the upper Fort under Capt. Samuel Davidson. Subsequent commanders at the Fort were Capt. (James) McFarland and Capt. (Daniel) Smith.

In March of 1780, Brown volunteered for a tour of duty in a company commanded by Capt. Price in Col. Elijah Clark's Regiment. They were marched to South Carolina and were engaged against a Tory force commanded by Major Dunlap. In his pension statements, Brown mentioned skirmishes at Broad River, Wofford's Iron Works and Thicketty Fort. He also related that Dunlap was was taken prisoner.

His tour ended in October 1780. Brown returned home just at the beginning of the battle of Kings Mountain. He left Burke County intending to join the patriot forces. Instead he met them in Rutherford County shortly after the battle had been fought. Brown mentioned the hanging of the Tory partisans at Bickerstaff's. He specifically mentioned Col. Ambrose Mills and Capt. John McFalls as being victims of the hanging.

Brown returned to Burke County and enlisted in a final tour of duty in early 1781 under Col. Joseph McDowell. He served against the Cherokee Indians. He was an Indian spy (scout) in a company commanded by Capt. Daniel Smith.

SUMMARY OF LATER LIFE

Brown applied for federal pension in January 1833 (or Jan. 1834?) In Warren County, TN. He was awarded a pension of $80.00 per annum. He was then age 75 years. After the Revolution he lived in Hawkins, Knox, Smith and Warren County, TN. He is buried at Viola Graveyard, Warren County.

CENSUS LOCATIONS

1840 Warren County, TN

REFERENCES

U.S. National Archives Pension Statements No. S3057
Roster of Soldiers and Patriots of the American Revolution buried in Tennessee.

Bates, Published by Tennessee Society DAR 1979, revised by Helen
C. March, p. 24
Various printed census indices.

BROWN, SAMUEL

SUMMARY OF EARLY LIFE

Samuel Brown was perhaps Burke County's most recognized Loyalist, not because of his "loyalty", but because of his bad habits of stealing and pilfering. One of Burke County's (then Rowan County) earlier settlers, he and his wife Elizabeth lived on the west bank of the Catawba, now Catawba County. John Oxford and John Perkins were close neighbors. Evidence of Brown's pugnacious nature is described in Rowan County minutes. In an altercation with his neighbor John Oxford, Brown suffered the humility of having a portion of his ear bitten off. Draper mentions that his wife Mary may have left him prior to the Revolution, due to his bad habits.

SUMMARY OF PARTISAN ACTIVITY

A rather complete, though somewhat biased, description of Browns partisan activity is found in L. C. Draper's book <u>Kings Mountain and Its Heroes</u>, Chapter VII. It seems that Brown (occasionally accompanied by his sister, Charity) established quite a reputation in the Catawba Valley for stealing -- mainly household items such as dishes, pewter items, silver and the like. With the onset of increased hostilities, Brown chose to be "Loyalist". He carried his activities to South Carolina, avoiding the military whenever possible. On one occasion he hid out "in the bushes" with the notorious David Fanning. This occurred during the early part of Fanning's career (c.1778) but Fanning recorded it in his notable Memoirs, published years later.

Eventually Brown carried things a little too far, insulting the family of David Culberson of Fair Forest area of S. C. Culberson and his friends laid an ambush for Brown, shot him in the back, killing him instantly. According to Draper, this occurred somewhere around the summer of 1780. Though Draper intimates that Brown was a Tory "Captain", the British records do not confirm that he was either a soldier or an officer.

LAND HOLDINGS AND TRANSACTIONS

1. Granville Grant to Samuel Brown (Rowan Co.NC) 144 acres west side of Catawba River. 7 Jan 1761 Proven in Rowan Court 1762.
2. Granville Grant to Samuel Brown (Rowan Co.NC) 640 acres south Buffalo Creek adj. to Robert Thompson. Proved October Court 1760.
3. Samuel Brown and wife Elizabeth to John Kennedy 100 acres on south Buffalo. Granted 22 Aug 1759 proved Sept 1770. Rowan County.
4. Samuel Brown and wife Elizabeth to Elisha Perkins of Craven County S.C. 144 acres west side Catawba River. Granted 7 Jan1761 (#1 above). Proved May Court 1774. Rowan Co.

5. John Perkins, a Burke entry shows, entered land formerly deeded to Samuel Brown -- 740 acres south side Catawba "on Brown's Creek", adj. to Perkins land and that of Andrew Fullbright (32 above ?).
6. William Davidson, in a 1778 Burke County entry, entered land on Glady Creek, 350 acres including "old improvements by Samuel Brown". (Land records suggest Brown selling out to Perkins c. 1774 and then heading west into what is now McDowell County and then into South Carolina).

REFERENCES

Draper, Lyman C. Kings Mountain and Its Heroes Reprint copy of original 1881 edition, Baltimore GPC 1967 pp. 136-139.
Burke County land records by Huggins, Edith Vols I-II 1977.
Fanning, David "The Narrative of Colonel David Fanning" Reprint of 1865 edition, Reprint Co., Spartanburg, S.C. 1973 p.6.
Rowan County "Abstracts of Minutes of the Court of Pleas and Quarter Session" 1763-1774. Abstracted by Jo White Linn 1979, Salisbury, N.C.
"Abstracts of the Deeds of Rowan Co., N.C." 1753-1785. Abstracted by Jo White Linn, Salisbury, N.C. 1983.
Clark, Mertie June Loyalists of the Southern Campaign In The Revolutionary War Vol I GPC Baltimore 1981.

BROWN, THOMAS

SUMMARY OF EARLY LIFE

During the Revolutionary period, Thomas Brown was living in Western Burke Co., now McDowell County. Neighbors included William and John Davidson. There were improvements by Joseph and Jacob Brown, possibly relatives.

SUMMARY OF PARTISAN ACTIVITY

In late 1782, as a consequence of the Confiscation Acts, Thomas Brown was cited to appear in Burke County Court on charges of being a Tory. He was to show cause as to why his property should not be confiscated, for being disloyal to the American cause.

SUMMARY OF LATER LIFE

A Thomas Brown died in Burke Co. prior to 1797, the date of inventory and estate process by the Courts. Another Thomas Brown is listed on subsequent records.

LAND HOLDINGS AND TRANSACTIONS

1. 400 acres Burke Co. both sides of the Catawba River and including a portion of Cane Creek near Sidwell's Ford, adj. to land of John Davidson.
Ent. Nov 16,1778 #1042 Grant No. 1041 Iss. Aug 7, 1778
Book 65 p. 396.
2. 331 acres Burke Co., N.C. on both sides of Catawba River bounded on east by William Davidson and on the west by John Davidson. The land originally belonged to William Latta (purchased from Col. Osborne) and contained improvements of both Joseph and Jacob Brown.
Ent. 16 Oct 1778 # 902 Grant No. 1384 Iss. 16 Nov 1790
Book 77 p. 150.

REFERENCES

Burke County Records, Huggins Vol I-II&III
Land Grant Data, Burke County, N.C. Morganton/Burke Library Morganton, NC.
AIS Census Indices

BIGGERSTAFF, JOHN (Bickerstaff)

SUMMARY OF EARLY LIFE

John Biggerstaff, according to DAR Records, was born 1720. He was probably related to Samuel and Aaron Biggerstaff of Rutherford County, N.C. (Loyalists). John Biggerstaff, at the beginning of the Revolutionary War, was living on Clark's Little River (now East Caldwell-Alexander Counties, NC). He was living in the area as early as 1763, according to Rowan County records.

SUMMARY OF PARTISAN ACTIVITY

John Biggerstaff was one of the early members of the Rowan Co., NC Committee of Safety. He appears in the September 1774 minutes.

In 1776, Biggerstaff received a commission as an Ensign in the N.C. Continental line, 2nd Regiment. He was subsequently promoted to Lieutenant. Later in the war, Biggerstaff served as a Captain of militia in Lt. Col. Robert Holmes' Regiment of Burke militia. Much of his company's activities were directed against local Loyalists.

SUMMARY OF LATER LIFE

According to DAR records, Biggerstaff was married to Cynthia Pollard. Biggerstaff was involved in several court cases in Burke county between 1783 and 1789. He also served on several juries. John Biggerstaff died c. 1800.

LAND HOLDINGS AND TRANSACTIONS

1. Burke County, NC 50 acres on branch that flows into Clark's Little River (upper Little River), north side, above Scott's development. c.c. John Dacear and William Constable. Ent. 29 December 1778 #1367 Grant. No. 679 Iss. 11 Oct. 1783 Book 50 p. 252
2. Burke County NC 100 acres on both sides of the main fork of Clark's Little River (upper Little River), including Scott's improvement. Ent. 29 Dec.1778 #1366 Grant No. 663 Iss. 11 Oct. 1783 Book 50 p. 244 c.c. William Daifer, William Constable.

Biggerstaff purchased in 1763, 120 acres on Third Creek in Rowa County, NC from Matthew Long, but sold it later in the same year to William Armstrong.

CENSUS LOCATIONS

None listed.

REFERENCES

Colonial and State Records of North Carolina.
IX p. 1073,1074 (Goldsboro and Raleigh 1909)
Huggins, Edith Burke County Records Vol III
Dar Patriot Index National Society DAR, Washington 1966 p.59
N.C. Revolutionary Army Accounts: 1. Vol V p.175 #370
2. Vol I Book 5 Folio 32 #1949
3. Vol IV Book G Voucher 370.
(Above from Haun, Weynette P., N. C. Revolutionary Army Accounts Durham 1990, 1992).
Burke County NC Land Records Morganton Burke Library
   Morganton, NC.
U.S. National Archives Revolutionary War Pension Declarations
   of John Chapman, Adam Rainboult, Samuel Steele.
Roster of Soldiers from North Carolina in the American Revolution
N.C. DAR Reprint issue 1967. (original 1932) pp. 29,210
Linn, Jo White, Abstracts of the Deeds of Rowan County, NC.
   (Salisbury, NC 1983)
   175301785 pp. 65, 145.
→

BURCHFIELD, JOHN

SUMMARY OF EARLY LIFE

John Burchfield was born in Guilford County, NC June 6, 1765. was living in Burke County, NC at the time of the American Revolutionary.

SUMMARY OF PARTISAN ACTIVITY

John Burchfield first entered Revolutionary service in April 17 under Capt. Joseph McDowell, Lt. Joseph McKinzie and ensign Her Highland. He marched from Burke County NC to Ninety Six, SC ar from there to White Ponds. Later his unit joined with Gen, Daniel Morgan's troops in early 1781. On January 17, 1781 Burchfield fought in the battle of Cowpens. During this engagement, he received a sword wound of the forehead. After t battle he recalled seeing Col. William Washington and General Morgan. They had come to "view the wounded". He also stated that Highland was appointed Captain after the battle. Under Highland he marched back to Quaker Meadows and was discharged having served ten months. His final tour of duty was served on the Catawba frontier as an Indian spy or scout. He served in t Turkey Cove area of the North Catawba at Wofford's Fort. His commanding officer was Capt. William Johnson.

SUMMARY OF LATER LIFE

John Burchfield applied for Revolutionary War pension in Frankl County, Indiana February 14, 1833 at age 67 years. In his declarations, he stated that after the Revolution he lived for thirteen years in Abbeville District, SC and then for twenty-or years in Warren County, KY. He said that he moved to Indiana i 1812 having lived first in Rush County and then in Franklin County. He was awarded a Federal pension of $32,66 per annum.

John Burchfield married on December 22, 1815, Mary Patterson. her later pension declarations she stated that John Burchfield also served in the War of 1812, first as a Private and then as Sergeant. (18th Regiment, Capt. Henry C. Guest). John Burchfie died in Jefferson County, Indiana December 28, 1849. His widow gave her age as 52 years when applying for a pension in Septemb 1850. She was residing in Hamilton County, Ohio, but applied i Dearborn County, Indiana.

CENSUS LOCATIONS

1790 Pendleton County, SC (?)
1800 Pendleton County, SC (?)
1810 Warren County, KY
1820 Owen County, KY
1830 Franklin County, IN

REFERENCES

AIS Census Indices
US National Archived, Pension Data, # W8175

BURCHFIELD, MESHACK

SUMMARY OF EARLY LIFE

Meshack Burchfield was born in Baltimore County, MD in 1762. When a child, he came with his father and family to Burke County NC, near Pleasant Gardens (now McDowell County, NC).

SUMMARY OF PARTISAN ACTIVITY

Meshack Burchfield first entered military service in western Burke County in the summer of 1776 at about age 14 or 15. The Indians had broken through on the Catawba frontier, killing 30 or 40 settlers. Burchfield was joined together with the remainder of the inhabitants and sent to Quaker Meadows, home of Col. Charles McDowell. Later he was stationed at Cathey's Fort on the North Catawba. He remained here on garrison duty at the time of Rutherford's Cherokee Expedition of August and September 1776. Burchfield then served intermittently on the Catawba frontier as an Indian scout or "spy". He served on two punitive raids against the Cherokees, headed up by Maj. Joseph McDowell.

In early 1780 Burchfield enlisted in the horse company commanded by Capt. Robert Patton. They left Burke County and advanced toward Charleston. Later they joined in with troops commanded by Gen. Huger.

Burchfield stated in his pension declaration that they arrived near the outskirts of Charleston at about the same time that Cornwallis had arrived with his troops. On April 14, 1780, Huger's forces were overwhelmed by the attacking British under Tarleton, Webster and Ferguson. The Americans were thrown into confusion and scattered. The attack occurred in the pre-dawn hours. Later Several of the troops, including Burchfield, attempted to join up with the horse Company of Col. William Washington. By the time they arrived at his camp, he had left.

Burchfield then went to Camden, S.C., joining the militia units of Col. Charles McDowell and Gen. William Caswell. They again advanced toward Charleston to Wateree River and encamped. They were here when Charleston surrendered on May 12, 1780. After the surrender they retraced their steps to Camden and were joined by soldiers of Abraham Buford's command. Upon hearing of the British advance, the Americans decided to split - Buford continuing due North - Caswell and McDowell to the east toward Cross Creek. (The British chased after Buford, allowing McDowell and Caswell to go uncontested to Cross Creek. Buford was later defeated at the Waxhaws). The American forces, according to Burchfield, numbered about 1800 men (before they separated).

Continuing westward from Cross Creek, McDowell and his men arrived at Ramsour's Mill just after the battle of June 20, 1780 From Ramsour's, the soldiers then returned to Burke Court House. After a few weeks, Burchfield joined in with those militiamen crossing "the ridge" into Watauga. Later he took part in the Kings Mountain Campaign, culminating in the battle of October 7, 1780. Burchfield mentions the taking of many persons and names three of them. Col. (Ambrose) Mills, John McFalls and William Douglas.

Burchfield, in the spring of 1781, accompanied Joseph McDowell on a Spring Cherokee raid. He stated that there were about 180 soldiers engaged. (This might have been the raid of March 1782). While in Watauga on a business trip in 1782, Burchfield joined up with a unit commanded by Col. John Sevier and Maj. Tipton. On a two month tour, they were engaged against the Chickamaugas near Tellico, killing about 100 Indians.

SUMMARY OF LATER LIFE

Meshack Burchfield's name was present in several Court Records in Burke County extending from 1792-1798.

Meshack Burchfield applied for Revolutionary War pension in Marion County, MO on May 7, 1833. He was then age 71 years. He was awarded a pension of $69.72 per annum.

LAND HOLDINGS AND TRANSACTIONS

Burke County, N.C. 1793 Tax Lists show Meshack Burchfield with 240 acres, Capt. Casion's Co.

CENSUS LOCATIONS

1790 Burke County, NC
1800
1810 Warren County, KY
1820 Warren County, KY
1830 Lincoln County, MO

REFERENCES

U.S. National Archives Pension Data # S 16668
AIS Census Indices
Land Grant Data, Morganton-Burke Library, Morganton, NC
Huggins, Edith, Burke County Land Records, Vol. II p. 128

BURCHFIELD, NATHAN

SUMMARY OF EARLY LIFE

Nathan Burchfield settled in upper Burke County, N.C. on a branch of Linville River. He was a close neighbor of Greenberry Wilson. He was father of Revolutionary War soldiers Meshack and Robert Burchfield.

SUMMARY OF PARTISAN ACTIVITY

Nathan Burchfield was a Loyalist of Burke County. In 1782 he was subpoenaed to Burke County Superior Court to show cause as the why his property should not be confiscated, for being disloyal the American cause. Witnesses against him included Col. Joseph McDowell, Joesph Dobson and Capts. James Morris and Robert Patton.

SUMMARY OF LATER LIFE

Nathan Burchfield's wife was Aberilla Burchfield (Eberelia). They were pioneers on the western frontier and there were many stories concerning their encounter with the hostile Cherokee Indians. Apparently Nathan Burchfield was killed by the Indians ca. 1783. Burke Court records mention his administrator, Eberelia Burchfield, April 23, 1783.

LAND HOLDINGS AND TRANSACTIONS

1. Land entry Burke Co., NC #1419 28 Dec 1778. 150 acres on branch of Linville River sd. Br., "empties into river on North Side, joining former entry...". Entry discontinued.

2. Land entry Burke Co., NC #135 200 acres main Catawba River, above James Moffett's, known as "Cormey's Bottom", both sides of river. 5 Feb 1778.

3. Land entry Burke Co., NC #443 300 acres Linville River between Daniel Gowen and Henry Ernest "up Linville River and improvement in possession of Burchfield". 28 May 1778.

REFERENCES

Huggins, Edith, Vol II, pp. 149, 163
Burke County Land Grant Records, Morganton-Burke Library, Morganton, NC

BURCHFIELD, ROBERT

SUMMARY OF EARLY LIFE

Robert Burchfield was born December 18, 1759 on Pipe Cree, Maryland. He and his family were living in Western Rowan County at the commencement of hostilities, later Western Burke County.

SUMMARY OF PARTISAN ACTIVITY

Robert Burchfield first entered military service in the spring of 1776, (his records say 1775, probably in error). He was stationed at Cathey's Fort on the western Frontier and acted as an Indian Scout, or Ranger. He served in Gen. Rutherford's Brigade, Col. Matthew Locke's Regiment and in a Ranger Company commanded by Capt. George Cathey. Other officers were Lt. Robert Scott and Sgt. William Steele. His first tour expired in June, but he re-enlisted the same month for another three month tour. On this assignment he served at Davidson's Fort, again as a frontier Ranger, guarding against the incursions of the Cherokee Indians. He mentions his superiors as being Maj. William Davidson, Capt. Samuel Davidson, Lt. James Davidson.

Burchfield volunteered for a third term of duty in November 1778. This was brought about by the British invasion of Georgia and the threatening of Savannah. He was marched from Salisbury through Charlotte to Camden, SC, over the High Hills of Santee to Eutaw Springs and then to Ten Mile House above Charleston, and finally to Purysburg. Burchfield was part of Rutherford's Brigade, but was later assigned to a Light Infantry regiment commanded by Col. Archibald Lytle of the Continental Line. Other officers named were Maj. John Nelson, Capt. Robert Alexander, Lt. John Baxter and Sgt. Jesse Wethers. There was also Capt. James Richardson.

Initially they worked their way up and down the east side of the Savannah River to keep the British from crossing. Later they crossed the Savannah and joined the American Units under Gen. John Ashe. Burchfield took part in the disastrous defeat of Ashe at Brier Creek by the British on March 3, 1779. Burchfield was forced to swim several streams before finding safety. He rejoined Gen. Rutherford's Brigade and was shortly afterwards discharged home in April 1779 at Turbyville.

Burchfield's next duty was a short tour of one month in November 1781. He fought against the Cherokees (battle of Boyd's Creek) in the area of Tennessee. His superior officers included Col. John Sevier, Maj. Jesse Walton, Maj. Jonathan Tipton, Col William Trimble and Lt.Jesse Wethers.

In May 1782 he was stationed at Wofford's Fort on the North Catawba, again as an Indian Scout or Ranger. His superior officers included Charles McDowell, Col. Joseph McDowell (QM), Maj. Jos. McDowell (P.G.), Capt. James Davidson and his brother Ens. Meshack Burchfield.

His last tour of duty was as a part of a reprisal action against
the Cherokee - who had raided western Burke County. The
Cherokees in this raid had killed Burchfield's father. He gives
the date as March 1783. Officers listed included the McDowells
Maj. Cleveland, Capt. George Cathey, Lt. Thomas Lytle, Ens.
Richard Reed.

Burchfield, in his pension declaration, describes how (in one of
the Indian actions) he ..."killed and scalped an Indian who was
aiming a death shot at one of the American soldiers..."

SUMMARY OF LATER LIFE

Robert Burchfield lived first in North Carolina, moved shortly
after the Revolution to Kentucky and finally to Ripley County
Indiana. He applied for Revolutionary War pension in Riepley
County, Ind. On November 13, 1832. He was awarded $60.00 per
annum.

Burchfield married in March 1787 Elizabeth Hill, daughter of Co
Hill of Rowan County. By this union were the following childre

Mary Roberts	Nancy Whitarn
Sally Kelly	Kitty Smith
Betsy O'Neal	Robert Burchfield, Jr.
John Burchfield	

Robert Burchfield died on October 29, 1844 in Ripley County,
Indiana. His widow, applying for pension in February 1845 gave
her age as 77. She died the same year, September 20, 1845.
Hatcher gave burial site as Whitham Cemetery, Wabash County,
Ind., Brum Township.

LAND HOLDINGS AND TRANSACTIONS

1. Burchfield received an N.C. Land Grant for 350 acres in Burk
County, N.C. on both sides of Isaac Creek, that runs into the
Catawba (on south side), and about "a half a mile from the main
river", including said Burchfield's improvements".
Ent. October 20, 1778, No. 352, Grant No. 208 Book 28, p. 207
Issued March 14, 1780.

2. Burchfield received an NC Land Grant in Burke County, NC for
290 acres on Isaac Creek, adjacent to his own former survey and
near John Olwand's Road.
Ent. November 29, 1778, No. 703, Grant No. 123, Book 28, p. 123
Issued March 15, 1780.

3. KY Deed (Ct. Of Appeals) Henry Co., 1802, 133 acres on
Butler's Fork.

CENSUS LOCATIONS

1790

1800
1810 Franklin County, KY
1820
1830 Ripley County, Indiana
1840 Ripley County, Indiana

REFERENCES

U.S. National Archives Pension Data # R 1444
AIS Census Indices
N. C. Land Grant Data, Morganton-Burke Library, Morganton, N.C.
Hatcher, Patricia L., Graves of Revolutionary War Patriots
Vol. I Dallas 1987 p. 133.

CAPPS, WILLIAM   (Caps)

SUMMARY OF EARLY LIFE

William Capps was a native of Chatham County, NC and was born ca 1764-65 (age 81 in March 1845). By the time of the American Revolution, he was living in Burke County, NC. He seems to have been related to William Capps. Sr. and Barney Capps (a Loyalist of Burke County).

SUMMARY OF PARTISAN ACTIVITY

William Capps was drafted for a 3 months tour of duty in late 1780, McDowell's Burke militia, and placed in a company commanded by Capt. Mordecai Clarke. They marched to Grindall's Shoals on the Pacolet River in SC. They joined with American units under the overall command of Brig.Gen. Daniel Morgan. A few days later they took part in the American military victory at Cowpens, SC (Jan. 17,1781). It is interesting that Capps commented (in his pension declaration) that Capt. Clarke became an instructor in swordsmanship under Col. William Washington.

After returning to Burke Co., Capps served a tour of duty on the Carolina frontier, at Wofford's Fort (now McDowell Co., NC).

His Commander was Capt. James Neill. After serving this tour of duty he migrated to Montgomery Co., VA and again was drafted for a tour of duty. His commanding officer was a Capt. Simpson

SUMMARY OF LATER LIFE

At the conclusion of the Revolution, Capps moved back to Burke Co. for a short while. He then moved to Edgefield District and Greenville District, SC. In the early part of the century, Capps moved to Buncombe Co., NC, later Henderson Co. He remained there for the remainder of his life.

His wife was Nancy Capps. Other members of Capps family listed on military and census records include Hiram Capps, Lucina Hammond
(daughter), Cornelius Capps, Barney Capps, John Capps.

William Capps applied for Revolutionary War pension in 1845 and was awarded a pension in the amount of $20.00 per annum. He died shortly afterwards. Both he and his widow were deceased by 1857.

LAND HOLDINGS AND TRANSACTIONS

Buncombe County NC Deeds
1. 6 Dec 1799   100 ac Green River, State of NC # 711

```
2. 6 Dec 1799   100 ac Green River, State of NC # 711
3. 6 Dec 1799   200 ac Fall Creek    State of NC # 712
4. 6 Dec 1799   200 ac Fall Creek    State of NC # 712
5. 8 Dec 1801   100 ac Big Cove of Green River (Philip Guise
   and wife)
6. 8 Dec 1801   100 ac Green River (Philip Guise & Wife)
7. 23 Oct 1806  200 ac  Green River State of NC # 1310
```

CENSUS LOCATIONS

```
1790   Edgefield Co., SC
1800
1810   Buncombe Co., NC
1820   Buncombe Co.,NC
1830
1840
```

REFERENCES

US National Archives # S8133
AIS Census Indices
Buncombe Co., NC Index to Deeds, 1783-1850 Wooley, J.E.
SHP 1983 p.80

CATHEY, WILLIAM

SUMMARY OF EARLY LIFE

William Cathey was born in Augusta County, VA in 1741. He was the son of Andrew and (?) Rebecca Cathey. He was a brother to Mary, James, Margaret and Ann Cathey.

William Cathey was married c. 1769 to Rebecca Holeman, possibly in Burke County. He was living on the Catawba frontier at the beginning of the Revolutionary War.

SUMMARY OF PARTISAN ACTIVITY

William Cathey was a builder of "Cathey's Fort", a major fronti outpost during the Revolutionary War. Here, William Cathey. joined by his kinsmen and neighbors assisted in the defense of the Catawba Frontier against the hostile Cherokee Indians. The fort played a major role at the onset of the Cherokee War of July and August 1776. It was here that Charles McDowell, along with the frightened inhabitants of the frontier, were sequestered until of General Griffith Rutherford's army. There were numerous incursions during the remainder of the war, requiring constant staffing of the fort. The site of the fort is just north of present day Marion, NC, off US Highway 221.

SUMMARY OF LATER LIFE

William and Rebecca Cathey were the parents of eleven children as follows:
Jacob, John, Thomas, George, James, William, Ann, Margaret, Elizabeth, Sarah and Daniel.

William Cathey died on Richland Creek, Haywood County, NC in 1812, another source says 1814.

CENSUS LOCATIONS

1790 Burke Co., NC 1st Co.
1800 Buncombe Co., NC
1810 Haywood Co., NC

REFERENCES

Cathey, Boyt H., Cathey Family History and Genealogy Vol.I
  Franklin, N.C. 1993. pp. 70-71
AIS Census Indices
Land Grant Data, Morganton-Burke Library, Morganton, NC

CHAPMAN, NICHOLAS

SUMMARY OF EARLY LIFE

Nicholas Chapman was born in 1758 in Baltimore County, Maryland. He was the son of John and Eurith Chapman. By the time of the American Revolution, he had moved to Rowan County, NC. He continued to live there for about eight years following the Revolution. In his pension declaration he makes mention of a "Common Prayer Book as used by the Church of England". He was a brother of John Chapman, Jr., also a Revolutionary War veteran. (See Vol. I).

SUMMARY OF PARTISAN ACTIVITY

Nicholas Chapman entered Revolutionary Service in 1778 as a militiaman in James Nichol's Company of Col. Francis Locke's Rowan Regiment. He enlisted for a term of six months. From Rowan County, they were marched to South Carolina, joining Gen. Benjamin Lincoln's Army. Their Brigade Commander was Gen Griffith Rutherford.

They approached Charleston as the British were threatening the city. Later the British withdrew toward Savannah and the Americans followed. Nicholas was marched first to Purysburg and then to the "Two Sisters". A part of the brigade joined Gen. John Ashe and were in the American defeat at Brier Creek, March 3, 1779. Chapman was in the group that remained at the Two Sisters. He was discharged in early May 1779.

His next tour of duty was in 1781. He served for a period of two months as a wagon driver for the Continental Line. His Commanding officer was Capt. Yarboro of Salisbury.

His final tour of duty was that of a guard, under Capt. John Johnson. He was assigned to guard the prisoners taken by Gen Morgan at Cowpens. From Salisbury, the prisoners were marched north to the Virginia line and turned over to Virginia authorities. Chapman served for about three or four weeks on this tour, "just before the battle of Guilford". (March 1781).

In 1783, Nicholas Chapman was subpoenaed to Rowan Court on charges of being a Tory, and to show cause as to why his property should not be confiscated.

SUMMARY OF LATER LIFE

Chapman lived for about eight years in Rowan County, in Rutherford County for about a year, in Burke County for about three years and then in Lincoln County for about twenty to twenty one years. He finally moved to Burke County and remained there the rest of his life. His wife was Sarah Seely (Sealey) Chapman, daughter of George Seely of Burke County. Nicholas Chapman applied for federal pension in Burke County, NC on July 22, 1833, age about 75 years. He was awarded an annual pension of $20.00

In 1852 a son, James Chapman, was given power of attorney for collecting pension awards due Nicholas Chapman. Other family members named included George Chapman, James Chapman, Robert Chapman, Joshua Chapman, John Chapman, and Mary Hoil (Hoyle) - probably the children of Nicholas and Sarah Chapman. Nicholas Chapman died in Burke County, NC July 25, 1851.

LAND HOLDINGS AND TRANSACTIONS

Deed, Burke County, NC to Nicholas Chapman from John Smith, 100 acres on Sealey's Mill Creek, from Grant of 1796.
Witness: George Chapman, Abraham Hoyle. (From Huggins, Vol.II p.103a).

CENSUS LOCATIONS

1790 Burke County, NC 13th Company
1800 Lincoln County, NC
1810 Lincoln County, NC
1820 Burke County, NC
1830 Burke County, NC
1840

REFERENCES

U.S. National Archives, Pension Statement, No. 58193
Chapman, Thomas C., Article on Nicholas Chapman in The Heritage of Burke County, Winston Salem, 1981,pp.138-138.

CLARKE, ALEXANDER

SUMMARY OF EARLY LIFE

Alexander Clarke lived in the Alamance area of old Orange County, NC prior to the Revolution. Shortly after the battle of Alamance in 1771, he came to western Rowan County in company with Veazey Husbands. He settled in the Lower Creek area (later Burke, now Caldwell County). He apparently was a "Regulator" along with Husbands. During the Revolution, he was a Loyalist.

SUMMARY OF MILITARY SERVICE

Alexander Clarke was subpoenaed in Burke County Court to show cause as to why his property should not be confiscated ... for being disloyal to the American cause. November 12 session, 1782. Witnesses against him were Benjamin White, James Taylor White.

SUMMARY OF LATER LIFE

Clarke settled on Little's Fork of Lower Creek. He was the father of Jeremiah Clarke, a well known Loyalist. Also father of Cornelius Clarke?

LAND HOLDINGS AND TRANSACTIONS

Alexander Clarke received a NC Land Grant for 318 acres of land on Husband Creek adjacent to land belonging to Henry Pearson, Thomas Whitson, Thomas Littlejohn; c.c. Thos. Littlejohn, Abraham Littlejohn.
Ent. December 19, 1778 No. 1372, Grant No. 1181, Iss. May 18, 1789, Book 71 p. 51.

REFERENCES

Article in The Heritage of Caldwell County (Winston Salem) 1983. Rev. I.W. Thomas pp. 290-291
Huggins, E. W. Vol. II, p. 148

CLARKE, JEREMIAH

SUMMARY OF EARLY LIFE

Jeremiah Clarke was the son of Alexander Clarke. The Clarkes lived on Husbands Creek, a tributary of Lower Creek. His father was a former Regulator and closely associated with Col. Veazey Husbands.

SUMMARY OF PARTISAN ACTIVITY

Jeremiah Clarke was a member of a well known Loyalist family of Burke County, now Caldwell County, NC. In November 1782, he was cited to appear in Burke County Court as a suspected Tory and to show cause as to why his property should not be confiscated, for being disloyal to the American Cause. Witnesses against him included Silence Fares (Fears), Charles Wakefield.

SUMMARY OF LATER LIFE

Jeremiah Clarke married Eleanor Boone, daughter of Jonathan Boone. They had the following children:

John
Cornelias W., m. Susan Bogle
Nathan
Jehu
Thomas
Morning, m. Levi Hartley
Susan, m. (1) David Crawford, and
        (2) McIntosh, (3) Wilson

Morgan District court records of 1793 mention "heirs of Jeremiah Clarke", indicating that he had died sometime prior to this date."

CENSUS LOCATIONS

1790 Burke Co., NC   ("Eloner Clarke")

REFERENCES

Huggins, Edith. W. Burke Co. Records Vol. I-IV
Burke Co. Land Grant Records, Morganton Burke Library, Morganton NC
Thomas, I.W. Rev., Article in Caldwell County Heritage p. 290-291
Burke Co. Surviving Will and Probate Records 1777-1910, 1983
Turner and Philbeck #104
AIS Census Indices
Morganton District, NC Superior Court of Law and Equity (Edited by W.P. Haun) 1779-1806 (1987)

CLARKE, SAMUEL

SUMMARY OF EARLY LIFE

Samuel Clarke (or Clark) was living in the Lower Creek area of Burke Co., now Caldwell Co. during the Revolutionary period. He was the son of Alexander and Joanna Clarke and a brother of John Clarke.

SUMMARY OF PARTISAN ACTIVITY

According to family members in a Federal Pension application, Samuel Clarke was a private militiaman of Burke Co., NC and served under Major Joseph McDowell and Capt. Peter Fore (or Ford). (See separate biography on Capt. Fore, this volume).

SUMMARY OF LATER LIFE

After the Revolution, Clarke moved to Floyd Co., KY, living there at least 25 years and possibly longer. Earlier in 1792 he had married Margaret Hayes. They were married by Albert Corpening, a Justice of Burke County. Three children are listed. Alexander and Margaret are listed in the pension declaration and Samuel, Jr. in the 1830 Kentucky census of Floyd Co.

The family stated that Samuel Clark was an overseer of the McDowell property, prior to his departure to Kentucky. Samuel Clarke died Nov. 27, 1845. His wife applied for federal pension in 1852 but the pension was disallowed. Note: The failure of Samuel Clarke himself to apply for federal pension during his long life time is itself somewhat suggestive evidence that he may have had some Loyalist leanings.

LAND HOLDINGS AND TRANSACTIONS

1. Joanna Clarke to Samuel Clarke 122 acres Burke Co., NC per deed, 20 Feb. 1793.

2. Samuel Clarke in tax lists, is listed as having 150 acres of land in 1792 and 1795 (Capt. Highland's and Capt. England's Companies).

3. Samuel Clarke to Peter Spainhour 100 acres Burke Co. NC per deed 19 May 1797.

4. Kentucky Land Warrants - Samuel Clarke
    100 acres Little Mud Creek Sept. 1834, Floyd Co., KY
    200 acres Johns Creek 12/24/1835 Floyd Co., KY

CENSUS LOCATIONS

1790 Burke Co., NC 7th Co. (Joanna Clarke)
1800 Burke Co., NC

```
1810    Burke Co., NC
1805    Tenn. Tax lists Grainger and Roane Co's. -- 2 Samuel Clark
1820    Floyd Co. KY
1830    Floyd Co. KY (Samuel Clarke, Jr. also listed)
```

REFERENCES

Caldwell Co. Heritage 1983 Winston Salem, NC article by Rev.
   I.E.Thomas, p. 290-291
US National Archives Pension Data #R2000
Huggins, Edith Burke Co. Records Vols I-IV
AIS Census Indices; Heritage Collection Ky. Census
<u>Early Tennessee Tax Lists</u> by Byron and Barbara Sistler.
   Evanston, Il. 1977
<u>The Kentucky Land Grants</u> by Jillson Part I. GPC 1971 p. 505
Burke County Court Minutes 1795-98 Abstracted by Rev. Dan Swink
   1987.

CLINE, CHRISTOPHER

SUMMARY OF EARLY LIFE

Christopher Cline was born c. 1741, the son of Sebastian (Bostian) and Elizabeth Beaver Cline. The family, of Palatinate origin, moved from Pennsylvania to North Carolina ca 1740. The family settled near Elk Creek in what is now Catawba Co. Christopher Cline, after marriage, moved to Clark's Creed also in present day Catawba Co.

SUMMARY OF PARTISAN ACTIVITY

In early 1782, during the court martial trial of Col. Charles McDowell, there was sworn testimony that Cline had been treated preferentially as a Tory and had been sent on "easy" duty to Fort Charles on the Catawba frontier (stated as "Christian" Cline). In late 1782 his name appears on a Burke County Court Docket as a suspected Tory. Those listed had to show cause as to why their property should not be confiscated, for being inimical to the American Cause.

SUMMARY OF LATER LIFE

Christopher Cline married (1) Margaret Ramsour and (2) ?. _____. Children by his first marriage were as follows:

John b. c. 1763 m. Catherine Shuford
Henry b. c. 1765 m. Elizabeth Carpenter
David b. c. 1769 m. Mary Conrad
Suzannah b. c. 1773 m. John Butts
Leonard b. c. 1775 m. Elizabeth Deal
George b. c. 1777 m. Polly Peterson
Easter b. c. 1779 m. Jonathan Starr
William b.c. 1781 m. Sally Rader

LAND HOLDINGS AND TRANSACTIONA

1. 144 acres Burke C., NC on Clark's Creek adjacent to land belonging to James Hanon, Conrad Burns, Richard West, John Benfield and Samuel Steele. The land included part of the wagon road. Entry states "improvements whereon he lives". c.c. John Benfield, Samuel Steele. Ent. 20 Nov 1779 #1787 Grant No. 792. Iss Nov 9, 12784 Book 57 p. 20.

His father Sebastian Cline had received a Crown Grant for 350 acres on Lyle's Creek, now Catawba Co. Iss. 28 April 1768.

CENSUS LOCATIONS

1790 Lincoln Co., NC 3rd Co.

REFERENCES

Court Martial Trial Minutes of Col. Charles McDowell, from a facsimile given to the author by Miss Eunice Ervin, Morganton, N.C.
Genealogy by articles in Catawba County Heritage (Winston Salem,NC. 1986). by Pansy J. Currin and Martha S. Henry.
Huggins, Edith Burke County Records Vol.II
Hofmann, Margaret Colony of North Carolina 1765-1775 Abstracts of Land Patents. Weldon, NC 1984 p.485
Cline, Ciscero "The Klein or Cline Family" Newton, NC 1915 with additions by JoAnn Mercer 1978 p.3.
→

COFFEY, BENJAMIN

SUMMARY OF EARLY LIFE

Benjamin Coffey was born 1745 in Spotsylvania County Virginia. Later, with his family, he moved to Rowan County North Carolina, later Burke County.

SUMMARY OF PARTISAN ACTIVITY

Benjamin Coffey entered Revolutionary War service in Burke County, NC in 1776 in a company commanded by Capt. Thomas Whitson of McDowell's Regiment. He served on the Catawba frontier guarding against the hostile Cherokee Indians. Coffey also assisted in the building of Crider's Fort on Lower Creek now Lenoir, Caldwell County, NC. Coffey moved from Burke County to Wilkes County during the war. In 1780 he enlisted in Capt. John Barton's Company of Col. Benjamin Cleveland's Wilkes Regiment. He was engaged briefly in subduing Tory activity in Burke and Wilkes Co. In September and October of 1780 he participated in the Kings Mountain Campaign and battle. He was furloughed home about the first of November 1780 because of ankle problems.

SUMMARY OF LATER LIFE

After the Revolution, Coffey moved from Wilkes County, NC to Hawkins County, TN. Coffey applied for Revolutionary War pension while in Hawkins County, TN on May 25, 1833 at age 86 years. He was awarded a pension of $40.00 per annum.

Benjamin Coffey died in Hawkins County on January 4, 1834.

LAND HOLDINGS AND TRANSACTIONS

1. 200 acres from John Dyer both sides of the Yadkin River, Wilkes Co., NC adjacent to land of James Coffey, Thomas Coffey and James Dyer. 6 October 1785.

2. NC Land Grant 88 acres, Stillhouse Branch, Wilkes Co., NC 13 December 1799.

3. NC Land Grant 45 acres South Fork Yadkin, Wilkes Co., NC on Miller's Creek -- Humphries Old Camp. 24 December 1798.

4. 100 acres North side Yadkin River, Wilkes Co., N. C. at mouth of Soloman's Branch adjacent to Michael Israel. 9 March 1780.

REFERENCES

Wilkes County Deed Book A-1, B-1, C-1. 1778-1803 abstracted by Mrs. W. O. Absher of North Wilkesboro.
AIS Census Indices

"Roster of Soldiers and Patriots of the American Revolution Buried in Tennessee". by Bates (March 1979) p. 39
N.C. National Archives Pension Data # S1655

COFFEY, REUBEN

SUMMARY OF EARLY LIFE

Reuben Coffey was born in Albemarle County, VA September 16, 1759. When a young boy of four or five, his family moved to Amherst County, VA. They lived there about fifteen years and moved to Wilkes County, NC, near the head of the Yadkin River. Coffey was living in Wilkes County at the beginning of the American Revolution.

SUMMARY OF PARTISAN ACTIVITY

Reuben Coffey first entered military service in the Spring of 1780, in a horse company commanded by Capt. Moses Guest. Other officers included Lt. Thomas Ferguson, Major Hartgrove, Major Joseph Winston, Adjutant Jesse Franklin and Col. Benjamin Cleveland.

Under Guest, they marched to Ramsour's Mill, arriving there a day after the battle of June 20, 1780. His regiment then returned to Wilkes County and was engaged in local anti-Tory activity. In September and October 1780, they joined with the Over Mountain men headed by John Sevier and Isaac Shelby. Coffey marched with them and on October 7, 1780 participated in the great American victory of Kings Mountain, SC.

Coffey, after the Battle, was a witness to the hangings at Bickerstaff Old Fields. Nine Tories were hanged, three at a time. On the march back toward the Moravian Towns, Coffey and several others were detached to serve against local actions by Loyalists. They were commanded by Ens. Benjamin Guest. They were engaged against Tories in Guilford County, at Hunting Creek in Rowan County, in the hollows of the Yadkin in Surry County and in Wilkes and Burke Counties. He was discharged at his home in Wilkes County by Capt. Guest after having served for at least a year.

SUMMARY OF LATER LIFE

Reuben Coffey continued to live in Wilkes County for several years. He moved to Burke County and lived there for twenty two years. Finally he moved to Wayne County, KY. Coffey applied for Revolutionary War pension in Wayne County, Ky on August 28, 1832, age 72 years. He was awarded a pension of $40.00 per annum. Reuben Coffey was married to Sally Scott. He died March 24, 1842.*

*Another Reuben Coffey died in Burke County, NC prior to 1817, date of will probate, Exec. Jesse Coffey, Witness, Jason Gragg.

LAND HOLDINGS AND TRANSACTIONS

1. Reuben Coffey received a Burke County, NC land grant for 250

acres of land on Coffey's fork of Johns River in an area called the "Little Globe". Chain carriers were Jesse Moore and John Sellars.
Ent. Dec 7, 1779, # 1701, Grant No. 1289, Iss Nov 16, 1790
Book 77, p. 126.

2. Coffey received a Burke County land grant for 40 acres of la on Lower Creek. The land was adjacent to land belonging to Jas Greenlee, Elias Powell, Jr., Samuel McDaniel and John McGimpsey
Ent. Oct 4, 1798, # 3448, Grant No. 2639, Iss. Dec 6,1799
Book 107, p. 33.

3. 100 acres of land in Burke County, NC on Chestnut Mountain a the head of Steppe's Creek, joining the Wilkes County Line.
Ent. Dec 1, 1826, # 9090, Grant No. 5321, Iss. Dec 13, 1828.

4. 80 Acres Wilkes Co., NC, deed from Benj. Coffey S. Side Yadk River, Warrior Fork, Absher Deed Abstract. 55 Deed BK. A1/139 1 Oct 1789.

5. 40 acres Wilkes Co., NC deed from Robert Whitesides south si Yadkin River, Mouth Warrior Fork, 4 Nov 1788 Deed BK. A1/145 Absher Deed Abstr./56.

6. Sale of land to Abraham Strange 28 Jul 1794 40 acre tract, above A1/417-418.

7. Sale of land 120 acres, part of tract inherited from his father, Jas. Coffey, to Ambrose Coffey 20 Nov 1795. Deed BK A1/384, Wilkes Co., NC

CENSUS LOCATIONS

1790 A Reuben Coffey listed in Burke Co., NC 5th Co. And in
     Wilkes Co., NC 1st Company
1800 Burke County, NC
1810 Burke County, NC
1820 Burke County, NC
1830 Wayne County, KY (A Reuben Coffey and Reuben Coffey, Jr.
         Listed in Burke County, NC)
REFERENCES

DAR Patriot Index Washington 1966 p. 141
U. S. National Archives, Pension Data # S 46916

CONRAD, RUDOLPH

SUMMARY OF EARLY LIFE

Rudolph Conrad was living in Eastern Burke County, (now Catawba County), during the Revolutionary period. He resided on Pinchgut Creek.

SUMMARY OF PARTISAN ACTIVITY

Rudolph Conrad was commissioned by the Rowan County Committee of Safety early in the war. He was made a Capt. of a militia company in the Second Rowan Regiment under Col. Christopher Beekman and Lt. Col. Charles McDowell. Subaltern officers who served under him were John Sigman, Jr. and B. Smith.

In March of 1776, he led his company on the Cross Creek Expedition against the Tories of the southeastern part of the state. This action finalized the Moore's Creek Bridge campaign in which Loyalist activity in that part of the state was suppressed.

In the summer and fall of 1776 he again led his company in the Cherokee Expedition of Gen. Griffith Rutherford. This action lasted about two months.

After the creation of Burke County from Rowan in 1777, Conrad continued on in the Burke Militia under Col. McDowell. In 1781 he was acting as a deputy contractor for military supplies. He testified in the Court Martial action of Col. McDowell in early 1782.

SUMMARY OF LATER LIFE

Rudolph Conrad was married to Christiana Stockinger. The 1790 and 1800 censuses list three minor boys and one girl. DAR records show two earlier marriages to (1) Catrout Shuford and (2) - Shell.

Conrad was active in Lincoln County Court actions in and about the turn of the century. He served on jury duties and also as a Constable.

LAND HOLDINGS AND TRANSACTIONS

1. Burke Co., NC 200 acres on Wortman's Branch adjacent to land belonging to George Lutes (Lutz), formerly George Hefner's. (near Pinchgut Creek, now Catawba Co.) c.c. John Hasselbarger and Peter Eigert, Jr. (Icard). Ent. 11 Dec 1778 #1169 Grant No. 410 Iss. 28 Oct 1782 Book 44 p. 166.

2. Burke Co., NC 321 acres on N. side Pinchgut Creek adjacent

to land of George Lutes (Lutz), Bullingers, Hose (Haues) and to his own land. c.c. Jacob Lutes, John Arnts.
Ent. 11 March 1779 #1171 Grant No. 147 Iss. March 15, 1780 Book 28, p. 146.

3. Lincoln Co., NC sale of land to Conrad Tipps 400 acres 13 Aug 1791.

4. Lincoln Co., NC purchase of land from Richard West 250 acres 2 Sept 1790.

5. Lincoln Co., NC sale of land to Henry Shell 250 acres 2 Oct 1792,

CENSUS LOCATIONS

1790 Lincoln Co., NC 1st Co.
1800 Lincoln Co., NC

REFERENCES

US National Archives, Pension statements of Andrew Shook, Conrad Tippong, Jacob Tipps, Philip Anthony.
DAR Patriot Index p. 149 (National Society DAR, Washington, D.C. 1966)
Burke Co., NC Land Grant Data, Morganton Burke Library, Morganton, NC
Lincoln Co., N.C. Minutes of Quarterly Courts as summarized by McAllister-Sullivan, Lenoir, NC 1789-1796 and 1796-1805 (1987-88).
Revolutionary Army Accounts, Journal "A" Cross Creek Expedition as edited by Weynette P. Haun, Durham, NC 1989 p. 5
Huggins, Edith W., Burke Co. Records 2 Vols. I-IV SHP 1987.

COOK, ISAAC

SUMMARY OF EARLY LIFE

Isaac Cook was born in Charlotte County, VA in 1759. He was living in Wilkes County, NC at the beginning of the Revolutionary War. He had moved there with his parents at about age 13 or 14 years.

SUMMARY OF PARTISAN ACTIVITY

Isaac Cook first entered military service as a militiaman in Benjamin Cleveland's Wilkes Regiment. He entered as a substitute and later as a volunteer.

His initial tour was served in a light horse company commanded by Capt. John Cleveland and Lt. Thomas Isbell. Other regimental officers included Col. Elisha Isaacs and Major Francis Hardgrove. Cooks outfit was mainly engaged in action against local Tory opposition. In this tour, there were skirmishes on two occasions near the Deep River. Several prisoners were taken. He served in a second tour as a voluntary militiaman under Capt. John Keys and Lt. Thomas Isbell. Other officers included Capt. Samuel Johnson, Capt. Beverly and Lt. Samuel Merrell. Again, their activities were directed against the Deep River Tories. He also served as a guard. He was guarding prisoners at the time of the Shallowford Ford skirmish in October 1780. (Surry County). He mentions in his pension declaration that a Col. Elrod of the Tories was killed. Cook was stationed for a while at the home of Major Micajah Lewis on the Yadkin River in Surry County.

SUMMARY OF LATER LIFE

Isaac Cook continued to live in Wilkes County until just before the turn of the century. He then moved to Burke County, NC and lived there until about 1830. In his old age, he moved to Yancey County, on the South Toe River.

Isaac Cook applied for Revolutionary War pension in Yancey County, N.C. June 21, 1834 at "about age 75." Pension claim was rejected. An appeal apparently was being filed in 1852 by a daughter, Elerner Riddle. She was listed as "daughter of Isaac Cook, deceased."

LAND HOLDINGS AND TRANSACTIONS

1. Wilkes Co., NC Deed records show sale of 75 acres on Beaver Creek, part of a 150 acre tract received from John Cook (dec)...grant, adjacent to land of Thos. Lewis. Deed Bk. B1/349-50. Abstract by Absher p. 74. Oct 29, 1784. Remainder of tract, 75 acres, conveyed to Martha Dotson on Aug 12, 1794. Deed Bd B1/514, Absher p. 89.

2. Wilkes Co., NC, NC Land Grant, 100 acres on Swan Creek

1 Feb 1803 #2504, conveyed by deed to James Denny 7 Nov 1807. Absher p. 281, Deed Abstracts Book F1.

CENSUS LOCATIONS

1790 Wilkes County, NC 9th Company
1800 Burke County, NC
1810 Burke County, NC (Cooke)
1820 Burke County, NC
1830 An Isaac Cook listed in Macon County, NC but
     none in Burke or Buncombe Counties.

CRESSON, ANDREW (Crisawn, Creasman)

SUMMARY OF EARLY LIFE

Andrew Cresson was born ca. 1750. At the beginning of the American Revolution, he was a resident of Surry County, NC.

SUMMARY OF PARTISAN ACTIVITY

Andrew Cresson first entered military service in March 1775. He had enlisted for the duration of the war. He was placed in the North Carolina Continental Line, 4th Regiment. He served in Capt. John Armstrong's Company. The Regimental Commander was Col. Alexander Martin. In 1776, he was transferred to the South Carolina Line, 5th Regiment, Col. Isaac Huger commanding. He was discharged in 1778, and later substituted in the 5th Regiment, Virginia Continental Line, Col. William Russell commanding. He enlisted for a term of three years. He was sent to Charleston, then under siege. He was captured by the British in May 1780. Later Cresson escaped his captors, having remained a prisoner for about six weeks. After returning to North Carolina, he continued to serve in the North Carolina Continental Line, Col. Henry Dixon's Regiment. He remained in service until 1782. Cresson, in his pension statements, stated that he took part in the following battles, Camden (Aug 16, 1780), kings Mountain (Oct 7, 1780), Guilford Court House (March 15, 1781) and Eutaw Springs (Sept 8, 1781).

SUMMARY OF LATER LIFE

Andrew Cresson married Lucy _____. By this union were the following children: Josiah, John, Nancy, Rebecca, David, Polly (m. William Walker), Thomas, and Elijah.

Andrew and Lucy Cresson were married in Orange County. Later they lived in Surry County. From Surry County, NC they moved to Burke County, remaining there the remainder of their lives. Andrew Cresson died in 1824. Lucy Cresson died on November 1, 1843.

Andrew Cresson had applied for Revolutionary War pension in Burke County NC on October 22, 1820. He was awarded an annual pension of $96.00 per annum. At that time he was age 69, his wife age 58 years. At the time of his pension application, Cresson stated that he was old and infirm and unable to work. They lived on the farm belonging to his son-in-law (William Walker).

CENSUS LOCATIONS

1790
1800 Burke County, NC
1810 Buncombe County, NC (Andrew Crisson)
1820 Rutherford County, NC

REFERENCES

AIS Census Indices
U.S. National Archives, Pension Data, # W 6767
Moss, Bobby G.; <u>Roster of SC Patriots in the American Revolution</u>
  GPC 1983 p. 217

CULBERSON, DAVID (Culbertson, Cuthbertson)

SUMMARY OF EARLY LIFE

David Culberson was a resident of Burke County during the Revolutionary period. In 1792 affidavits by R. McGomery, J.H. Stevilie and John Carson stated that Culberson "Has lived in Burke County for some time, soberly and honestly".

SUMMARY OF PARTISAN ACTIVITY

David Culberson made application for Revolutionary War final settlement in 1792. Captain Daniel Smith made a deposition confirming the service record of Culberson.

David Culberson joined the North Carolina Continental Line for a period of nine months beginning in late 1778. He was placed in Captain Micajah Lewis' Company of the 4th Regiment. They marched to South Carolina, joining the army of Gen Benjamin Lincoln. On June 20, 1779 he took part in the battle of Stono Ferry, SC. By this time, Culberson had obtained the rank of Sergeant. He was discharged in August of 1779.

SUMMARY OF LATER LIFE

Culberson was a resident of Burke County when applying for Revolutionary War final settlement on July 3, 1792.

LAND HOLDINGS AND TRANSACTIONS

David Culberson received a North Carolina land grant of 50 acres on south east side of Honeycutt's Creek and akjacent to his own land.
Ent. Nov 18, 1840 Grant No. 6064 Iss. Dec 15, 1842 Book 14-8 p.165
1815 Burke County NC Tax lists shows 100 acres on Paddys Creek adjacent to Wm. Cuthbertson, Capt. Morler's Company 1817 and 50 acres Bradshaw's Creek adjacent to William Murphey 1817. Marler's Company.

CENSUS LOCATIONS

1790 Burke Co., NC 1st Co.
1820 Burke Co., NC
1830 Burke Co., NC

REFERENCES

Revolutionary War Final Settlements, NC State Archives, Comptroller's Papers boxes 14-20 as listed in Huggins, Edith Burke County records Vol. II, p. 158
Revolutionary Army Accounts, Vol. II 1792 Box ZZ Voucher #331

CURTIS, THOMAS

SUMMARY OF EARLY LIFE

Thomas Curtis was born in London, PA (Laurel Hills) in 1742. He was living in Hillsborough, Orange County, NC, at the beginning of the Revolutionary War. Census records show a Thomas Curtis (Jr. & Sr.) Of Randolph County, NC

SUMMARY OF PARTISAN ACTIVITY

Thomas Curtis first entered military service in early 1776. He enlisted in Col. James Thackston's Regiment and was placed in a company commanded by Capt. Hugh Tinnin. Thackston's Regiment then took part in the Cross Creek Expedition in February and March 1776. This was the sequel to the Moore's Creek Bridge Campaign and battle of February, 1776. They were joined by the troops commanded by Gen. Griffith Rutherford, conducting "mop-u activities, taking prisoners and conveying them to confinement, etc. Curtis served for three months as a drum major. He makes mention of the British Flag being displayed at Cross Creek. Co Thackston ordered it cut down and the America flag substituted.

The prisoners taken at Cross Creek were taken to Hillsborough a placed under the jurisdiction of Capt. Archibald Lytle. Curtis joined his detachment after his first term had expired. O ther officers included Lt. James Armstrong and Ens. Ralph Williams.

In the summer of 1776, Curtis enlisted in Col. Ambrose Ramsey's Regiment and took part in Rutherford's Cherokee Expedition. Curtis was placed in a company commanded by Capt. William Williams. Curtis makes note in his pension declaration that independence was declared during the assembly phase of the campaign. The regiment was at Hillsborough at the time. Col. Ramsey led his Regiment to Salisbury and then to the head of th Broad River. Here it was learned that enough troops had alread embarked and Ramsey was ordered to march back to Hillsborough a disband. Curtis again served as a drum major.

His next tour of duty was in the summer of 1780. He enlisted as substitute for a Henry Mason. He again joined Col. Ambrose Ramsey's (or Ramsay) Regiment in a company commanded by Capt. James Farguler. Ramsey's Regiment joined Gen. Horatio Gates' command, then headed toward Camden, SC.

At the beginning of the march, Curtis was asked to "give up the drum" and accept a promotion to the Orderly Sergeant. He accepted and served in this capacity for the remainder of the Campaign.

Col. Ramsey's Regiment marched to Lynches Creek, Black Swamp, Hanging Rook, and then to Rugeley's Mill. While at Rugeley's Curtis mentions seeing Gen. Gates, Gen. DeKalb, Gen. Smallwood and Gen. Williamson. At this time he was appointed to inspect some new recruits. Before this could be finished, he stated that he heard the "drum beat of battle." He was ordered to a light infantry group under Gen. Williamson and took part in the disastrous battle of Camden on August 16, 1780. He stated he was near Gen. Williamson when he was killed. After the battle, Curtis, like most of the other participants," made his way home the best way he could." He arrived home on the last day of August.

SUMMARY OF LATER LIFE

Thomas Curtis married Mary Allison of Orange County in 1776. He continued to reside in Orange County for another sixteen years. He moved to the head of the Broad River for a year and then to Burke County, NC. He lived in Burke County thirteen or fourteen years and moved to Buncombe County, then back to Burke County and then to Buncombe County again. Still later he moved to Blount County, TN and to White County, TN. He was living in White County when he applied for Revolutionary War pension in October 1833, at age 92 years. He was awarded $30.83 per annum.

Thomas Curtis died in White Co., TN on June 28, 1836. His widow continued to receive his pension following her application in 1838, at age 80 years.

LAND HOLDINGS AND TRANSACTIONS

Thomas Curtis received the following NC Land Grants:

1. Orange County, 112 acres on lead branch of Lytle River (Little River) "including his improvements."
Ent. Dec 21, 1779, No. 1161, Grant # 554, Book 47, p.330. Iss. Oct 9, 1783.

2. Randolph County, 150 acres on both sides of Carraway Creek.
Ent. # 225, June 1780, Grant No. 197, Book 6, p. 257 Iss. Nov 2, 1784.

3. Randolph County, 250 acres both sides of Carraway Creek.
Ent. # 186, May 10, 1780, Grant No. 145, Book 6, p. 239, Iss. Nov 2, 1784. Adjacent to land of Col. John Collier and Samuel Lowe.

4. White Co. TN (with Wm. Martin & Jas. Allison) 200 acres, May 6, 1828. # 7895 TN Grant Bk. 3 p. 287.

CENSUS LOCATIONS

1790 Randolph County, NC
1800 Burke County, NC
1810
1820 Burke County, NC
1830 Burke County, NC

REFERENCES

US National Archives Pension Data # W 6748
"Roster of Soldiers and Patriots of the American Revolution
Buried in TN." (Bates-March 1979) p. 47
AIS Census Indices
Tennessee State Archives and Library, Nashville   Land Grant Data

DALTON, WILLIAM

SUMMARY OF EARLY LIFE

William Dalton was living in Albemarle County, VA at the beginning of the American Revolution. (He was age 78 in 1832). He was living with his father and family.

SUMMARY OF PARTISAN ACTIVITY

William Dalton first entered military service in 1776 as a private soldier in the Virginia Continental Line. He served a two year tour in Capt. John Moore's Company of Col. Nelson's Regiment. He was marched with his regiment to Fredericksburg, Alexandria, Baltimore and back to Charlottesville. At Charlottesville, they were assigned to duty guarding prisoners at the main barracks. His tour of duty ended in 1778. Some time later, probably 1779 or 1780, his father and family moved to Burke County, NC. ..."in the very hottest part of the Indian and Tory War...".

In Burke County Dalton volunteered as a militiaman serving in Joseph McDowell's mounted battalion. He describes the retreat to the Watauga Settlements at the beginning of the Kings Mountain Campaign, and the re-crossing back into Burke County (Sept. and Oct 1780). In Rutherford County he joined up with a company commanded by John McClain, serving on the Carolina frontier.

In 1781, he became a member of Capt. James McDaniel's company and served at the siege of Ninety-Six, S. C. in June 1781. He, in his pension declarations, described how he suffered from heat and cold, and that it "settled in his bones".

SUMMARY OF LATER LIFE

From census records, it appears that William Dalton was living in Rutherford County, N.C. after the Revolution. William Dalton applied for federal pension living in Rutherford County, N.C. in 1832. He was awarded a pension in the amount of $80.00 per annum.

CENSUS LOCATIONS

1790 Rutherford Co., NC (1st Co.)
1800 Rutherford Co., NC
1810 Rutherford Co., NC
1830 Rutherford Co., NC

REFERENCES

US National Archives Pension Data #S8295
AIS Census Indices

DAVIDSON, JAMES

SUMMARY OF EARLY LIFE

James Davidson was born in 1741, Rockbridge County, VA and was the son of Pioneer Samuel Davidson. He was a brother of Benjam. Davidson and a first cousin of George, Samuel and William Davidson. The Davidsons were early settlers of the upper Catawb River Frontier.

SUMMARY OF PARTISAN ACTIVITY

James Davidson was commissioned a Captain in Charles McDowell's Burke County Militia. He was stationed on the Catawba River frontier, guarding against the incursions of the hostile Cheroke Indians. Capt. Davidson, at various times, was in command at Fort Charles, Wofford's Fort, and Davidson's Fort.

In 1781, he, along with Capt. William Neill of Burke County brought charges against their commanding office, Col. Charles McDowell. Based on these charges, McDowell was court martialed in early 1782. According to Davidson, McDowell showed partiali in the treatment and sentencing of Loyalists. He also related how McDowell used "strong arm" tactics against any opposition to his command. McDowell was convicted and relieved of his comman but later restored to command and promoted (to Brigadier Genera and in command of newly created Morgan District). On creation Burke County from Rowan County in 1777, James Davidson was on a commission to select a site for the new Burke County Courthouse and jail. He was also a Court Magistrate. In 1786-88, he serv as Sheriff of Burke County.

LAND HOLDINGS AND TRANSACTIONS

1. Burke County North Carolina 453 acres north side of Catawba River at the mouth of Buck Creek and adjacent to land belonging to John Carson, John Chambers, Edward Dawson and Elijah Patton. Ent. 9 Oct 1778 No. 413 Grant No. 76 Iss. 20 Sept 1779 Book 28 p.76. C.c. John Carson, William Cathey.
2. Burke County North Carolina 250 acres on Flat Creek, a branc of the Swannanoa River and adjacent to land surveyed by Ephraim McLean on the three forks of the Swannanoa.
Ent. 1783 Grant Iss. 1789.
3. Burke County North Carolina 300 acres on Flat Creek, a tributary of Swannanoa River and at the mouth of a small stream known as Bridge Creek. It lay adjacent to his own property. Ent. 1786 Grant Iss. 1789.
4. Burke County North Carolina 200 acres on Long Branch, a tributary of Flat Creek.
Ent. 1784 Grant Iss. 1790.
5. Burke County North Carolina 640 acres on Swannanoa River at Three Forks, presumably surveyed by Ephraim McLean.
Ent, 1783 Grant Iss. 1792.
6. Burke County North Carolina 100 acres Flat Creek, a tributar

Of Swannanoa River and adjacent to his own land.
Ent. 1784 Grant Iss. 1793.

Buncombe County North Carolina, James Davidson received land grants in Buncombe County between 1787 and 1803. These grants mainly lay on Flat Creek, on French Broad River, Sandy Mush, Swannanoa River, Turkey Creek and Hominy Creek.

CENSUS LOCATIONS

Burke Co., NC 11 th Co.

REFERENCES

Data on Davidson family submitted to Author by George S. Reynolds, Jr. of Tallahassee, FL.
Burke County Land Grant data, Morganton Burke Library, Morganton, NC.
Charles McDowell Court Martial records facsimile presented to Author by the late Miss Eunice Ervin of Morganton, NC.
Buncombe County Index of Deeds 1783-1850 (Wooley-1983)
US National Archives Pension Statements of Arthur McFalls, Andrew Neill.

DAVIDSON, SAMUEL

SUMMARY OF EARLY LIFE

Samuel Davidson was born in Ulster in 1736, the son of John and Jane Davidson. The Davidsons came to this country in ca. 1739 settling in Rockbridge Co., VA on Beverly Patent land. They became members of the Tinkling Springs Presbyterian Church The siblings who came over with Samuel included brothers George and Thomas Davidson along with his twin brother William Davidso In Virginia were born sisters Rachel, Margaret and Elizabeth and brothers Robert and John. John Davidson sold his Virginia lands in 1747-48 and came to Anson Co. (later Rowan then Iredel Co.). He died shortly afterwards and his lands were obtained by the oldest son George Davidson. Jane Davidson, his widow, late married William Morrison.

SUMMARY OF PARTISAN ACTIVITY

By the beginning of the American Revolution, Samuel Davidson had procured land in western Burke Co. at the head waters of the Catawba river. There he erected a frontier fort known as "Davidson's Fort" or "Sam Davidson's Fort". This would be one of the main outposts used against the hostile Cherokee Indians during the war. Here Samuel Davidson was elected Captain of militia in McDowell's Burke Regiment. He subsequent led raids against the Cherokees and against local Loyalists. He shared command of the frontier outpost with Captains Daniel Smith, James McFarland, James Davidson and others. AS late as 1781 Davidson was still conducting forays against hostile Indians.

SUMMARY OF LATER LIFE

Samuel Davidson was married to Mary Smith. The site of Davidson's Fort was at present day Old Fort, NC in McDowell County.

In 1784, Samuel Davidson was killed on an isolated Indian raid. (Or 1783? See entry below)

LAND HOLDINGS AND TRANSACTIONS

1. Burke Co., N.C. 400 acres on Byers Fork of Crooked Creek (now McDowell Co., N.C.) adjacent to land of William McCafferty David Vance and Byers improvements.
c.c. William Woods, Samuel Forgery.
Ent. 12 May 1778 #186 Grant No. 156 Iss. 15 Mar 1780
Book 28 p. 155.
2. Entry of 1 Aug 1783 "The legal representatives of Samuel Davidson deceased 440 acres on Swannano River including his improvement, up and down river for complement". Warrant issued.

REFERENCES

Data on Davidson family submitted to Author by George S. Reynolds, Jr. of Tallahassee, FL.
Burke Co. Land Grant Data Morganton Burke Library, Morganton, N.C.
DAR Patriot Index National Society DAR Washington, D.C. 1966 p.178
U.S. National Archives Pension Records of Josiah Brandon, Michael Cline, John Davidson, Robert Brown.

DAVIS, CLEMENT

SUMMARY OF EARLY LIFE

Before and during the Revolutionary War, Clement Davis was livi
in the western part of South Carolina.

SUMMARY OF PARTISAN ACTIVITY

Clement Davis first entered Revolutionary service in Newberry
District, SC in a company commanded by Capt. Charles King in Co
John Lindsey's Regiment, Brig. Gen. Williamson's Brigade. He
served against the Cherokee Indians in 1775-76.

In 1779 he served in a company commanded by Capt. Levi Cersey,
Casey, of Col. John Lindsey's Regiment. He served in the siege
of Augusta, Ga. And Fort Granby, SC. On his return home he was
made prisoner by the British and Tories under Col. Tarleton.
After his release, he served in 1780-81 in Capt. James Stark's
Company of Col. Jared Smith's Regiment. Overall Commander was
Gen. Nathaniel Greene. He served in South Carolina, and mentio
action at Cowpens (Jan. 17, 1781), Ninety-Six (June 1781) and
Eutaw Springs (Sept. 8, 1781). He was discharged at Dorchester

SUMMARY OF LATER LIFE

Clement Davis applied for Revolutionary War pension in Buncombe
County, N.C. October 17, 1832, age 77 years. He was awarded a
pension of $80.00 per annum.

He moved from S.C. to Lincoln County, NC (Or Burke Co. ? .. See
census records, below) after the war and lived there until 1806
when he moved to Buncombe County, NC. He married in Lincoln
County, Elizabeth Flemming in 1785, (she was age 75 in 1841).

Clement Davis died in Buncombe County NC on October 29, 1838.
His widow continued to receive his pension and was later living
in Cherokee County, NC.

LAND HOLDINGS AND TRANSACTIONS

1. Clement Davis on 1796 Burke County NC Tax lists.. incompl...
prob. Capt. Bradshaw's Co.

2. 100 acres Turkey Creek, Buncombe Co., NC acquired from Goldm
Ingram. Ca. 1805-1806, Book 9 p. 90 (to Reason Davis 1809)

3. 200 acres in two tracts, Flat Creek, Buncombe County, NC fro
Thomas Revis, et.al. June 16, 1814 (6/2/1812) Book G p. 201.

CENSUS LOCATIONS

1790 Burke Co., NC 4th Co.
1800 Burke Co., NC.
1810 Buncombe Co., NC
1820 Buncombe Co., NC

REFERENCES

US National Archives, Pension Data, W4936
Buncombe County, N.C. Index to Deeds 1783-1850, by Jason E. Wooley, Easley S.C. 1983.
Moss, Bobby G. <u>Roster of SC Patriots in the American Revolution</u> GPC 1983 p. 235

DAVIS, SNEAD

SUMMARY OF EARLY LIFE

Snead Davis was born in Prince Edward County, Va. on August 31, 1752. At the beginning of the Revolutionary War he was living with his father in Wilkes County, N.C. on the Yadkin River. He continued to stay with his father off and on throughout the Revolution and for several years after the war. AT the early part of the conflict his father moved from Wilkes Co., NC to Burke Co., NC and remained there for the duration.

SUMMARY OF PARTISAN ACTIVITY

Snead Davis in a nutshell typifies the tough, resilient but affable Revolutionary. In his pension statements, at age 81, he relates in extrodinary detail his Revolutionary duties and exploits -- and there were many.

He first entered military service in the Wilkes County militia in Capt. Richard Allen's Company. He marched with Allen and joined an NC Regiment under Col. Archibald Lytle. They marched to the vicinity of Charleston, SC. His tour apparently expired before the surrender and he returned home in early 1780. After returning home Davis volunteered to serve in the South Carolina State troops under Gen. Thomas Sumter (SC authorities were allowed to actively recruit in NC, offering bounties, etc.). He was placed in Capt. John McKenzie's Company and participated in the military activities in the South Carolina low country near Cooper River, Edisto River and Orangeburg. He was engaged in a skirmish at Monck"s Corner. During this tour he related how, as an orderly sergeant, his group surprised a party of Tories who were "drinking and carousing after having perpetrated outrages". There were seven of them and they killed them all. They released a frightened old farmer and his two daughters who were being held by them. He was wounded twice in this action, once by a rifle butt to the head. Later when engaging some of Lord Rawdon's troops on their way to Ninety Six, he received a saber cut across the side of his head and forehead.

After his tour expired and his wounds were healed Davis went to the High Hills of the Santee below Columbia and enlisted in Capt. Thurman's Company of Gen. Francis Marion's South Carolina Brigade. He described how they routed a British force at Georgetown and how "one officer was dragged down out of a chimney in which he had concealed himself." He served for about five months. After returning home from South Carolina Davis again joined the militia under Capt. Becknel and took part in the King's Mountain campaign and battle of September and October 1780. (The chronology of these events may be somewhat mixed). He witnessed the hanging of the Tories at Biggerstaff's following the battle. He described how Tory Col. Ambrose Mills, before being hanged, "made his wife tie the handkerchief over his eyes"

Davis assisted in escorting the prisoners to the Moravian towns and assisted in conveying the prisoners from Cowpens to Virginia authorities. Afterwards Davis remained in service and was at the battle of Guilford Courthouse on March 15, 1781. About five weeks after his tour expired he joined a Georgia regiment under Col. John Clark and saw action in the Oconnee River section. There was also action against the Indians on the South Carolina frontier at Walton's Station. He served the remainder of the tour as an Indian spy or scout.

SUMMARY OF LATER LIFE

Burke County, NC Court records showed a Snead Davis in Burke County in 1786. Still living with his father after the War he accompanied him to Powell's Valley in southwest Virginia. Davis left his father in Powell's Valley and moved to Warren County, KY. near the Dripping Spring. Tax lists show him being there in 1800. Still later he moved to Livingstone County, KY and applied for federal pension there in 1834. He was awarded a pension in the amount of $92.50 per annum. There was a supporting statement by a fellow soldier of the area, Soloman Hicks. His last known residence was McLeansboro, Hamilton County, Il. in 1837. Also listed was a sister, Polly Adams. He mentions his son John, of Amite County. Ms.

CENSUS LOCATION

1800 Warren Co., KY
1820 Livingston Co., KY

REFERENCES

U.S. Nation Archives Pension Data #S32205
Volken, Lowell 1820 Census Index of Kentucky
AIS 1800 Census Index Kentucky
Moss, Bobby G., S.C. Patriots in the American Revolution, GPC, 1983, p. 239.

DAVIS, SAMUEL

SUMMARY OF EARLY LIFE

Samuel Davis was born October 12, 1753. He was a resident of Albemarle County Va. before and during the Revolutionary War.

SUMMARY OF PARTISAN ACTIVITY

Samuel Davis first entered Revolutionary service in August 1778 in the Albemarle County, Va. militia. This tour was commanded Capt. Isaac Davis. His unit marched from Albermarle County to Williamsburg. They were stationed in the Williamsburg vicinity for the remainder of the tour. He was discharged at Richmond i November 1778.

Davis' next tour of duty was for a three month duration in April 1780. He was marched to the York peninsula, in the vicinity of Half Way House. (between Williamsburg and Hampton). There his unit joined the forces of General La Fayette. There was no significant action during this tour.

His next tour took place in - August 1781. He stated that he joined up ..."soon after Cornwallis had passed through Charlottesville...". Their object was to pursue Cornwallis. Davis' commanding officer was Capt. Robert Sharpe. They followe after Cornwallis, who had taken the Three Notch Road"...toward Richmond. They came up against Cornwallis near Richmond, but were forced to retreat. His unit crossed the Rapidan River at Raccoon Ford, and later countermarched and followed Cornwallis once again. Davis' tour expired at this time and he was discharged.

His last tour of duty began in September 1781. His commanding officer again Capt. Isaac Davis. They again marched to the Yor Peninsula joining the forces of General George Washington. A month later he was present at the surrender of Cornwallis (Oct. 1781), after which he was discharged home.

SUMMARY OF LATER LIFE

Shortly after his war service, Davis moved to Burke County, NC, living there for about thirty years. After being pensioned in Burke Co., he moved to Macon County, NC for about three years a finally to Cass County, Ga. where he spent the remainder of his life (about seven years).

Samuel Davis applied for Revolutionary War pension in Burke County, NC on October 23, 1832. He was awarded $33.33 per annu

Samuel Davis died on October 31, 1838 in Cass County, Georgia. His wife predeceased him. His children included Nathan Davis, Sarah Bright, and Samuel Davis, Jr.

LAND HOLDINGS AND TRANSACTIONS

1. Samuel Davis in Burke Co., NC 1795 Tax Listings is listed as having 200 acres land in Capt. Bradshaw's Co. This would be in the Muddy Creek - Young's Branch area near the Rutherford County line. Same acreage appears later in Capt. Laughron's Co., pre-1800.

CENSUS LOCATIONS

1800 Burke County, NC
1810 Burke County, NC
1820 Burke County, NC
1830 Burke County, NC

REFERENCES

US National Archives, Pension data. No. S2499
AIS Census Indices
Huggins, Edith W., Burke Co. Records Vol. IV pp. 112, 131 (1987)

DAWSEY, WILLIAM SPENCER (also as Dorsey and Dossy).

SUMMARY OF EARLY LIFE

William S. Dawsey was born c. 1760. William S. Dawsey may have been related to an Endymion Dawsey, who left a will in Rowan County in 1777. (The name survives later in Burke County as Dimion.) Early in the Revolutionary period he entered land on the Jumping Run, now Catawba County.

SUMMARY OF PARTISAN ACTIVITY

Wiliam S. Dawsey enlisted an a militiaman in the Burke Regiment in 1782. At this time he was given as being age 22, 5'6" tall, light hair. By occupation he was a farmer.

Dawsey served in Robertson's Company, Burke militia.

SUMMARY OF LATER LIFE

Dawsey served as a juror, Burke County Court in 1796. He is listed on the 1800 census of Burke County. Family members by this name lived south of Morganton and were brick makers. Some were active in the Gilboa Methodist Church.

LAND HOLDINGS AND TRANSACTIONS

Burke County, NC, Ent. 100 acres Jumping Run adjacent to the line of Joseph Lawrence. 3 Nov 1779. Discontinued.

CENSUS LOCATION

1800 Burke Co., NC

REFERENCES

Huggins, Edith W. Burke Records Vol. I &II.
Phifer, Edward W., Burke Morganton 1977 pp.110,249
NC DAR Roster of Soldiers from N.C. in the American Revolution p. 7.
Swink, D.D., Minutes of the Court of Pleas and Quarter Session Burke Co. 1795-98.
Pierce's Register, "Dawsey, William, S." #91424

DEAL, MICHAEL

SUMMARY OF EARLY LIFE

Michael Deal, judging by names in inventory listings, appears to have been related to William, Jacob and Peter Deal. They resided in eastern Burke County, now Catawba County.

SUMMARY OF PARTISAN ACTIVITY

Michael Deal served in the South Carolina regiment of Col. Charles Starke Myddleton. Deal was a dragoon in a mounted company commanded by Capt. Francis Moore. This unit saw service in middle South Carolina during the siege operations in and around Ninety Six, S.C. (June 1781). The record shows that he was dead around August 1781. It should be mentioned that numerous North Carolina militiamen of Loyalist sentiment served in this regiment.

The estate of Michael Deal was inventoried on September 12, 1781 in Burke County Court by Capt. Rudolph Conrad. This would correspond to the death period as given by military records.

REFERENCES

Huggins, Edith W., Burke County Records SHP 1987 Vol. II p.164.
Moss, Bobby G., Roster of S. C. Patriots in the American Revolution. GPC 1983 p. 244.

DEMENT, JOHN

SUMMARY OF EARLY LIFE

JOhn Dement, during the Revolutionary War, lived on a 500 acre tract on Crooked Creek, Burke County, NC, now McDowell County. A Henry Dement also lived in the same area.

SUMMARY OF PARTISAN ACTIVITY

In November of 1782 John Dement was cited to Burke County Court to show cause as to why his property should not be confiscated, for being inimical to the American cause. Witnesse include Jane and Recebba Cooper, Joseph Dobson, Col. Joseph McDowell, Robert Patton and James Morris.

SUMMARY OF LATER LIFE

John Dement apparently died in late 1782, as his will was being probated in the January 1783 Burke County Court. Mary Dement (widow?), James Davidson and George Cathey, Jr. gave administrative bond.

LAND HOLDINGS AND TRANSACTIONS

1. 500 acres Burke County, NC on Crooked Creek, a tributary of the Catawba River, and adjacent to land belonging to George Davidson.
Ent. 20 Oct.1778 #4185 Grant No. 282 Iss. March 15, 1780.
Book 28, p. 281.   c.c. James Forgy, Henry Cross.

2. 100 acres Burke County, NC on Crooked Creek, adjacent to land of George Davidson.
Ent. 20 Oct. 1788 #486 Grant No. 112 Iss. 15 Mar. 1780
Book 28, p. 112. c.c. James Forgy, Henry Cross.

CENSUS LOCATION

1790 Burke County, NC, 4th Company (Mary Dement)

REFEREBCES

Huggins, Edith. Burke County Records Vo. I and II
Burke County, NC Land Grant Data, Morganton Burke Library
Morganton, NC
AIS Census Indices

Eberhart, David (Everhart)

SUMMARY OF EARLY LIFE

David Eberhart was living in Burke County, NC during the Revolutionary period. A Jacob Eberhart, Sr., lived on Silver Creek (Father?). They could possibly be related to those of the same name from Abbotts Creek, Davidson County, NC.

SUMMARY OF PARTISAN ACTIVITY

David Eberhart entered military service as an enlistee in the North Carolina Continental Line in 1778. He served under Col. James Thackston and Major John Armstrong. Their units were marched to South Carolina so as to oppose the threatened British offensive against Charleston. His group took part in the battle of Stono Ferry, SC on June 20, 1779. There were affidavits as to his service by fellow soldier James Mackie of Burke County.

SUMMARY OF LATER LIFE

By 1792, Eberhart had moved to Georgia, Elbert County. Later occurrences of this name is seen in nearby Madison and Hall Counties Georgia.

REFERENCES

Affidavit of Capt. James Mackie as cited in Huggins, Burke County Records Vol. II.
Revolutionary Army Accounts Vol. II, Book 22, No. 339 as cited in Roster of North Carolina Soldiers in the American Revolution NC DAR Reprint copy page 197.
Burke County Land Records, Morganton Burke Library, Morganton, NC.
Haun, Weynette P.," NC Revolutionary Army Accounts, Secretary of State; Treasurer and Comptrollers papers, Vol I, II part II." Durjam 1990. P. 281.

FEARS, EDMUND   (Fair, Fairs)

SUMMARY OF EARLY LIFE

Edmund Fears was living in Burke County, NC during the Revolutionary period. He had received land grants on Jumping Branch, on the north side of the Catawba River.

SUMMARY OF PARTISAN ACTIVITY

Edmund Fears was commissioned as a Lt. and later Captain of militia in McDowell's Burke Regiment.

In the actions preceding the battle of Kings Mountain, Fears and his men joined Col. Benjamin Cleveland's Wilkes Troops. They participated in the skirmish at Lovelady Ford on the Cataw River on September 30, 1780. (near present day Rutherford College, N.C.). During this action, Lt. Larkin Cleveland, Col. Cleveland's younger brother, was badly wounded.

Capt. Fears and his company then joined with the mounted troops of Maj. Joseph McDowell of Burke County. He and his men then fought in the battle of Kings Mountain on October 7, 1780. After the battle, they were witnesses to the trial at Bickerstaff's In Rutherford County (after which several Tories were hanged).

At the conclusion of the war, Capt. Fears was a witness against members of the Murray family. The Murrays were their main antagonists at Lovelady Shoals earlier.

SUMMARY OF LATER LIFE

After the war and for about twenty years or so, Edmund Fears was active in Burke County affairs. He served on various trial juries, on road juries, as a witness in several cases, and on one occasion was involved in a court action against John Murray

At about the turn of the century, Fears migrated to Kentucky, settling on Green River in Casey County.

Edmund Fears died in Casey County ca 1825, Will probate in June 1825. There was a person in Burke County records "Silence Fear his wife?

Children of Edmund Fears were as follows:
Sarah (m Winkler)
Rebeccah (m Gwin)
James (m Elizabeth May)
Edmund (m (1) Sophia Joslin (2) Catherine Bell)
Nary (m Mason)
Hannah (m Smith)
Margaret (m Whittle)

Jane (m Vandaver)
Aaron (m Leah Smith)

CENSUS LOCATIONS

1790 Burke County, NC 7th Company
1820 Casey County, Kentucky

LAND HOLDINGS AND TRANSACTIONS

Burke County, NC, 300 acres north side of Catawba River adjacent to John Knox. The property included portions of Smokey Creek. cc Arthur Hicks, Robert Ballew. Ent. 22 Oct 1778 No. 412, Grant #449, Iss. 28 Oct 1782, Book 44 p 192.

Burke County, NC, 50 acres north side of Catawba River at mouth of the Jumping Branch. cc Arthur Hicks, Robert Ballew. Ent. 31 March 1778, #394, Grant #466, Iss. 28 Oct 1782, Book 44, p 203.

Burke County, NC 50 acres north side of Catawba River near mouth of Jumping Branch.
Iss. 11 Oct 1783.

Burke County, NC, 300 acres on north side of Catawba River adjacent to old surveys of Knox and Harshaw.
Ent. 10 March 1779, No. 1774, Grant #901, Iss. 7 Aug 1787. Book 65 p 354, cc James Prichard, Sr., & Jr.

Kentucky Land Warrants:
A. 18 acres 1820 Green River, Casey County.
   Book H, p 539.
B. 100 acres 1825, Green River, Casey County.
   Book Q, p 412 (Edmund, Jr.?)

Kentucky land grant south of Green River.
A. 200 acres 1798, Lincoln County, (later Casey County)
   Boox 27, p 107.

REFERENCES

AIS Census indices.
Burke County land grant records, Morganton Burke Library, Morganton, NC.
The Kentucky Land Grants Vol (part) I Jillson, Willard R. reprint issue GPC 1971.
US National Archives pension declaration S15305 Ballew, Richard.
Fair, Tim Huntsville, Alabama.
 Data in vertical files, Morganton Burke Library
Huggins, Edith, Burke County, NC records.
White, Katherine K., The Kings Mountain Men, (reprint issue GPC) Baltimore 1970 p.172.
Swink, Daniel D., "Minutes of the Court of Pleas and Quarter Sessions" (1791-1795) and (1795-1798) Burke Co. NC Lawndale, NC

FLEMING, ABRAHAM

SUMMARY OF EARLY LIFE

Abraham Fleming, from land records, appears to have been residing in Burke County, NC (now Caldwell County) on the north side of the Catawba River on Freemason's creek and adjacent to land belonging to John Burke and William James and across from Joseph Ballew (near Castle Bridge). Later, after 1790, he may have moved to the Morganton vicinity.

SUMMARY OF PARTISAN ACTIVITY

Abraham Fleming was cited to Burke County court in late 1782 to show cause as to why his property should not be confiscated for being inimical to the American cause. Witnesses included Ezekial Springfield, William Bailey, Jane and Rebeccah Cooper, Ann Hughes, Francis Kennedy, James Prichard, and John Harper.

There is some evidence that Fleming may have also served on the American side as shown by a later court case involving the delivery of salt near Wilmington on orders by Capt. (Alexander) Erwin (probably relating to the Wilmington Expedition of 1781).

SUMMARY OF LATER LIFE

Abraham Fleming was married to Frances ("Frankey")-. There were older children, Abraham, Jr. and Samuel ? or John ?. The younger children included David, Thomas, Rebecca and Betsy, (all under age 14 in 1799) and Tarleton. Fleming appears to have been a rather substantial citizen. His occupation is listed both as a hatter and a planter. His land holdings included tracts on both sides of the Catawba in eastern Burke County and also land in western Burke. The 1790 census lists him as an owner of eight slaves. His will indicated extensive household and personal property. Fleming was involved in many court cases in the post revolutionary period, mainly involving property. Fleming died, apparently prematurely, in either late 1798 or early 1799. His will was being probated in mid 1799. His widow appealed for financial support for her orphaned children, through the courts as well as guardianship. Heirs listed a Betsy, Abraham, David, Francis, Tarleton, John and Rebeccah Fleming.

LAND HOLDINGS AND TRANSACTIONS

Abraham Fleming received 125 acres on the Catawba River via deed from the estate of Conrad Michael of Rowan County, NC Original owner, Thomas Kerr of Berks County, PA., had obtained the land from Lord Granville in 1761 and sold it to Michael in 1763.

Burke County court records indicate the following deed transactions.

A. William James to Abraham Fleming 70 acres 14 Mar 1796.
B. John Blanton to Abraham Fleming 500 acres 1 Oct 1797.
C. Thomas McIntyre to Abraham Fleming 400 acres 29 Oct 1797.

Land grants as follows:

1. 48 acres Burke County on north side Catawba River adjacent to his own land and that of William James. Grant Iss. 28 Oct 1782, Book 44 p 142. cc John Rutherford and Richard Bryant.

2. 640 acres Burke County on Davidson's Creek adjacent to land of Thomas and Sluyter Bushell. (Bouchelle) Iss. 21 Dec 1798, cc James Harbison and Joseph Curtis.

3. 300 acres in Burke County on Freemason Creek including the Healing Spring. Iss. 7 June 1799, Book 102, p 44.

4. 100 acres Burke County on south side Catawba River near the mouth of Bucks Creek adjacent to the land of Humphry Montgomery. Iss 7 June 1799, Book 101, p 69.

5. 640 acres Burke County on Freemason's Creek on north side of Catawba River. Iss. 12 March 1798, Book 106, p. 393.

6. 300 acres Burke County on north side Catawba River. Iss. 12 Mar 1800, Book 106 p. 395.

CENSUS LOCATIONS

1790 Burke County, NC 7th Co.

REFERENCES

Burke County, NC Land Grant Records, Morganton- Burke Library, Morganton, N.C.
Huggins, Edith W. Burke Co. NC; Records Vols. I-III.
SHP
Phifer, Edward *Burke* 1977 edition p. 391
Swink, Daniel D. "Minutes of the Court of Pleas and Quarter Sessions, 1791-95 and 1795-98". Burke Co. NC, Lawndale, NC 1986-87.
AIS Printed Census Indices.
Linn, Jo White. "Abstracts of the Deeds of Rowan County, NC 1753-1785. Salisbury, NC 1983. P. 122.

FLOYD, ABRAHAM

SUMMARY OF EARLY LIFE

Abraham Floyd was born in Camden area of South Carolina in 1756. He was living in South Carolina at the beginning of the Revolutionary war.

SUMMARY OF PARTISAN ACTIVITY

Abraham Floyd first entered military service in 1776 in a milit. Regiment of Col. Thomas Neel. He served in Capt. William Byers Company. Gen. Andrew Williamson commanded the Brigade. Floyd participated in the Cherokee Expedition of 1776 and was in the skirmish at "Black Hole" in the French Broad basin.

He served a second tour of duty under Capt. (Wm.) McCullough an Major Thomas Ross. At the battle of Brier Creek, Georgia, Marc 3, 1779, Floyd was captured. After enduring great hardships in captivity at Savannah, Floyd managed to escape. He then return to the Camden area of South Carolina.

SUMMARY OF LATER LIFE

After the end of the Revolutionary War, Abraham Floyd moved to Burke County, NC and remained there until after the turn of the century.

In 1801 he moved to Madison County, KY. He stayed there until 1828, when he moved to Decatur County, Indiana. He applied for Revolutionary War Pension in Decatur County on April 28, 1834. He was awarded a pension in the amount of $35.55 per annum.

LAND HOLDINGS AND TRANSACTIONS

1. Abraham Floyd entered 50 acres Burke County, NC on both side of Crooked Creek, a tributary of the Catawba River, "joining own land on North including house he lives in...". Transferred to William Julian. #103 undated, possibly 1788.

2. On 1793 tax list, Floyd id in Capt. Carson's Company (1st Co. Burke County 240 acres.

CENSUS LOCATIONS

1790 Burke Co., NC 1st Co. (Abrm Flord)
1800 Madison Co., HY
1810 Pulaski Co., KY ?
1820 Madison Co., KY (Aron)
1830 Bartholomew Co., IN

REFERENCES

US National Archives Pension Data #S32251

AIS Census Indices
Clift, Glenn "Second Census of Kentucky" GPC 1076
Volkel, Lowell Index 1820 Census of KY Thomson, IL 1975
Smith, Dora W. Kentucky 1830 Census Index, Thomson, IL 1973
Moss, Bobby Gilmer Roster of South Carolina Patriots in the American Revolution GPC Baltimore 1983. Pp. 131,319,611,612,719

FORD, PETER (Fore)

SUMMARY OF EARLY LIFE

During the Revolution, Peter Ford was living near the junction Avington's Creek and Lower Creek, Burke County, NC (Now Caldwell County).

SUMMARY OF PARTISAN ACTIVITY

Peter Ford was commissioned a Captain in the Burke County Militia, Col. Robert Holmes's Regiment. In late 1779, his men were marched to the Charleston area of SC in order to counter t British threat. His duty ended in March just two months prior the surrender in May 1780.

SUMMARY OF LATER LIFE

Peter Ford's name disappears from Burke County records at the close of the Revolution. Though not clear, there are reference to possible estate settlements in 1784 ("Peter Ford administrators William Moreland and wife Sarah vs William Sumpter").

LAND HOLDINGS AND TRANSACTIONS

1. Burke County NC 150 acres pm Avington's Creek, a tributary of Lower Creek adjacent to land of William Sumpter. The land was portion of the tract sold ny William Sharp to William Sumpter, Peter Holt; James Jack.
Ent. 7 June 1778 No. 266, Grant #18 Iss. Dec 10, 1778 Book 28 p 18.

2. Burke County, NC on Avington's Fork and Lower Creek at mouth of Avington's Creek. 350 acres cc Peter Holt, James Jack. Ent. 7 Jan 1778 No. 268, Grant #32, Iss. Dec 10, 1778 Book 28 p. 32.

3. Burke County, NC 50 acres on Lower Creek at mouth of Moses Creek adjacent to his own land. Cc John Bates and John Baddis. Ent. 26 Dec 1778 No. 793, Grant No. 163, Iss. Mar 15, 1780 Book 28 p. 162.

4. Burke County, NC 100 acres on Ross'es Branch that empties int Lower Creek. It included part of a path that led from Craig's place to James's Mill, adjacent to land of Conrad Korns (Kerns). Cc Matthew Sharp, Edward Craig.
Ent. 11 Dec 1778, No. 764 Grant No. 194 Iss. 12 Mar 1780 Book 28, p. 193.

REFERENCES

Burke County NC Land Grant Records, Morganton-Burke Library, Morganton, N.C.
Huggins, Edith W., Burke County NC Records Vol.III SHP 1987

p. 95.
US National Archives, Rev. War Pension Data, Pension Declarations, Sherwood Bowman # S 6678.
Phifer, Edward.   <u>Burke</u> 1977 ed. P. 310 Morganton, NC

FRANKLIN, SR, JOHN

SUMMARY OF EARLY LIFE

John Franklin was born ca 8/1727 - 1730. During the period of the French and Indian War, Franklin was in Virginia and for awhile at a place known as Stump's Fort. Colonial militia records indicate a John Franklin serving in Captain Thomas Waggener's Company 1756-1758. In 1756 he was listed as being a sailor from New England, about 5'6" tall and age 26 years. Family members state that he was of the family of Benjamin Franklin, though this is strongly disputed by a Franklin chronicler, Dorsey W. Franklin.

There is a possibility that he may have lived for a while in Tryon County since a Crown Grant was issued to him on Clark's Creek in 1768. During and after the Revolution, Franklin was living on Lower Creek, Burke County, now Caldwell County, NC.

SUMMARY OF PARTISAN ACTIVITY

John Franklin, Sr. saw military service during the initial phases of the Revolutionary War. In early 1776 he was appointed Adjutant of Christoper Beekman's 2nd Rowan Regiment. He participated in the Cross Creek expedition of March 1776. This was a clean up activity following the battle of Moore's Creek Bridge. After returning home, he again saw service in the Cherokee expedition of mid 1776.

SUMMARY OF LATER LIFE

John Franklin was married to Phoebe Parker (c. 1724 - 1821). By this union were born the following children:

John	Pheba
David	Anna
Moses	Lydia
Jonathan	Mary
Samuel	Rachel
Jemima	

John and Pnoebe Franklin continued to live in the Lower Creek area for the reaminder of their lives. They lived in close proximity to their son, John Franklin, Jr.

John Franklin died probably ca. 1818, as his will was probated i the January 1819 Court. The will was dated 1813. The widow, Pheobe Franklin, lived at least until 1820, the date of her will She also appears on the 1820 Federal census.

LAND HOLDINGS AND TRANSACTIONS;

1. Burke Co., NC; 320 ac on a branch of Lower Creek that said Franklin now lives on including said Franklin's improvements. Th

land lay adjacent to that to that of James McKenney. CC James McKinney, John Franklin, Jr. Entry #330 3 Jun 1778 Grant No. 106 15 March 1780 Bk. 28 p. 106.

2. Burke Co. NC: 200 ac that Franklin purchased from Adam Dayberry (Derryberry). The land was on Lower Creek and adjacent to that of Thomas Wilsher, James McKinney and to his own land. CC John Blackwell, John Franklin, Jr. Entry # 331 19 Oct 1778. D
Grant No. 150 15 Mar 1780. Bk. 28 p, 150.

3. Burke Co. NC; 180 ac Lower Creek adjacent to land of John Franklin, Jr. CC Moses and David Franklin. Entry #911 1 Apr 1789 Grant No. 1478 16 Nov. 1790 Bd. 77 p, 140.

CENSUS LOCATIONS;

1790 Burke Co. NC (7th Co.)
1800 Burke Co. NC
1810 Burke Co. NC

REFERENCES

Clark, Murtie J.; Colonial Soldiers of the South; GPC; Baltimore
  1983 p. 419.
Franklin, T. Earl; Art. In Burke Co. NC Heritage; 1981 W.Salem
  Pp 89-90
Haun, Weynette P., NC Revolutionary Army Accounts Secretary of
  State Durham 1988 p. 4 Journal "A" 1775-1776
AIS Census Indices
Land Grant Data Morganton-Burke Library, Morganton NC
Hofman, Margaret; Colony of NC 17650-1775 Abstracts of Land
  Patents p. 538 Weldon NC 1984.
Turner, Grace and Philbeck, Miles; "Burke Co. NC Surviving
  Will and probate Abstracts 1777-1919" (1983) No. 201
Franklin, Dorsey Wayne; John Franklin/An American Hero and
his Progeny Springfield MO 1987,

FULLWOOD, WILLIAM

SUMMARY OF EARLY LIFE

William Fullwood was born on October 10, 1762 (family Bible say November 10, 1764), in Sumter District, SC, Pudding Swamp on waters of Black River. He was the son of William Fullwood, Sr. and Sarah Fullwood. He continued to live in this area until aft the Revolutionary War. His father was a Major in the SC Troops

SUMMARY OF PARTISAN ACTIVITY

William Fullwood, at about age 17, first entered military servi in the spring of 1780. He, along with about twentyfive or thir others joined the Whig forces then commanded by Capt. John Armstrong and Lt. William Lewis. They were called upon to suppress a body of Tories who had organized in the vicinity of Lynches Creek, SC. Fullwood, in his pension declaration, described in detail as to how they surprised the Tories, chased them for some distance. Later it was discovered that several mounted Tories were nearby. Fullwood volunteered under Lt. Lew to go after them. Instead, they were surprised by several of Tarleton's Dragoons and routed. Fullwood then returned to his home, which was nearby, and later advanced to Brittain's Neck, between the Great Pee Dee and Little Pee Dee Rivers. He joined up with Gen. Francis Marion's troops, staying with them several weeks. After being assigned to a South Carolina division, Fullwood served as a guard at Lenew"s (Lannou's) Ferry, SC. His superior officer was Lt. William Bennett.

His next tour of duty was in the summer of 1780, under Gen. Marion and Lt. Thomas McFaddin. He served south of the Santee River. As Gen. Gates was approaching Camden in August of 1780, Fullwood and several others were ordered to drive a herd of cattle to Gates' Army. They were only a few miles away when the heard of Gates' total defeat at Camden on August 16, 1780. Afte this he "made for home".

Fullwood's last tour of duty was for three months, beginning in the Spring of 1781. He served "south of the Santee" under Gen. Marion, Capt. John Nelson, Lt. McFaddin, Lt. Bennett. Fullwood was appointed quartermaster of Col. Richardson's Regiment. This was his final duty assignment.

SUMMARY OF LATER LIFE

Fullwood continued to live in South Carolina until about age 30 when he moved to Burke County, NC. He continued to live there for the remainder of his life. He was a Clergyman by occupatio (Methodist). William Fullwood applied for Revolutionary War pension in Burke Co., N.C. on January 18, 1844. He was awarded $33.33 per annum.

In a letter written concerning his military service, Fullwood eloquently stated ..."I was trying to guard the tree of liberty, which had been planted by some of the master spirits of our highly favored country...".

Fullwood died after November 4, 1850 (date of last codocil in his will). The children listed in the will include:

Samuel Fullwood
William Fullwood, Jr.
Martha m. William Howard
John M. Fullwood (predeceased his father) m. Elizabeth_____.
Ann m John Estes

No probate given.

LAND HOLDINGS AND TRANSACTIONS

1. Approximately 47 acres on Flat Creek, Buncombe County, N.C. acquired from Towry Ledford and John Lackey in four tracts, Feb. 18, 1807. Buncombe County Deeds, Book 7 pp. 510-515.

2. 385 acres Burke Co., NC by deed from Joseph Dobson. Proved in court on May 5, 1798. 1815 Tax listings show property on Paddys Creek adjacent to land belonging to William Gibbs.

3. 100 acres Burke Co., NC by deed from _____ Baker dated Dec. 20, 1795.

CENSUS LOCATIONS
1790 Clarendon County, SC
1800 Burke County, NC
1810 Buncombe County, NC
1820 Burke County, NC
1830 Burke County, NC
1840 Burke County, NC

REFERENCES

AIS Census Indices
Swink, Daniel D. "Minutes of the Court of Pleas and Quarter Sessions, 1794-98 Burke Co., NC" p. 103. Lawndale, NC 1987.
US National Archives, Rev. War Pension Data # S 18829
Moss, Bobby Gilmer. Roster of South Carolina Patriots in the American Revolution   GPC Baltimore 1983 p. 337.

GASPERSON, JOHN

SUMMARY OF EARLY LIFE

John Gasperson was born in Gloucestershire, England in 1744. At the beginning of the American Revolution, he was soldier in the British army under Lord Howe. He served in the early Campaigns in the Northern Department.

SUMMARY OF PARTISAN ACTIVITY

By 1781, Gasperson had been transferred to the Southern Theater and was stationed at the British Garrison at Ninety Six, S.C. under Col. Cruger. According to Gasperson in his pension declarations, he was treated unfairly by his superiors and subsequently deserted, along with two other soldiers. He went to the Tyger River section of SC, living among the Whigs for about six months. He then migrated to Burke County, NC where he enlisted in a Horse Company commanded by Capt. Thomas Kennedy of Lt. Col. Joseph White's Regiment. The subaltern officer was Lt. Henry "Harry" Highland. Under Capt. Kennedy he embarked on the Wilmington Expedition in the late fall and early winter of 1781, which ultimately freed Wilmington from British. During this action, he took part in the skirmish at the "Brick House" and was wounded by a bayonet.

During the return march, Gasperson along with Capt. Kennedy and several others were captured by the noted Tory Partisan, Col. David Fanning. Gasperson managed to escape (Kennedy was later paroled by Fanning). Lt. Highland and Sergeant Hezekiah Hargraves also escaped with Gasperson.

SUMMARY OF LATER LIFE

After the war, Gasperson lived in Rutherford and Burke Counties NC and for a short while in Georgia and South Carolina. Still later he moved to east Tennessee, first Knox County and finally to Anderson County. He applied for federal pension in Anderson County, TN, August 29, 1832, age about 89 years. He was awarde a pension in the amount of $20.00 per annum. John Gasperson died February 26, 1835.

CENSUS LOCATIONS

1810 Spartanburg Co., SC
1820 Buncombe Co., NC
1830 Anderson Co., TN

REFERENCES

US National Archives Pension Data # S1818
AIS Census Indices
Fanning, David. <u>The Narrative of Colonel David Fanning</u> Reprint from 1861 publication. Reprint Publishers, Spartanburg

GINGER, HENRY

SUMMARY OF EARLY LIFE

Henry Ginger was born in Cumberland County, PA on April 4, 1758. He was living in Pennsylvania during the Revolutionary War.

SUMMARY OF PARTISAN ACTIVITY

Henry Ginger enlisted for a term of three years in 1776, in the fall of the year. He was placed in Capt. Walter Denny's Company of the Pennsylvania Regiment commanded by Col. Butler. Under Denny, they were marched to the Delaware, joining the army of Gen. George Washington. Ginger participated in the crossing of the Delaware. Under Washington he fought in the battles of Trenton, Brandywine, and Germantown. He was with Washington at Valley Forge in the winter of 1777-78. At Doylestown, PA, they were engaged against the British and Indians. Ginger, along with about forty others, was captured. Capt. Denny was killed. Ginger was taken to New York and imprisoned in a church for three months. Later, he was exchanged. This was at the conclusion of his enlistment period and thus ended his military service.

SUMMARY OF LATER LIFE

Ginger remained in Cumberland County, PA for about fifteen or twenty years and then he moved to Burke County N.C., remaining there twelve years. He then moved to East Tennessee, West Tennessee, and finally to Fayette County, IL. (About 1825).

Ginger applied for Federal pension in Fayette County, IL on October 19, 1832. He was awarded a pension of $80.00 per annum.

Henry Ginger married Chauncey Luster before moving to Illinois. He died February 8, 1842. He was buried in the Britton Cemetery southeast of Vandalia, IL, Fayette County.

LAND HOLDINGS AND TRANSACTIONS

Henry Ginger probably lived on or near the western Catawba in the vicinity of Joseph Dobson. His name appears on a Road Committee in that area in October, 1793.

CENSUS LOCATIONS

1790 (Landewich Ginger; Cumberland Co., PA)
1800 Burke County, NC
1810
1820 Maury Co., TN
1830 Fayette Co. IL
1840 Fayette Co., IL .. A Lewis Ginger listed.

REFERENCES

Swink, Dan D. "Minutes of the Court of Pleas and Quarter Sessions", Burke Co., NC 1791-1795 (1986 p. 16)
US National Archives Pension Data S 31064
<u>Soldiers of the American Revolution Buried in Illinois</u> (Springfield 1976) p. 87
AIS Census Indices

GRAY, WILLIAM

SUMMARY OF EARLY LIFE

During the Revolution, William Gray lived on the North bank of the Catawba River, now Caldwell County. He was a neighbor of the Bradshaw family. (See also land entries, South side Catawba River).

SUMMARY OF PARTISAN ACTIVITY

In late 1782 William Gray was cited to Burke County Court on charges of being a Tory and should show cause as to why his property should not be confiscated, for being disloyal to the American Cause. Witnesses included Jane and Rebecca Cooper, Joseph Dobson, Col. Joseph McDowell, Robert Patton and Capt. James Morris.

SUMMARY OF LATER LIFE

William Gray most likely met his demise during the later part of the Revolutionary War as his estate was probated in April 1783. Administrator Lydda (or Lydia) Gray.

LAND HOLDINGS AND TRANSACTIONS

1. In 1778, William Gray entered two tracts of land in Burke Co., NC, Nos. 814 and 815, 30 Sept 1778 on South Side of Catawba River...including "improvements where he live...", including mouth of Cainey Branch.

2. 61 Acres north side Catawba River, Burke County, NC including a small island in the river, adjacent to land belonging to Joel Bradshaw. The property included improvements where a William Bracker once lived. Cc Field Bradshaw, John Gray. Ent 24 Oct 1778 No. 804 Grant #1295 Iss, 22 Aug 1795 Book 88 p.24.

3. 30 acres Burke County, NC on north side of Catawba River including mouth of a branch "where said William Gray then lived...". In survey of description Branch is called "Rock Shole Branch". The land also included an improvement by John Moore. Ent 22 May 1780 No. 951 Grant #1347 Iss 22 Aug 1796 Book 88 p.42

CENSUS LOCATIONS

1790 Burke C. NC 6th Co. (Lydia Gray)

REFERENCES

AIS Census 1790 North Carolina
Huggins, Edity Warren, Burke Co NC Records SHP and Raleigh. Vols I, II.
Burke Co NC Land Grant Records, Morgnton-Burke Library, Morganton, NC

GREEN, JOHN

SUMMARY OF EARLY LIFE

John Green was born on Rocky Creek, State of South Carolina (he was approximately 70 years of age in 1832, when applying for government pension). He moved with his family to Tryon County, NC "as a small child". He returned to South Carolina to enlist as a Revolutionary soldier, at about age 16.

SUMMARY OF PARTISAN ACTIVITY

John Green first entered military service in the summer of 1781 at the Cherokee Ponds in South Carolina. He was placed in Capt Jesse Johnson's company of Col. Samuel Hammond's South Carolina Regiment. Green stated in his pension declaration that he entered service at the "time the British were in the town of Ninety Six"...i.e. June 1781. Green enlisted for a twelve month tour of duty. From the time of his enlistment until 17 Sept. 1781 he and his follow soldiers were engaged in "harassing the British and Tories." At the time of the battle of Eutaw Spring (Sept. 8, 1781), Green was sick and was left with the baggage wagons near Augusta. Later, after recuperating, he assisted in tending to the sick and wounded. He continued to serve in the Savannah River area until the time of discharge. He was discharged home by Col. Hammond.

SUMMARY OF LATER LIFE

Shortly after the Revolution, Green returned to Rutherford County, NC (Formerly part of Tryon County). He was married the and lived in Rutherford County for about eight years. He then moved to Burke County, N.C. and lived there for about thirty years.

John Green applied for Revolutionary war pension in Burke Count NC in October 1832, age 70. Green was awarded $33.33 per annum

Green, in his later years, moved to Yancey County, NC He died Madison County, NC June 2, 1853. (Madison County was created from Buncombe and Yancey Counties in 1851).

Green's wife predeceased him. At Green's death, the following children survived:

James Green   Aaron Green
Joseph Green   Isabella Green
Arthur Green

LAND HOLDINGS AND TRANSACTIONS

1. John Green received a NC Land Grant for 100 acres of land Rutherford County on Shoaly Branch of Hinton's Creek, adjacent land of William Wilson. Entered for Thomas Thompson, transfer

to John Green.
Entry No. 365, Ent. February 14, 1793, Grant # 955 Book 82 p. 423.
Iss. July 9, 1794. Entry also made for 50 acres adjacent to above land. Ent. Oct 12, 1795. Grant not issued.

2. A John Green received an NC Land Grant for 100 acres of land, Burke County, N.C., adjacent to land belonging to "Buchanan". Cc were John McKinney and Joseph Buchanan. The land was on Gouge"s Creek that flowed into Cane Creek.
Ent. Jan 25, 1797, No. 3227, Grant No. 2382 Book 100 p. 215. Iss. December 21, 1798.

A John Green received grants for 50 acres and 100 acres on Johns River, Burke County, NC in 1829 and 1830 (Grant Nos. 5347, 6749). Another John Green received and N.C. Grant, Burke County, NC for 100 acres on Clark's Little River in 1798. (Grant No. 2399).

CENSUS LOCATIONS

1790 Rutherford County, NC 9th Company
1800 Burke County, NC 1810 Burke County, N.C.
1820 Burke County, NC
1830 Burke County, NC
1840 Yancey County, NC
1850 Yancey County, NC

REFERENCES

US National Archives: Pension data # S 6914
AIS Census Indices
Land Grant records: Morganton-Burke Library, Morganton, NC
Moss, Bobby G. <u>Roster of SC Patriots in the American Revolution</u>
GPC 1983 p. 383

HANEY, CHARLES

SUMMARY OF EARLY LIFE

Charles Haney was a resident of Pennsylvania on enlisting for service in the American Revolution.

SUMMARY OF PARTISAN ACTIVITY

Charles Haney first entered military service at York, PA in Jun 1776 in Capt. Benjamin Savage's Company. Other officers include Colonels McAllister and Kennedy. They were marched to Philadelphia and then sent up the Delaware River to Trenton. Later they marched to Paulus Hook, N.J. and then to Fort Lee, N He was present when Fort Washington was taken, and Fort Lee evacuated. Washington then marched through New Jersey back int Pennsylvania. At about this time Haney became ill and was sent down the Delaware River to Philadelphia. He remained there unt after the battle of Trenton. He was discharged in January 1777 and moved shortly afterwards to Prince Edward County, Va. He w drafted for a term of six months duty and was placed in Capt. Jesse Owen's Company in a regiment headed by Cols. Lucas and Downman. They marched to Hillsborough, NC joining the Virginia troops of Gen. Edward Stevens in Gen. Gates Army. From Hillsborough they marched to Rugeley's Mill, SC north of Camden. On August 16, 1780, Haney took part in the battle of Camden, SC a total defeat for American forces. Haney, in his pension statement, said..."we were scattered all over the country withou any regulations or orders...".

From Camden he made his way back to Hillsborough, and then home to Virginia.

SUMMARY OF LATER LIFE

Charles Haney applied for Revolutionary War pension in Burke County, N.C. on October 22, 1832. He was awarded a pension of $31.10 per annum. Statements on his behalf were made by Edward Goode and Andrew Hunter. Goode stated that he had known Haney Pennsylvania.

LAND HOLDINGS AND TRANSACTIONS

1. 1815 Tax Lists of Burke Co., N.C. gives Haney as owner of a 136 acre tract on Muddy Creek.

2. Deed from Jesse Stroud to Charles Ha(I)ney, 99 acres reg in open court January session, 1798. Burke Co., NC.

CENSUS LOCATIONS

1790
1800
1810 Burke County, NC

1820 Burke County, NC
1830 Burke County, NC
1840 (Hannah Haney, Burke Co., NC)

** A Charles Haney is listed on 1840 Guilford Co., NC census; a Charles Haney received TN land grant Giles Co., 1844, relationship to soldier, if any, unknown.

REFERENCES

AIS Census Indices
US National Archives Revolutionary War Pension Data # S 8661
Swink, Daniel D. "Minutes of the Court of Pleas and Quarter Sessions, (1795=1798)" Burke Co., N.C., Lawndale NC 1987 p.81
Pittman, Betsy Dodd 1815 Burke Co.,N.C. Tax Lists. 1990 Valdese N.C. p. 13.
Tennessee State Library, Nashville, Misc. Land Records.

HARSHAW, ABRAHAM (ABRAM)

SUMMARY OF EARLY LIFE

According to Gibson, Abraham Harshaw came to Burke County, NC in 1780, having emigrated from France. He settled in Burke County near the confluence of Smokey Creek and the Catawba River.

SUMMARY OF PARTISAN ACTIVITY

A Loyalist during the Revolutionary War, Abraham Harshaw was cited to Burke County Court in 1782. He was to show cause why his property should not be confiscated, for being disloyal to the American cause. Sworn witnesses were Capt. Edmund Fares (Fears) and Silence Fares (neighbors in Smokey Creek areas.)

SUMMARY OF LATER LIFE

Abraham Harshaw married Ann Bradshaw. Ann Bradshaw was born in Bedford County, VA and was a sister of William Bradshaw. (She died in 1835, age 77). Abraham Harshaw's will was presented for probate in 1806.

Their children were as follows:

Jacob Harshaw (1786-1868) m. Barbara Weaver (1790-1868)
John Harshaw - never married
Annie Harshaw - drowned
Elizabeth Harshaw (1781-1868) m. David Repatoe
Aaron Harshaw
Isaac Harshaw m. Powell
Alladin Harshaw - died young
Joshua Harshaw m. Elizabeth Metchim
Abraham Harshaw m. Catherine Baker
Moses Harshaw m. Nancy English

LAND HOLDINGS AND TRANSACTIONS

1. NC Land Grant for 200 acres of land lying north of the Catawba River at the mouth of Smokey Creek. The land lay adjacent to property belonging to Edmund Fears and John Mattocks The entry states "...including the improvements he lives on being ye land said Harshaw purchased from John Knox..."
Ent. Dec. 12, 1778, No. 766, Grant Co. 423, Iss. Oct. 28, 1782
Book 44, p. 176

CENSUS LOCATIONS

1790 Burke Co., NC 2nd Co.
1800 Burke Co., NC

REFERENCES

Gibson, Randy; article in The Heritage of Burke County, N.C.

(Winston Salem 1981) pp. 221-2
AIS Census Indices
N.C. Land Grant Data; Morganton-Burke Library, Morganton, N.C.
Huggins, Edith Warren, Burke Co. NC Records Vol. II p. 149
Raleigh, NC 1977

HAWKINS, JOHN

SUMMARY OF EARLY LIFE

John Hawkins was born December 22, 1762 in the Hyco Creek section of North Carolina (now Person and Caswell Co. area). With his father and family, he moved to Burke County, NC and was living there when the Revolutionary War began.

SUMMARY OF PARTISAN ACTIVITY

John Hawkins first entered Revolutionary service in 1779 as a seventeen year old. He was placed in a Company commanded by Capt. James Brittain of McDowell's Regiment. He entered in the spring of 1779 and saw service against the Cherokee Indians. After a short tour, he re-enlisted in a Company commanded by Capt. Thomas Kennedy, again serving against the Cherokees. Returning from this tour he served in the frontier Forts -- Brown's Fort under Capt. Josiah Brandon and Davidson's Fort under Capt. James McFarland and Capt. Daniel Smith. In the summer of 1780, Hawkins served in a light horse battalion under Maj. Joseph McDowell of Quaker Meadows. They served in the South Carolina actions against Ferguson, under the overall command of Col. Charles McDowell.

In the late 1780's he again served in the light horse under Maj. McDowell and saw action at Cowpens though he did not participate in the battle itself of January 17, 1781. His last tour of duty was in the summer and fall of 1781. He served again under Capt. McFarland at the frontier forts. Later his company took part in the Wilmington Expedition under Gen. Griffith Rutherford, late 1781.

SUMMARY OF LATER LIFE

John Hawkins continued to live in Burke County for about seventeen years after the war. In 1797 he moved to Missouri. In Missouri he was known as "Major" John Hawkins. John Hawkins applied for federal pension on July 8, 1833, age 71 years. He was awarded and annual pension of $71.67.

John Hawkins was married to Rebecca Kester. The soldier John Hawkins died July 24, 1840. He is buried at Potosi, Washington County, Missouri.

LAND HOLDINGS AND TRANSACTIONS

1. Burke Co., NC 250 acres Beaverdam Branch. The land lay adjacent to that of Robert Birchfield and James Hamby. The property was crossed by a road.
Ent. 20 May 1779 #688 Grant No. 458 Iss. 28 Oct 1782
Book 44, p.198. "included improvements in which he now lives".
c.c. William Allen, Robert Birchfield.

CENSUS LOCATIONS

1830 Washington Co., Missouri

REFERENCES

US National Archives Pension Data # S16857
AIS Census Indices
DAR Patriot Index National Society DAR, Washington,DC 1966 p.314
Revolutionary Army Accounts (N.C.) Vol X Voucher #4909
Hatcher, Patricia L. Graves of Revolutionary Patriots
Vol II p.132 Dallas 1987.

HAWKINS, JOSEPH

SUMMARY OF EARLY LIFE

Joseph Hawkins was born June 7, 1765 near Baltimore, Maryland. During the American Revolution, he was living with his father and family in Burke Co., NC.

SUMMARY OF PARTISAN ACTIVITY

Joesph Hawkins first entered military service in 1781 as a volunteer militiaman in Capt. James McFarland's Company of Col. Charles McDowell's Burke Regiment. He spent two months on the Catawba frontier in service directed against the hostile Cherokee Indians.

In September of 1781 he was again a volunteer serving again in McFarland's Company. On this occasion he took part in the Wilmington Expedition in the last half of 1781, directed by Gen. Griffith Rutherford.

After his return from the Wilmington Expedition, Hawkins volunteered for a short period of duty on the Holston River (NE Tennessee). He was in Nicholas Hale's Company of Sevier's Regiment.

His final tour of duty was in Joseph McDowell's spring Cherokee raid of April 1782. He served as a substitute for Hugh Woods, who had been drafted.

SUMMARY OF LATER LIFE

Joseph Hawkins continued to live in Burke Co., N.C. until 1806. He had married by this time. He and his family moved to Jackson County, Tennessee.

Joseph Hawkins applied for federal pension in Jackson Co., TN on March 18, 1834. He was awarded an annual pension of $33.33.

LAND HOLDINGS AND TRANSACTIONS

Jackson Co. TN Joseph Hawkins reveived multiple small land grants in 1814 (10,15, & 16 ac.) Bks. 5,6

In Burke County NC, there was the conveyance of land from William Hawkins to Joseph Hawkins, by deed, 140 ac., dated June 20, 1790

CENSUS LOCATIONS

1790 Burke Co., NC 10th CO.
1820 Jackson Co., TN
1830 Jackson Co., TN

REFERENCES

US National Archives Pension Data #S 4322
AIS Census Indices
Tennessee State Archives and Library, Nashville, Land Grant Records
Swink, Daniel D. "Minutes of the Court of Pleas and Quarter Sessions" Burke Co. NC 1791-1795 (1986) .

HAYES, GEORGE

SUMMARY OF EARLY LIFE

George Hayes was born in Amherst Co., Virginia in 1760. During the Revolutionary period he was living in Burke Co., NC, Mulberry Creek area.

SUMMARY OF PARTISAN ACTIVITY

George Hayes first entered military service as a private militiaman in Burke Co., NC, McDowell's Regiment, in December 1780. He served in a Company commanded by Capt. Alexander Erwi

Under Capt. Erwin they advanced to Ramsour's Mill and then to Sugar Creek in Mecklenburg County, joining the brigade of Gen. William L. Davidson. His company escorted some prisoners to Salisbury and then rejoined the brigade on the Catawba River. At this time the British army under Lord Cornwallis was approaching the Catawba River from the west. Davidson advanced to Tuckaseegee Ford and then to Cowan's Ford. At Cowan's Ford (February 2, 1781) Gen. Davidson's force was completely routed by Cornwallis. Gen. Davidson was killed. Capt. Erwin may have been captured (as indicated by British records). Hayes later joined up with a company commanded by Capt. Robert Brown and served the balance of his six month tour at the head of the Catawba River on the Carolina frontier.

SUMMARY OF LATER LIFE

After the war, Hayes moved from Burke County to Hawkins Co., TN (later Carter County) and from there to Bledsoe Co., TN He applied for federal pension in Hawkins County, TN on April 29, 1833, age 73 years. He was awarded a pension in the amount of $20.00 per annum. There were supporting statements by George Hayes, Jr. and Benjamin Coffey.

LAND HOLDINGS AND TRANSACTIONS

1. Burke Co., NC 50 acres on a branch of Mulberry Creek. The land lay adjacent to that of Thomas Hayes.
Ent. 4 Dec 1801 #4167 Grant No. 3052 Iss. 4 Dec 1802
Book 114 p.352 c.c. Ransom and John Hayes.
(This may have been his son George Hayes, Jr.)
2. Wilkes Co., NC 13 Dec 1798 N.C. Grant #1750 George Hayes 25 acres both sides Yadkin River p.463.

CENSUS LOCATIONS

1790 Burke Co., NC 5th Co.
1800 Burke Co., NC (George Hayes, Jr.?)
1830 Hawkins Co., TN
 ** A Geo. Hayes on Tax Lists Knox Co. TN 1804.

REFERENCES

US National Archives Pension Data #S1668
Absher, Mrs. W.O. "Wilkes County, NC Deed Books D, F-1, G-H 1795-1815 SHP 1990 p.187.
AIS Census Indices
Huggins, Edith, Burke County Records Vols I-IV
Swink, Dan D., Abstracts of Burke County Court Minutes 1791-95 and 1795-98
Tennessee State Archives and Library, Nashville; Tax Lists.

HELDERMAN, NICHOLAS

Nicholas Helderman appears to have been the son of Christian and Mary Helderman and the grandson of Nicholas Helderman, Sr. During the pre Revolutionary period, Nicholas Helderman left Pennsylvania and settled near Seagle's Creek, Lincoln County.

SUMMARY OF PARTISAN ACTIVITY

Nicholas Helderman was a Loyalist in Burke County during the 1780-81 war time period. In the Charles McDowell court martial records, Capt. James Davidson, in command of Fort Charles on the Western frontier stated "...Samuel Robertson, Nicholas Helderman and Isaac Lockman came to my command". The charge against McDowell was that he sent known Loyalists to duty in the frontier forts as " mild punishment" (for their Tory activity). Earlier Thomas Wheeler had stated that he was present when Nicholas Helderman was "sentenced" to one year duty in the Continental Service.

In late 1782, Helderman's name appears on the well known "Tory List". This was a list of those persons who were subpoenaed to Burke County Court to show cause as to why their land should not be confiscated, being inimical to the American Cause. North Carolina Continental Line records show Helderman being enlisted on December 31, 1781 for the duration of the war in Armstrong's Company of the 10th Regiment (Tennessee records show Nicholas Helderman receiving 640 acres for service in the North Carolina Continental Line, 21 Nov. 1809, assigned to Andrew Durr, 10 March 1810).

SUMMARY OF LATER LIFE

Nicholas Helderman had three sons, two daughters by census records. He died, according to Hunter, in 1810 or early 1811. Wife's name not listed.

CENSUS LOCATIONS

1790 Lincoln County, NC 10th Company
1800 Lincoln County, NC
1810 Lincoln County, NC

LAND HOLDINGS AND TRANSACTIONS

Lincoln County, NC, 50 acres on Lockman's creek adjacent to John Taylor, Jacob Shuford, and "his own land".
Ent. July 8, 1794. Granted from other tracts, Helderman apparent owned land on Seagle's Creek.

REFERENCES

Huggins, Edith W., Burke County Records Vol II, page 154B

Pruett, A.B. Abstracts of Land Entries, Lincoln Co., N.C. 1783-1795
AIS Census Indices
NCDAR <u>Roster of Soldiers from North Carolina in American Revolution.</u> SHP Reprint Page 133, 356.
<u>Heritage of Catawba County</u>, Article by Rebecca Hunter, page 175-176. Hunter Publishing Company, Winston Salem, 1986.
Whitley, Edythe R., Tennessee Genealogical Records
GPC 1980, Page 38

HICE, CONRAD

SUMMARY OF EARLY LIFE

Conrad Hice was a brother of Geroge, Jacob and Leonard Hice. They lived in Mecklenburg County, NC At the beginning of the Revolutionary War, later Cabarrus County.

SUMMARY OF PARTISAN ACTIVITY

Conrad Hice served a total of nine months, consisting of three tours of duty, each lasting about three months. He served in a militia company commanded by a Capt. Starnes. In one of his du assignments, he was marched to Camden, SC And participated in t Battle of Camden on August 16, 1780. This was a disastrous defeat for the Americans. Hice lost his horse and all of his equipment. He was forced to hide in a nearby swamp for protection. Pension records indicated that Hice was a private for six months and a Captain of Calvary for two months.

SUMMARY OF LATER LIFE

Conrad Hice married Sophia _____. By this union were t following children:

Conrad Hice, Elizabeth Pearson, Peggy Winkle

Conrad Hice moved from Cabarrus County to Burke County, NC. He died in Burke County in 1816. Sophia Hice died in Tennessee, October 7, 1850. She was over a hundred years old at her death

His son Conrad Hice, applied for federal pension on behalf of h deceased mother. A pension amount of $70.00 per annum was awarded, retroactive to 1831.

LAND HOLDINGS AND TRANSACTIONS

1. 1815 Burke Co. Tax Lists show Conrad Hice as possessing a 1 acre tract on Upper Creek adjacent to property of Joseph Beck.

CENSUS LOCATIONS

1790 Mecklenburg Co., NC ("Hese")
1800 Cabarrus County, NC
1810
1820 Franklin County, TN (Conrad Hice, Jr.,?)

REFERENCES

US National Archives Pension Data # W 4453
Pittman, Betsy D., 1815 Burke Co., N.C. Tax lists, Valdese, NC 1990, p. 116.
AIS Census Indices

HICE, GEORGE (Hise)

SUMMARY OF EARLY LIFE

George Hice was living in Mecklenburg County, NC during the Revolutionary War. (Later Cabarrus Co.) He was a brother of Leonard, Jacob and Conrad Hice.

SUMMARY OF PARTISAN ACTIVITY

According to family statements (in applying for Federal benefits), George Hice was a Revolutionary War soldier and served in Capt. Martin Phifer's Company of Col. John Phifer's Regiment. The brigade commander was Gen. Griffith Rutherford. According to his son, George W.B. Hice, he also served under Col. William Campbell of Virginia at the battle of Kings Mountain on October 7, 1780.

SUMMARY OF LATER LIFE

George Hice married Catherine Starringer on February 14, 1780. Two sons are given...Jacob and George W.B. Hice. George W.B. Hice was from Union County, Ga. George Hice lived in Cabarrus County for about twenty six years and then moved to Burke County, N.C. (His brother also came to Burke County). No reason is given as to why he did not apply for Revolutionary War pension. George Hice died on November 9, 1846. His wife had died earlier, on August 11, 1838. *See footnote, below.

His sons applied for benefits in 1854. Claims were rejected.

LAND HOLDINGS AND TRANSACTIONS

330 Acres on both sides of Simpson Creek, between his own north line and that of Benjamin Rose. Burke Co., NC.
Ent. September 3, 1828, No. 9004, Grant No. 5290
Iss. Oct. 24, 1828, Book 137 p. 406
Chain carriers J.W. Scott; G.W.B. Hice.

CENSUS LOCATIONS

1790 Mecklenburg County, NC
1800 Cabarrus County, NC
1810 Burke County, NC
1820 Burke County, NC
1830 Burke County, NC

*Will of George Hice presented for probate Burke Co., NC, Jan. 1847 by George W.B. Hice, exec. Elizabeth Hice (2nd Wife?) contested will. Caveat entered Oct. 1847 by Joshua Fincher and wife, Elizabeth. Transcript of will in Fall 1849 Burke Co., N.C. Superior Court Minutes. Will dated 22 June 1843. Names son Jacob Hice. To Elizabeth Fincher. Son George W.B. Hice Dau. Salena A. Hice, under age. Wife Betsy Hice. Executor: Son

George W.B. Hice.

REFERENCES

US National Archives, Pension Data, # R 5044
AIS Census Indices
Burke Co. NC Land Grant Data, Morganton-Burke Library, Morganton NC.
Philbeck, Jr., Miles S. And Turner, Grace. "Burke Co. NC> Surviving Will and Probate Abstracts 1777-1910." Chapel Hill 1983. # 255.

HIGDON, LEONARD

SUMMARY OF EARLY LIFE

Leonard Higdon was born in Anson County, NC in 1754. He was a resident of Anson County when he first entered Revolutionary service.

SUMMARY OF PARTISAN ACTIVITY

Leonard Higdom entered military service in 1780 in Anson County under Col. Thomas Wade. He served in a militia company and took part in the skirmish at Gum Swamp. During this action a Capt. Wilson was killed. Later, Higdon served another three months tour of duty under Col. Wade and again opposed the British and Tories at Gum Swamp.

His last tour of duty was in the fall and winter of 1781, participating in Gen. Rutherford's Wilmington Expedition. The duty tour lasted six months. In his pension declaration, Higdon recalled the surrender of Cornwallis as having occurred at about the time of this tour.

SUMMARY OF LATER LIFE

Leonard Higdon married Susanah Harris. (She was age 69 years in 1845). They were married on March 31, 1791.

After the Revolution Higdon moved from Anson County to Georgia, He lived there one year and then came to Burke County. He lived in Burke County for many years. In his later life he moved from Burke County, NC to Macon County, NC.

Leonard Higdon applied for Revolutionary War pension in October 1832, Macon County, NC, age 78 years. In 1845, Susanah Higdon applied for Federal pension. In her declaration, she stated that Leonard Higdon died September 11, 1837.

LAND HOLDINGS AND TRANSACTIONS

1. 1815 Burke Co., NC Tax Lists show Leonard Higdon as possessing a 100 acre tract on South Fork of Catawba (probably on Jacobs Fork), adjacent to Leonard Higdon,Jr. and Peter Mull.

CENSUS LOCATIONS

1790
1800 Burke County, NC
1810
1820 Burke County, NC
1830 Macon County, NC

REFERENCES

DAR Patriot Index 1966, p. 327
Pittman, Betsy D., Burke Co., NC 1815 Tax Lists, Valdese, NC 19
p. 49.
U.S. National Archives Pension Data # R 4975
AIS Census Indices

HIGHLAND, HENRY ("HARRY")

SUMMARY OF EARLY LIFE

Henry Highland came to Burke County in the mid 1760's in the household of Hugh McDowell, older brother of Col. Charles and Maj. Joseph McDowell of Quaker Meadows. He grew up as a member of the McDowell household and was considered a member of the McDowell family.

SUMMARY OF PARTISAN ACTIVITY

Henry Highland began his military career during the middle part of the Revolution. Commissioned an Ensign in the Burke Militia, he led several short forays into hostile Indian territory. He also conducted activities against local Tories. Highland participated in the Kings Mountain Campaign of September and October 1780. After Kings Mountain he led a group of horsemen into South Carolina to the vicinity of the British garrison at Ninety Six. Later, after joining up with the troops of Gen. Daniel Morgan, Highland fought in the epic battle of Cowpens on January 17, 1781, a great American victory. Apparently Highland performed well, as he was subsequently promoted. In later 1781 Highland served with Capt. Thomas Kennedy on the Wilmington Expedition. After the liberation of Wilmington and on their return home, both he and Kennedy were captured by the notorious Tory Col. David Fanning. Highland managed to escape, Kennedy was paroled.

In March of 1782, Capt. Highland accompanied Maj. Joseph McDowell of Quaker Meadows on a short punative raid against the Cherokees.

SUMMARY OF LATER LIFE

Henry Highland remained a Captain of a military judicial company until about the turn of the century. He was active in civic affairs. He is listed on 1815 Burke records, but Tennessee census records indicate removal to Dickson County, most likely to the land on Harpeth River. Census records also suggest his demise prior to 1830.

LAND HOLDINGS AND TRANSACTIONS

1815 Burke County, N.C. Tax List show Henry Highland possessing 1,100 acres of land on Johns River. It was part of a tract shared with the Perkins family.

Davidson County, TN land deeds, 640 acres Davidson Co., TN on both sides of Harpeth River including the mouth of Jones Creek. Reg. May 21, 1790. (surveyed October 21, 1785 by Henry Rutherford, Warrant #555). The land lay adjacent to John Province, Thomas Malloy, Joel Lane, Shadrack Jones, Christopher Stump. It also lay adjacent to that of Joseph McDowell of Quaker Meadows.

CENSUS LOCATIONS

1790 Burke Co., NC (1795 tax lists)
1800 Burke Co., NC
1810 Burke Co., NC
1815 Burke Co., NC (tax lists)
1820 Dickson Co., TN
1830 Dickson Co., -- Probably Henry Highland, Jr.

REFERENCES

March, Helen and Timothy "Land Deed Genealogy of Davidson Co., TN.(1783-1803)in 3 Vols. SHP Greenville S.C. 1992
Pittman, Betsy D., Burke County, N.C. Federal Census 1810. p.29
Pittman, Betsy D., Burke County, N.C. Tax Lists 1815. p.92
Revolutionary War Pension Statements of William Smith, Joseph Ballew, Richard Ballew, John Chapman, John Littlejohn, John Birchfield, John Gasperson.
REvolution Army Accounts, Book "A" p.6 "Capt. Henry Highland and his Company. Himself and payroll."
→

HILDEBRAND, CONRAD

SUMMARY OF EARLY LIFE

Conrad Hildebrand (often spelled "Cunrod", because of German pronunciation of Conrad) was born in Pennsylvania, Lancaster County, on August 28, 1741. He was the son of Christian Hildebrand.

In 1768 Conrad Hildebrand received a Crown Patent for 640 acres on West side of the South Fork of the Catawba River, now Burke County (then Rowan County, but listed as a Mecklenburg County Crown Grant, due to indefinite Granville line west of the Catawba River). Henry Hildebrand also received Grants near by (brother to Conrad?). Moravian records of 1776 list a "Mr. Hildebrand" passing through from Philadelphia, traveling toward his home on the Catawba River (Bethabara Diary). By then, he was well established, owning both a grist and powder mill.

SUMMARY OF PARTISAN ACTIVITY

The first mention of Hildebrand's activities is in the minutes of the Committee of Safety of Rowan County in 1775. The Committee instructed its militia Captains to take possession of the powder, lead and flints in the possession of Hildebrand. In the event he refused, he would be arrested. Theis action somewhat suggested Hildebrand may of been of Loyalist sympathies. Some references state that Hildebrand may have served against the Indians. It is more probable that he may have provided much of the powder lead and flints that were so essential in frontier warfare.More indicting circumstances as to his loyalty came to light during the Kings Mountain campaign. Lt. Anthony Allaire, a British provincial officer (who was captured at Kings Mountain), kept a day by day diary of his activites during this period. In his diary, published after the war, Allaire goes into detail concerning his escape from Continental authorities at Salem. In his retrograde journey, he related the various persons whobefriended him. In his crossing of the Catawba, headed toward South Carolina and eventual freedom, Allaire stated ..."we arrived at Hilterbrine's (sic) about 6 o'clock in the morning of the 14th (Nov 14, 1780). He received us with great caution, lest we should be treacherous; but when he found that we were British Officers he was very kind."

Since Hildebrand furnished supplies and other items to the Americans he obviously was playing both sides of the fence. It seems that he was successful in his suppression of overt loyalist activites. He was not cited to the court or threatened in any way. Later he served Burke County in the North Carolina lower House.

SUMMARY OF LATER LIFE

Conrad Hildebrand was married to Elizabeth Mull (daughter of

John and Mary Mull) on December 17, 1782. By this union were
born the following children:
Conrad, Jr., born October 23, 1783
Henry, born February 27, 1791
Elizabeth, born April 27, 1793
Maria, born November 11, 1795
Johannas, October 31, 1798
George, born November 8, 1802
Katrina, born February 10, 1806

Hildebrand continued to operate a mill. He served in the lower
House of the North Carolina General Assembly in 1795 and 1797.

Hildebrand was recognized as one of the more prosperous citizens
of the Catawba Valley during and after the Revolutionary War.
Conrad Hildebrand died on July 24, 1824. Many of his descendent
still reside in Burke County.

CENSUS LOCATIONS

1790 Burke County , NC 13th Company
1800 Burke County, NC
1810 Burke County, NC
1820 Burke County, NC

LAND HOLDINGS AND TRANSACTIONS

1. Burke County, NC 140 acres on Henry Fork of South Fork
of Catawba. and also mouth of Queen's Creek, including "his
own improvements". cc Jacob Gortner, John Boreland.
Ent. #740, June 21, 1778, Grant #713 Iss. Oct 11, 1783
Book 50 p 265.

2. Burke County, NC 173 acres on north side of Henry Fork
of South Fort of Catawba River adjacent to George Walker. Land
contains improvements previously made by Leonard Patterson.
Entry #831 Oct 5, 1778, Grant #957 Iss. August 7, 1787
Book 65 p 371. Chain carriers John and Joe Howard.

3. Mecklenburg, NC Crown Grant "Conrode Hildebrand"
29 April 1768 #6767 "640 acres in Mecklenburgh County on the
west side of the South fork of the Catawba River and on Howard's
Creek above Potter's land, joining both sides of the South Fork
of Howard's Creek and on both sides of the South Fork of Howard'
Creek".

REFERENCES

AIS US Census Indices, Land Grant data, Morganton Burke Library,
Morganton, N.C.
Hofmann, Margaret M. Colony of North Carolina Abstracts of Land
Patents 1765-1777, 1984 Roanoke Rapids, NC page 508
The Lowman Story by Margaret Lowman Smith, Mildred Lowman
Speagle, and Ruby Lowman Young. Gateway Press 1992,

pages 30-33.

Draper, Lyman C. **Kings Mountain and its Heroes**, GPC, Baltimore 1967 (Reprint of original 1881 edition).
Allaire's diary and appendix, page 514.
Wheeler, John H., **Historical Sketches of North Carolina**
  RPC Baltimore 1764 reprint. Rowan County section, pages 364, 367. Burke County section, page 62.
Huggins, Edith W., Burke County North Carolina land records, Vol I & II.
Hildebrand, Ollie H., Article in **Heritage of Burke County** 1981 Winston Salem, pages 228-229.
Hildebrand, Abbie Seals, conversations with the author 1960-1980.
DAR **Patriot Index**, page 328, National Society of DAR, Washington, DC in 1966.

HOOD, JOHN

SUMMARY OF EARLY LIFE

John Hood was born in 1760. At the time of the American Revolution, he was a resident of Burke County, NC. John Hood w a brother to Andrew and Thomas Hood.

SUMMARY OF PARTISAN ACTIVITY

John Hood first entered military service in May 1781 for a tour of duty of ten months. He was recruited into the South Carolir troops, as was common practice at that time. (See biography of Charles McDowell Vol. I, concerning recruitment techniques).

Hood was placed initially into a company commanded by Capt. Godfrey Adams. Later he was transferred to Capt. Moore's Compar of Col. Myddleton's South Carolina regiment. From North Carolir they were marched to the confluence of the Broad and Saluda Riv (now Columbia, S.C.). From there they were marched to Pinetree (Camden), McCord's Ferry, and finally to Eutaw Springs. Their overall Commander was Gen Thomas Sumter.

On September 8, 1781 Hood took part in the battle of Eutaw Springs. During the Battle, he received a severe wound of the inner part of his left thigh (by a musket ball). He stated in his pension declaration, that Capt. Moore still commanded his company. He also recalled the death of Col. Richard Campbell. He stated that "he was not well of his wounds when he heard of the surrender of Lord Cornwallis." After recovery, he was marched "from one place unto another" until about April 1782, when he received his discharge. Though his tour was for ten months, he had (because of his wounds) served about a year. Fellow soldiers Richard Scott, George Brown and Richard Brown were mentioned in his application.

SUMMARY OF LATER LIFT

John Hood was living in Fentress Co. TN when he applied for Federal pension in April 1833, age 73 years.

LAND HOLDINGS AND TRANSACTIONS

1. Burke Co. NC 200 acres Middle Fork Lower Little River, adjacent to land of George Brown. Ent. 15 Oct 1778 ***

2. Burke County NC 1815 Tax lists show John Hood as possessing tract of 98 ½ acres on Lower Creek.

***Note: It seems almost certain that John Hood the soldier liv on Lower Little River. In his pension declarations, there were statements from George Brown and Richard Scott, both from the Little River area. This is important, as there were at least 3 persons in Burke named John Hood.

3. Burke Co. N.C. 3 tracts on Muddy Creek, adjacent to Caleb Barr.

4. Tennessee Land Grant # 2706 Fentress Co. TN 100 ac. Nov 6, 1832.

5. Tennessee Land Grant # 1231 Fentress Co. TN 100 ac June 3, 1829, Book C/159.

CENSUS LOCATIONS

1790 Burke Co. NC 8th Co.
1800 Burke Co. NC
1810 Burke Co. NC
1820 Burke Co. NC
1830 Burke Co. NC

REFERENCES

US National Archives Pension Data # S 1534
Burke Co. NC Land Grant Records, Morganton-Burke Library, Morganton, NC
Pittman, Betsy D., 1815 Burke Co. NC Tax Lists 1990 pp 29,88
AIS Census Indices
NC Rev. Army Accounts, Raleigh Vol X Book ZZ Voucher # 2934
Tennessee State Archives and Library, Nashville Land Grant Records.
Moss, Bobby G. <u>Roster of SC Patriots in the American Revolution</u> GPC 1983 p. 460

HUFFMAN, SAMUEL   (Hoffman)

SUMMARY OF EARLY LIFE

Samuel Huffman was born in Germany in 1747 and came to America in 1748. He was the son of George and Catherine Huffman of the Rhenish Palatinate. George Huffman came originally to Pennsylvania, but then joined in the great migration to the Carolinas. He settled first in what is now Catawba County, but later moved to lower Burke County. Samuel Huffman grew to maturity on the Carolina frontier.

SUMMARY OF PARTISAN ACTIVITY

In 1780, Samuel Huffman took part in the Kings Mountain Campaign. This culminated in the great American victory of October 7, 1780. He also saw service in the Gilbertown area, presumably during the campaign period. Kinsmen John and Jacob Huffman of Lincoln County also took part in the battle. Samuel Huffman proudly displayed his old flint lock rifle, used in the battle of Kings Mountain, for many years thereafter A son Fredrick Huffman, was a veteran of the war of 1812.

SUMMARY OF LATER LIFE

Samuel Huffman was married to Barbara Moser. Samuel and Barbara Huffman lived near the Henry River section of Burke County. Samuel Huffman died in 1809 and is buried at the Hoffman Hildebrand family cemetery on River Road, Burke County (near old Prospect Ridge Lutheran Church site). Samuel and Barbara Huffman had ten children as follows:

Eva m. Leonard Higdon
Mary Magdeline m. John Mosser (TN)
Abram m. Elizabeth
Fredrick moved to Haywood Co., NC
Burkhard moved to Ohio
Gasper
Catherine m. Elijah Roper
Barbara m. William Cornwell
Elizabeth m. Thomas Walker
Michael

CENSUS LOCATIONS

1790   Burke County, NC 13th Co.
1800   Burke County, NC

REFERENCES

Vertical file material, Morganton Burke Library, Morganton, NC.

Huffman, Samuel   P.2

Huffman, Frances Wellman and Swink, Lottie Huffman, Data in vertical files 1994.
Lane, Richard N., Lexington NC (1973) material in vertical files, Morganton Burke Library, Morganton, NC entitled "Hoffman Genealogy".
"Reflections on Huffman, Past and Present" vertical files Morganton Burke Library, Morganton, NC 1994 by Swink and Lottie Huffman.
Huffman, Gene and Frances, Rt. 4, Morganton, NC Data presented at annual reunion 1994.

HUGHES, FRANCIS

SUMMARY OF EARLY LIFE

Francis Hughes was born in Shenandoah County, VA in the year 1759. At the beginning of the Revolutionary War, he was living in Western Burke (then Rowan) County, NC. He later was "unsettled", but apparently residing in the Watauga area of east Tennessee, then North Carolina.

SUMMARY OF PARTISAN ACTIVITY

Francis Hughes first entered military service in Burke County, N.C. in June 1776. He served as a ranger on the western Catawba Frontier, scouting against the hostile Cherokee and Creek Indians. He served in Capt. Penland"s Company. In August 1776, Hughes joined up with Rutherford's troops and took part in the Cherokee Expedition of August-October 1776. In his pension declaration, he mentions an engagement in which eighteen Indians were killed.

In January 1777, he enlisted in Col. John Sevier's Regiment. Their purpose was to clear the Watauga Settlements from Indian incursions. He helped to erect and garrison a fort on the Nolachuckey River (At Gallakers or Gallagher's). In September 1780, Hughes volunteered under Col. Sevier (Capt. Samuel William's company) and took part in the great Kings Mountain Expedition of September and October 1780. The march culminated in the American victory at Kings Mountain, S.C. on October 7, 1780.

His final tour of duty was for a period of one month under Col. Sevier. This consisted of a short march to Cherokee county and back.

SUMMARY OF LATER LIFE

Francis Hughes apparently moved from Burke County, NC to Watauga some time during the war. He continued to reside in East Tennessee for the remainder of his life.

On July 21, 1833, as a resident of Greene County, TN, age 74 years, he applied for Federal pension. He was awarded an annual pension of $51.66. In his pension application children are mentioned, but not by name. (See below).

Francis Hughes died January 25, 1841. His wife predeceased him. His heirs were as follows: John Hughes, Margaret Hughes, Ingabo Hixon and Rebecca Hixon.

LAND HOLDINGS AND TRANSACTIONS

1. Washington Co. TN NC Grant # 262 99 ac Oct. 24, 1782. Watauga Bk. 252

2. Washington Co. TN NC Grant # 362 99 ac. Oct. 24, 1782 Bk. 1 p. 567, probably same grant as per above.

3. Greene Co. TN NC Grant # 1115 640 ac. July 12, 1793 Bk. 6 p.463.

REFERENCES

U.S. National Archives Pension Data # S 3075
Bures, Robert. _Tennessee Genealogical Records_ Baltimore 1980 p.190.
"Roster of Soldiers and Patriots of the American Revolution Buried in Tennessee" Bates 1979 p. 88
Tennessee State Archives and Library Nashville Land Grant Records.

HUSBANDS, VEAZEY

SUMMARY OF EARLY LIFE

The Husbands family of Burke County, NC (now Caldwell County) was closely related to the noted Herman Husbands of Regulator fame (1765-1771). Many of Husbands followers eventually wound up living in Caldwell County, Lower Creek area. On a petition (1771-1773) to establish a new county from Rowan, the name of Veazey Husbands appears as well as those of Laommi, Robert and William Husbands. The Husbands had lived earlier in Anson, Randolph and Richmond Counties of central North Carolina. Like many of the former Regulators, Veazey Husbands was a devoted Loyalist from the beginning. He lived on a branch of Lower Creek known as Husbands Creek.

SUMMARY OF PARTISAN ACTIVITY

Veazey Husbands quickly rose to prominence as leader of the Burke County Tories obtaining the rank of Colonel of Militia. He was said to have commanded a regiment of about 700-800 men during the 1779-1780 period. Capt. William Lenoir mentioned the action against the Loyalists in 1779 (or ? 1780). This wou be in the same area that Husbands held his command.

In 1780, Col. Veazey Husbands led his troops in the Kings Mountain campaign, ending in the Loyalist disaster of October 7, 1780.

The records are not clear as whether or not Husbands was killed or captured. A Veazey Husbands was included on the Tory docket of late 1782, possibly his son or nephew. At any rate, he was dead by 1783 since there are administrative actions in Burke County Court records of January 1784.

An Elsa Husbands is listed in 1790 census records (his widow?) Veazey Husbands was also listed (son or nephew?)

LAND HOLDINGS AND TRANSACTIONS

1. 300 acres Burke County, NC on Pierson's Fork of Lower Creek, both sides, and adjacent to land belonging to John Sharp Ent. 24 May 1778, No. 268 Grant #1463 Iss 4 Jan 1792, Book 75, p 436. Entry data states "and included the aforesaid Husbands improvements and also improvements said Husbands lives on."

***Authors Note

Much more information is needed on the life of this foremost Loyalist of Burke County. This information should include his exact relationship with Herman Husbands and the Regulation and of his military command and role during the dark days of

1779-1780. And certainly it should include more about his family following the war. It is also hoped that British War records may reveal something as they have for other North Carolina Loyalist leaders.

REFERENCES

AIS 1790 Census North Carolina
Phifer, Edward. _Burke_ 1977 ed. Pp. 310,360
U.S, National Archives Pension declaration of William Lenoir # S 7137.
Burke County NC Land Grant Records, Morganton-Burke Library, Morganton, NC.
Huggins, Edith Warren, Burke Co. NC Records Vols. I-IV

INMAN, SHADRACK

SUMMARY OF EARLY LIFE

Shadrack Inman was born in 1747. The Inman clan, from Virginia had settled in western Burke County. Hezekiah and Ezekial Inman lived on Linville River. Shadrack lived on the Catawba River, near Charles McPeters and John Montgomery.

SUMMARY OF PARTISAN ACTIVITY

Shadrack Inman was a Loyalist sympathizer, along with his neighbors in upper Burke County. These included the Hodge family, McPeters family and the Hyatt family.

According to court martial records involving Col. Charles McDowell of Burke County, Inman was allowed to serve on duty in the frontier forts, rather than being sent to South Carolina ("partial" treatment by McDowell).

In November 1782 Shadrack Inman was cited to Burke County court to show cause as to why is property should not be confiscated, for being disloyal to the American Cause. Witnesses included Maj. Joseph White, Capt. William Moore, John Armstrong, Thomas Wilson et al. During the war, Inman did sign the Oath of Allegiance. North Carolina Revolutionary Army Accounts verify his service in the North Carolina militia.

It is not known at this time the relationship between the above Shadrack Inman and another (Capt.) Shadrack Inman killed at Musgrave's Mill in 1780.

SUMMARY OF LATER LIFE

For several years after the Revolution, Inman was involved in a court case with his neighbor John Montgomery, possibly related to confiscated property.

In 1783 he had acquired property in Greene County, TN, later Jefferson County. He lived in Jefferson County for the remainder of his life.

Shadrack Inman was married to Mary Jane McPheeters, or McPeters (1749-1830). They were married ca. 1767. Children include:

Shadrack	Hannah
Daniel	Sarah
Ezekial	Suzanna
Charles	Rachel
Thomas	Anne
John	Prudence
Jeramiah	Margaret
Elizabeth	

Inman, Shadrack

Shadrack Inman died in Jefferson County, TN on October 7, 1831.

LAND HOLDINGS AND TRANSACTIONS

1. Burke County, NC entry records of Charles McPeters "300 acres south side of Catawba River opposite John Montgomery's including improvements by Shadrack, Inman...."

2. Greene Co. TN NC Grant # 172 200 ac. Sep 20, 1787 Bk. 2 p.123.

3. Jefferson Co. TN (E. TN Grant #11194) May 30, 1825 150 ac. Bk. 12 p. 421.

CENSUS LOCATIONS (Including tax listings

1783 Greene County, TN (tax list) (probably later Jefferson County).
1800 Jefferson Co., TN (tax list)
1822 Jefferson Co., TN (tax list)
1830 Jefferson Co., TN

REFERENCES

Huggins, Edith W. "Burke County Land Records" Vols I-IV SHP
Sistler, Byran and Barbara "Early Tennessee Tax Lists" Evanston, Ill 1977
N.C.DAR ROSTER OF N.C. SOLDIERS IN THE AMERICAN REVOLUTION
1931 ed. p.392
AIS Census Indices
Phifer, Edward Burke 1977 ed. p.362
Court Martial Records of Col. Charles, McDowell (1782) facsimile. Copy presented to author by the late Miss Eunice Ervin of Morganton.
Tennessee DAR "Roster of Soldiers and Patriots of the American Revolution Buried in Tennessee." Rev. by Helen Marsh 1979,p.90

JACKSON, JAMES

SUMMARY OF EARLY LIFE

James Jackson was born in Orange County, Virginia in 1757. Before the Revolution, he was living in Burke County, NC. He continued to live there until about 1800.

SUMMARY OF PARTISAN ACTIVITY

James Jackson first entered military service in Burke County, NC in Capt. Thomas Whitson's company of Col. Charles McDowell's Burke Regiment. In his pension statements it is somewhat unclear as to when he entered. He gives the date as "1779"; however, his description of events are identical to those that occurred in the summer of 1776, namely the action of the North Catawba River which resulted in the death of Capt. Reuben White and the wounding of Capt. Thomas Whitson. Jackson then described a retaliatory raid under Col. McDowell - probably the Cherokee Expedition of fall 1776.

Jackson then describes his duties on the Catawba frontier. He was stationed at Davidson's Fort, first under Capt. Whitson and later under Capt. Henry Wakefield. There were numerous skirmishes with the Indians. This tour was mainly in 1778 and 1779.

During the Kings Mountain campaign, he was still stationed at the fort where they "were frequently annoyed by the Tories, and they had several running fights with them."

In 1781, Jackson was sent south to join the army of Gen. Nathaniel Greene in South Carolina (along with the rest of Whitson's command). He was placed in a regiment commanded by the Frenchman, Col. Malmedy. Under Malmedy, he took part in the battle of Eutaw Springs, SC on September 8, 1781.

Later, under a Capt. Gordon, he was marched back to Towan County, NC near "Bell's Brave." There he was discharged by Col. Locke in November 1781.

SUMMARY OF LATER LIFE

Jackson remained in Burke County until about the turn of the century. He then moved to Pike County, KY. He was still residing there when he applied for Federal pension in November 1833, age 76. He was awarded an annual pension of $80.00.

LAND HOLDINGS AND TRANSACTIONS

*None under James Jackson. A "Joseph" Jackson entered two tracts of land on Cane Creek, a tributary of Catawba River, 1778. Warrant transferred.

CENSUS LOCATIONS

1790 Wilkes County, NC 1st Co.?
     Rutherford Co., NC 2nd Co.?

REFERENCES:

AIS 1790 Federal Census, North Carolina
US National Archives Pension Data # S 38077
Huggins, Edith Warren, Burke Co., NC Land Records Vol. I
Raleigh 1977 p. 97

JAMES, JOSEPH ROGERS

SUMMARY OF EARLY LIFE

Joseph R. James (also known as "Joseph Rogers") was born near Lynchburg Ferry, Campbell County VA. He was age 80 when applying for federal pension in 1836. His mothers name was Rogers, for whom he was named.

SUMMARY OF PARTISAN ACTIVITY

Joseph James first entered military service in Burke County, NC in June 1780 as a volunteer militiaman in Capt. Galbraith Falls' Company of mounted horsemen, Col. Charles McDowell Burke Regiment. Under Capt. Falls he fought in the battle of Ramsours Mill on June 20, 1780. During this battle Capt. Falls was killed and his place taken by Capt. John Harden of Burke County. His company picked up seventeen prisoners after the battle.

Later, in mid August, he again enlisted under Capt. Harden. They rendezvoused at Quaker Meadows in Burke County and later joined with the over mountain men under Col's. Campbell and Shelby. On October 7, 1780 he took part in the epic battle of Kings Mountain. During this battle he received flesh wounds of both calves but was able to continue riding his horse. James was a witness to the hangings at Bickerstaff's and mentions a neighbor of his by the name of Sharpe that was hanged. After this his Company assisted in conveying the prisoners to the Moravian Towns (Winston Salem). In December of 1780, James, as a horseman, joined the mounted battalion of Major Joseph McDowell of Burke. They went from Burke County to the upper part of South Carolina on Pacolet River. They joined forces with Gen. Daniel Morgan and fought in the battle of Cowpens on January 17, 1781. During the battle James was charged by a British Dragoon, struck on the head by a sword and stepped on by his horse. Severely wounded, he was taken to a Mr. Saunders' home to recuperate.

Later James served a short tour of duty on the Catawba Frontier in late 1781. The same year he enlisted as a ten month Continental in South Carolina troops in Capt. Nesbitt's company of Col.(William) Hill's regiment, all under the command of Gen. Thomas Sumter.

SUMMARY OF LATER LIFE

After the Revolutionary War, James moved from Burke County, NC to Carter County, TN, Clay County, KY, Preble County, Ohio, Monroe County, Indiana, Coles County, IL, Cass County Ind., White County, Ind. and finally to Owen County, Indiana. Joseph R. James applied for federal pension in Owen County, Ind. on November 17, 1836, age 80 years. He was awarded an annual pension in the amount of $32.20.

CENSUS LOCATIONS

1790 Burke County, NC (1795 Tax lists)
1800 Carter Co., TN (1798 tax lists)
1810 Clay Co., KY
1820 Clay Co., KY

REFERENCES

US National Archives Pension Data # S 32340
Huggins, Edith, Burke County Records Vol IV (tax lists)
Volkel, Lowell, 1820 Kentucky Census Index (1974)
AIS Census Indices

JAMES, ROLLINGS

SUMMARY OF EARLY LIFE

Rollings James was born in Maryland in 1762. At the time of the American Revolution he was living in Burke County, NC.

SUMMARY OF PARTISAN ACTIVITY

Rollings James entered military service in Burke County, NC in March 1780. James was placed in a South Carolina Line unit. (S.C. officers at this time were recruiting heaving in western N.C., along with the approval of local militia personnel). He was placed in Capt. John McKenzie's company of Col. William Hill S. C. Regiment - later being transferred to Capt. William McKinzie's Company. From Burke County his unit was marched to the vicinity of Congaree River, to Orangeburg, SC, and to Four Hole Bridge. James' duties were as a hospital steward and as an aide to the paymaster, Edward Hunter. His final duties were in the Congaree River area. He saw no specific action during his ten month tour of duty.

SUMMARY OF LATER LIFE

Rollings James applied for Revolutionary War pension in Campbell County, TN, where he resided. He applied in September 1832 and was awarded an annual pension of $33.33. At that time he was a 70 years. A statement on his behalf was made by Amos Richardson of Campbell County, a Revolutionary War soldier.

CENSUS LOCATIONS

1790 Burke County, NC 5th Co.
1800 Carter Co. TN (tax list, "Rawlings James") also 1796,1797.
1810
1821 Grainger County, TN (tax list)
1830 Campbell County, TN

REFERENCES

US National Archives Pension Data # S 2018
AIS Census Indices
Moss, Bobby Gilmer. <u>Roster of South Carolina Patriots in the American Revolution</u> GPC 1983 p. 494

JENKINS, CHARLES

SUMMARY OF EARLY LIFE

Charles Jenkins was living in Virginia during the duration of the Revolutionary War. There are indications that he was living in Burke County as early as 1784 (see land records).

SUMMARY OF PARTISAN ACTIVITY

Charles Jenkins enlisted in the Virginia State Troops in October 1779. He served in the Garrison Regiment of Lt. Col. (Charles) Porterfield and in a Company commanded by Capt. Thomas H. Drew. The regiment was designated to defend certain forts and harbors of the Tidewater section. After completing this tour he was discharged at Little York (Yorktown). His last tour under Capt. Beason, Col. (Christian) Febiger and Gen. (Peter) Muhlenburg. He was discharged in 1783.

SUMMARY OF LATER LIFE

Charles Jenkins, because of poverty applied for (in Burke Co., NC) federal pension in 1821, under the Act of 1818. His total inventory was worth $28.50. He was awarded a pension in the amount of $8.00 per month to commence on July 23, 1821. His age at time of pension was listed as being 88 years.

LAND HOLDINGS AND TRANSACTIONS

Burke County land records show Zachariah Downs acquiring 100 acres on Camp Branch, a tributary of Jacob's Fork "including Charles Jenkins' improvement". Ent. 21 Oct 1784 Warrant Issued.

CENSUS LOCATIONS

1820 Burke Co., N.C.

REFERENCES

US National Archives Pension Data #S41693
Huggins, Edith, Burke County Records Vol.II;IV
Sanchez-Saavedra, EM "A Guide to Virginia Military Organizations in the American Revolution 1774-1787" Virginia State Library 1978
AIS Census Indices
→

JEWELL, WILLIAM

SUMMARY OF EARLY LIFE

William Jewell was about 20 years of age at the commencement of the American Revolution. He most likely was related to James and John Jewell of Hunting Creek, near present day Morganton, Burke County, NC.

SUMMARY OF PARTISAN ACTIVITY

William Jewell first entered military service as a volunteer militiaman in Christopher Beekman's 2nd Rowan Regiment (later Burke County). He was assigned to a company of foot men commanded by Capt. John Hardin. The overall brigade commander was Brig. Gen. Griffith Rutherford of Rowan County. In February and March of 1776, Rutherford's brigade undertook the Cross Creek Expedition, which was part of the Moore's Creek Bridge action against the lower North Carolina Tories. This brigade was mainly involved in mop up activities following the main battle in February. The tour lasted about two months.

In 1779 Jewell served a short tour of duty under Col. Charles McDowell and Maj. Joseph White. Their group advanced to the Savannah River section of South Carolina undergoing some minor skirmishing. Jewell returned home with some discharged wagons. He mentions general officers Brig. Gen. Butler and Maj. Gen. Benjamin Lincoln.

Jewell's next service was in the summer and fall of 1780. Again he was in Capt. Hardin's company of Charles McDowell's Burke regiment. His first action was at Cane Creek in lower Burke County (now McDowell County). This skirmish occurred on Sept. 12, 1780 and was directed against the advance units of Ferguson' regiment, then progressing into western North Carolina. McDowell's men were scattered. During this encounter Maj. Joseph White was wounded and Peter Brank killed. After Cane Creek Jewell took part in the Kings Mountain campaign culminating in the epic battle of October 7, 1780, a great American victory.

After the battle Jewell assisted in conveying prisoners from the battle site to the Moravian Towns, a distance of about 200 miles. This ended his military experience.

SUMMARY OF LATER LIFE

After the Revolution Jewell moved from Burke County to Davidson County, TN. He applied for federal pension in Davidson County on October 17, 1832. He was awarded a pension of $20.00 per annum.

LAND HOLDINGS AND TRANSACTIONS

1. Burke Co. NC NC Land Grant #1519 Ent. #1275 Nov 27, 1792. 200 ac adjacent to Jas. Hemphill. cc's ... John McDowell, Jas. Jewell.

CENSUS LOCATIONS

1790 Burke Co. NC Jas. Jewell only 6th Co.
1820 Davidson Co. TN
1830 Davidson Co. TN

REFERENCES

US National Archives Pension Data # S 1837
Burke Co. Land Grant Records, Morganton-Burke Library, Morganton,N.C.
AIS Census Indices
Middle Tennessee Censun 1830 (Sistler, Byron, Evanston Il 1971)

JOHNSON, JOHN

SUMMARY OF EARLY LIFE

John Johnson was a resident of "Burke County, N.C.", according to pension statements. He was allied with soldiers from the Watauga area of east Tennessee and may have resided in that region (which was included for a brief period in old Burke County). He was born 1760's.

SUMMARY OF PARTISAN ACTIVITY

John Johnson first entered military service as a drafted militiaman in 1777 for a period of six months. He served on the Catawba frontier guarding again the incursions of the hosti Cherokee Indians. He served in the region of the French Broad and Toe Rivers. He was in Capt. Samuel Henry's company, Sevier's regiment.

In 1778, he served another six months tour of duty on the weste Catawba frontier. Charles McDowell of Quaker Meadows was the overall commander. Other officers under who he served included Col. Cocke, Col. Samuels, Capt. Blair, Col. Waugh, and Capt. William Nelson.

SUMMARY OF LATER LIFE

After the Revolution Johnson moved from North Carolina to Tennessee and finally to Kentucky, Pike County. He applied for federal pension in Pike County, KY on June 2, 1834 and was awarded a pension in the amount of $30.00 per annum.

LAND HOLDINGS AND TRANSACTIONS

Burke Co., NC a John Johnson entered 300 acres on Rutherford's Creek adjacent to Griffith Rutherford and William Moore. Ent. 29 January 1778.

CENSUS LOCATIONS

1830 Pike Co., KY

REFERENCES

US National Archives Pension Data #S30512
AIS Census Indices
Smith, Dora W., Kentucky 1830 Census Index 1974 Thomson, IL

JOHNSTON, ROBERT

SUMMARY OF EARLY LIFE

Robert Johnston, at the beginning of the American Revolution, was living in South Carolina, near Camden. (He was age 84 when applying for pension in 1834). He was born ca 1750.

SUMMARY OF PARTISAN ACTIVITY

Robert Johnston first entered military service in South Carolina in late 1775. He was placed in Capt. Drakeford's Company of Col. Richard Richardson's SC Regiment. Under Col. Richardson he participated in the "Snow Campaign" of November and December 1775, directed against the Scovellite Tories of upper South Carolina. After a tour of three months, Johnston then moved to Rowan County, NC and immediately enlisted in Capt. Samuel Young's company of Griffith Rutherfords Brigade. They marched to the Cross Creek area of North Carolina (now Fayetteville, N.C.)to counter the actions of the Tories and Highland Scotch, February and March 1776. They did not arrive in time to take part in the battle of Moore's Creek Bridge, but did assist in clean up activity (disposing of property and arms, conveying prisoners, etc).

After this tour, Johnston was married and moved to Burke County, N.C. near the Catawba River.

In 1781, he served a tour of three months and was stationed at one of the frontier forts of the upper Catawba in Burke County, He served in a company commanded by Capt. Walker (probably Capt. George Walker of Burke).

SUMMARY OF LATER LIFE

In 1783, Johnston left Burke County and moved to Madison County, KY (that part which was later Nelson Co., KY).

Johnson applied for federal pension in Nelson County on March 10, 1834, age 84. He was awarded a pension of $30.00 per annum.

LAND HOLDINGS AND TRANSACTIONS

Kentucky land Grant 500 acres Coxe's Creek (now Cox's Creek) Jefferson entry (Nelson Co. KY) Book A p. 246.

CENSUS LOCATIONS

1800 Nelson Co., KY
1810 Nelson Co., KY
1820 Nelson Co., KY
1830 Nelson Co., KY

REFERENCES

US National Archives Pension Data #15482
Volkel, Lowell, Index to the 1820 Federal Court of Kentucky 197
Smith, Dora W., Kentucky 1830 Census index
AIS Census Indices
Jillson, Willard D., Old Kentucky Entries and Deeds
 GPC 1972 Reprint p. 229.
Moss, Bobby G. Roster of SC Patriots in the American Revolution
 GPC 1983 p. 506

JOHNSTON, LEWIS

SUMMARY OF EARLY LIFE

Lewis Johnston was born ca 1767. He was born and raised in Halifax County, NC.

SUMMARY OF PARTISAN ACTIVITY

Lewis Johnston entered military service in the summer of 1780 as a draftee from Halifax District, (at an extremely young age - 13 years old). He was placed in a company commanded by Capt. John Williams, and in the regiment of Col. Benjamin Seawell. Brigade commander was Gen. Jethro Sumner.

They marched through Franklin and Wake counties into Cumberland County and then toward South Carolina. At Drowning Creek, they were in skirmishes with Tories. In his pension statements, Johnston describes how one Tory was captured and severely whipped(and later died). Advancing into South Carolina near Rugeleys Mill, they came in contact with the fleeing soldiers from Gates' command. (They had earlier been defeated and dispersed by Cornwallis and the British army at Camden on August 16, 1780).
He joined in with the disorderly retreat, but later regrouped near Charlotte. Here he saw the wounded from the bloody defeat of the Americans under Col. Buford at Waxhaw. After crossing the Catawba at the Shallow Ford, Johnston became ill and was later discharged after serving three months.

In July 1781 he served another tour of duty under Col. Nicholas Lury and was stationed at Halifax Town for three months.

Lewis Johnston's application for federal pension was rejected for lack of proof of service. (His appeals and letters total 45 pages). There is no question that he served, since paymaster documents support this. Several factors were against him - his extremely young age at time of service - his late application (1840) - and also due to the scandal involved with the Halifax office.

His wife predeceased him. They had the following children: Elizabeth, Nelly, Mary, Lewis, Jr., Abraham, Albertson, Sarah, Myra and John. Some time after the Revolutionary War, Johnston moved from Halifax to Burke County, NC, (he is listed on 1800 Burke Census).

He was living in Burke County, NC at the time of his application for federal pension in 1840 at age 77 years. He died in Burke County, NC on May 10, 1850.

CENSUS LOCATIONS

1790 Halifax Co., NC
1800 Burke Co., NC
1810 ?Wilkes Co., NC
1820 Burke Co., NC
1830 Burke Co., NC
1840 Burke Co., N.C.

REFERENCES

US National Archived Pension Data #R5643
AIS Census Indices

KILLIAN, DANIEL

SUMMARY OF EARLY LIFE

Daniel Killian appears to have been a son of Andrew Killian, Sr. pioneer settler of the Catawba Valley. Yates Killian, in a family history, stated that Daniel was possibly the oldest child in a second marriage to Mary Cline. The Killians lived in Burke County during the Revolutionary War, now Eastern Catawba County. A brother, Andrew Killian, Jr., was a well recognized Loyalist. A biographer, Mrs. J.R. Gladney, states that Daniel Killian was born ca 1757 (DAR says 1752).

SUMMARY OF PARTISAN ACTIVITY

In 1778-1779, Killian served for a period of 10 months in the NC Continental Line. He served in SC under Gen. Benjamin Lincoln. In 1781, Daniel Killian served in Col. Charles Starke Myddleton's Regiment, South Carolina Continental Line under the overall command of Gen. Thomas Sumter. Killian was a member of the 2nd Dragoons in a company commanded by Capt. Francis Moore. This unit took part in activities in and around middle South Carolina during the siege of Ninety-Six. Many soldiers from western North Carolina served in this campaign and often were of Loyalist sentiments. In late 1782 Killian was cited to appear in Burke County to show cause as to why his property should not be confiscated, for being disloyal to the American Cause.

SUMMARY OF LATER LIFE

Shortly after the Revolutionary War Daniel Killian moved to Buncombe County settling on Beaver Dam Creek. Daniel Killian was married to (1) Osly Baker, January 15, 1787 in Lincoln County and (2) Margaret Watts. Children by these unions included:
John, born Dec. 2, 1788
Joseph, born Oct. 22 1791
Daniel, born Dec. 22 1793
Nancy, born Feb. 5, 1796
William W., born Feb. 5 1800
George, born May 16, 1802
Lydia, born Oct. 29, 1805
Mary, born 1801 or 1806.
The last two children were probably by second wife since a note in Bishop Asbury's Journal October 26, 1803 stated "Sister Killian and Sister Smith are both gone to their reward and glory". Daniel Killian died ca 1830-36 and is buried at Asbury United Methodist Church cemetery, Asheville, NC.

LAND HOLDINGS & TRANSACTIONS

1. In November 1779, Burke County, NC, Daniel Killian entered 250 acres on Pinch Gut Creek on property occupied then by Nicholas Speagle.

2. Buncombe County, NC deeds as follow;
A. Land on New Found Creek 2/2/1791 from William Whitson.
B. Pigeon River 200 acres 5/30/1795 from State of NC.
C. Newfound Creek 100 acres 9/1/1800 from State of NC.
D. Beaver Dam Creek 200 acres 12/2/1797 from State of NC.
E. Pigeon River 400 acres 7/7/1803 from Andrew Killian.

CENSUS LOCATIONS

1790 Burke County, NC 11th Co.
1800 Buncombe County NC
1810 Buncombe County, NC
1820 Buncombe County, NC
1830 Buncombe County, NC

REFERENCES

Gladney, Mrs. J.B. in biographical sketch of Daniel Killian in **Old Buncombe Heritage Book** published Winston Salem, NC 1981 pages 249-50.
Sherrill, William L.,**Annals of Lincoln County**, NC 1937, Reprint, Page 416.
Wooley, James E., Buncombe County, NC Index of Deeds 1783-1850, SHP 1983, pages 274-5
AIS Census Indices
Huggins, Edith W., Burke County Record, Vol II, Page 34, 154,SH 1987.
Moss, Bobby G., Roster of South Carolina Patriots in The Americ Revolution, GPC 1983, Page 533
DAR **Patriot Index** 1966, National Society of DAR, Washington, D.C. Page 386.
N.C. Revolutionary Army Accounts Vol. X Book 22 Voucher #334.

KUYKENDALL, MATTHEW

SUMMARY OF EARLY LIFE

Matthew Kuykendall was born in Mecklenburg County NC Oct 24 1758. He was the son of Peter and Mary Kuykendall. The Kuykendalls were early settlers of the Catawba frontier in the mid 18th century. His family lived in York District, S. C. at the beginning of the conflict. Matthew Kuykendall was a nephew of Col. Joseph Hardin of Rutherford County, NC, then York District, SC.

SUMMARY OF PARTISAN ACTIVITY

Matthew Kuykendall first entered military service in York District as an infantryman in Col. Joseph Hardin's Company. He entered in the summer of 1776 and joined in Rutherford's Cherokee Expedition of the late summer and early fall. Kuykendall, in his pension papers, described the action as being somewhat subdued. It consisted mainly of destruction of Cherokee villages and crops. He stated that the Indians managed to avoid them.

After returning home from the Cherokee Expedition Kuykendall moved from York District to Burke County, NC and remained a resident there until after the Revolution.

He again entered service in 1780 in Joseph McDowell's Company of the Burke Militia. He took part in the battle of Ramsour's Mill on June 20, 1780. Following this action he served with the McDowells in the summer campaigns of 1780 which ended with the skirmish at Cane Creek on September 12, 1780. With the Burke troops he retreated to Cathey's Place on the upper Catawba and then over the Blue Ridge to the Watauga settlements. Kuykendall later returned across the Blue Ridge with the remnants of the Burke Militia and with the Over Mountain Men of Watauga and Virginia. In Burke County Kuykendall took a furlough to be with his family and because of this, he missed the action of the main battle of King's Mountain of October 7, 1780.

Kuykendall once again served in early 1781 in Capt. Murray's company of McDowell's Battalion. On January 17, 1781 he fought in the battle of Cowpens in South Carolina. During this action he received a serious wound of his right arm which left him partially disabled for the rest of his life. This also ended his military career.

SUMMARY OF LATER LIFE

Kuykendall lived a few years in Burke County after the war and then moved to Washington County, Tenn. for a few years and then middle Tennessee. He lived in Davidson County. Census records also show a Matthew Kuykendall in Sumner County, Tenn., adjacent to Davidson County. Kuykendall's last residence was in Logan

County, KY., that part which became Butler County. He applied for Federal pension in Butler County at age 74 in 1832. He was awarded a pension of $50.00 per annum. Matthew Kuykendall was married to Margaret Hardin, daughter of John and Elizabeth Hardin. Their children were as follows:

Josiah	Andrew	Peggy
Moses	Mark	
Matthew	John	

Margaret Hardin Kuykendall ws born c. 1768. She and Matthew Kuykendall were married in Burke Co. In 1781. She died after 1840 and before 1846. In Butler Co., KY the Kuykendalls lived near a Moses Kuykendall, who had been a resident in the area since c. 1800. Matthew Kuykendall appears to have moved into t area c. 1823.

Matthew Kuykendall died in October 1845.

LAND HOLDINGS AND TRANSACTIONS

1. Butler Co. KY Land Warrant 200 ac. Little Muddy Creek 12 Aug 1835 Bk. 1-2 p. 398.

2. Butler Co. KY Land Warrant 50 acres Little Muddy Creek 14 Ar 1825 Bk. Rp. 312.

3. Kentucky Land Grant Warrant South of Green River 100 acres Little Creek 11 Oct 1823 Bk. 26 p. 341

4. Gen. TN Land Grant #827 Franklin Co. 204 acres Feb 6, 1809 B B/ 403.

CENSUS LOCATIONS

1790 Sumner Co., TN .. Tax lists of 1789,1792,1793,1794,1795.
1830 Butler Co. KY

REFERENCES

US National Archives Pension Data #30518
Tennessee State Archives and Library, Tax Lists and Land Grants
Jillson, Willard R. The Kentucky Land Grants GPC Reprint,
  Baltimore 1971 Part I (orig. Louisville 1925).
Fullerton, Jane Hardin "Kuykendall-Hardin" 1964 Nashville. Pp 43 47. Copy in TN St. Arch. & Library.

LEATHERWOOD, EDWARD

SUMMARY OF EARLY LIFE

Edward or "Ned" Leatherwood, according to family data, was born in 1754. He was the son of John and Sarah "Sally" Hunt Leatherwood. The Leatherwoods were early settlers of Maryland, Anne Arundel and Baltimore Counties. At the beginning of the American Revolution, Leatherwood had settled in Burke County, N.C. on the upper Catawba River.

SUMMARY OF PARTISAN ACTIVITY

In late 1782, Edward Leatherwood was cited to Burke County Court to show cause as to why is property should not be confiscated, for being disloyal to the American Cause. Disposition of case not known. He was a neighbor to several well known loyalist families and possibly related to some of them.

SUMMARY OF LATER LIFE

Edward Leatherwood continued to live in Burke County for the remainder of the century. His name appears on various Burke County jury lists for 1793, 1795, 1796, 1798. Burke County records also list Samuel, John, James and Aquilla Leatherwood (see below).

Leatherwood appears to have moved briefly to Buncombe County, but then moved back into Burke County. His last census appearance was in 1820.

Edward Leatherwood was married to Elizabeth Walker, In Virginia, ca. 1774-1777. .she appears to have been related to Rev. War soldier, Jas. Reuben Walker of Burke. Children as follows:

John b. 1779 m. Sarah Burns
Samuel b. ca. 1774-1784 m. Elizabeth Ferguson
Elizabeth b. c. 1783 m. Benjamin Hyde
Aquilla b. 1786
Reuben, named for Reuben Walker, m. Betsy Carriah.

It is possible that the James listed in Burke records may have been "James Reuben" since Reuben Walker's full name was James Reuben Walker. (see biog. Vol I).

LAND HOLDINGS AND TRANSACTIONS

1. 100 acres Burke County NC on north side of main Catawba River adjacent to land of John Doty and William Gray. Land included "on old field." cc Azariah Doty, - Hyatt. Ent. 25 Sept 1778 #? Grant No. 179 Iss. 14 Mar 1780, Book 28 p.178.

2. 1815 Burke County NC tax lists Edward Leatherwood with 300

acres on north fork of Catawba in North Cove adjo8ining land of Davy Cox and John Clelan (McClellan?).

3. Buncombe Co., NC Deeds
Robert Rodgers to Edward Leatherwood 200 acres on Jonathan's Creek, 24 Jul 1800, recorded 18 Jul 1801.
Samuel Williams to Edward Leatherwood 100 acres Jonathan's Creek 23 Apr 1806.
(Edward Leatherwood conveyed 20 acres on Jonathan's Creek to Joh Leatherwood 18 Jan 1808.)

CENSUS LOCATIONS

1790 Burke Co., NC 6th Co.
1800 Buncombe Co., NC
1810 Burke Co., NC
1820 Burke Co., NC

REFERENCES

Huggins, Edith. W., "Burke County N.C. Land Records". Vols I,II
Vochko, Ethel Stroupe. Biography of Edward Leatherwood in The Heritage of Swain County (NC). Bryson City, 1988. Pp 208-9. The same article appeared earlier, 1987, in The Heritage of Old Buncombe County (NC).
AIS Census Indices
Pittman, Betsy D., 1990, "Burke County, N.C. 1815 Tax Lists" p.102
Woody, J.E. Buncombe County, N.C. Index to deeds 1783-1850 SHP 1983 p.294
Swink, DanD., 1986,1987 "Minutes of the Court of Pleas and Quarter Session", Burke County, N.C. 1791-1795 and 1795-1798"

LEDFORD, PETER

SUMMARY OF EARLY LIFE

Peter Ledford was born in Randolph County, NC in the year 1758. He continued to live in Randolph County until about the turn of the century, moving then to Burke County. He remained in Burke County for about thirty years, moving to Macon County, NC in his later years.

SUMMARY OF PARTISAN ACTIVITY

Peter Ledford first entered military service in Randolph County in March 1781, shortly before the battle of Guilford Court House (March 15, 1781). He served in Capt. John Knight's Company of Col. Thomas Dugan's militia regiment. He served as a mounted trooper.

Ledford served several tours of duty under Col. Dugan, usually from three to six weeks each. In each tour, their military activities were directed against the noted Tory partisan, Col. David Fanning. He mentions raids as far south as the South Carolina line and as far west as the "narrows of the Yadkin." In his pension declaration he stated that, " we were drawn up in battle array against Col. Fanning, who was infamous in the annals of Toryism and who each time refused to give battle..."

Ledford served off and on until the end of 1781, a total service time of six months.

SUMMARY OF LATER LIFE

Ledford moved from Randolph County to Burke County sometime before 1800 (land grant in 1794) and lived there for about 30 years. In his later years, he moved to Macon County, NC. Peter Ledford applied for federal pension in Macon County, NC on June 19, 1833, age 74 years. He was awarded an annual pension of $26.52.

LAND HOLDINGS AND TRANSACTIONS

1. 320 acres on North Fork Catawba River adjacent to land belonging to Thomas Knight. Previously entered by William Wofford September 5, 1778.
Grant No. 1883, Iss. July 7, 1794, Book 85, p. 128.

2. 100 acres on Tom's Creek adjacent to land belonging to Curtis and"...on both sides of the big road leading to the Turkey Cove..."
Ent. February 3, 1813, No. 3896, Grant No. 3658
Iss. Dec. 2, 1814, Book 128, p. 427.

CENSUS LOCATIONS

1790 Randolph County, NC
1800 Burke County, NC
1810 Burke County, NC
1820 Burke County, NC
1830 Macon County, NC

REFERENCES

US National Archives Pension Data # S 7146
Burke Co., NC Land Grant Data; Morganton-Burke Library, Morganton, NC
AIS Census Indices

LEWIS, WILLIAM

SUMMARY OF EARLY LIFE

William Lewis was living in western Burke County, near Muddy Creek, during the Revolutionary War period. He seems to have been related to the Lewis family of Hanover County, VA that settled in western North Carolina in Burke and Rutherford Counties.

SUMMARY OF PARTISAN ACTIVITY

William Lewis's name appears on the Criminal Docket of Burke County Court in November 1782, to show cause as to why his property should not be confiscated, for being inimical to the American Cause. See further notes in foreword, this volume, relating to this "Tory List" of 1782.

The name William Lewis appears in both North Carolina and South Carolina military records, exact relationship to the above unknown, if any. A well known Revolutionary War figure, William T. Lewis, Sr. and his son William T. Lewis, Jr. lived in Surry County, NC.

SUMMARY OF LATER LIFE

Burke County Court records show Lewis acquiring property on Muddy Creek in 1784 (Ent. 1778) but disposing of it in 1792. The same year he acquired a house in Morganton, formerly owned by Alexander Cummings and later selling it to James McIntyre (both in 1792). He appears on the 1790 census 1st Company but does not appear on the 1800 census or the 1815 tax lists. He does appear in Burke County Court records in 1795.

LAND HOLDINGS AND TRANSACTIONS

1. 370 acres Burke County, NC on Young's Fork of Muddy Creek, including his own improvements. The land lay adjacent to that of Joshua Young.
Ent. 1778 #441 Grant No. 796 Iss. 9 Nov 1784 Book 57 p. 12
c.c. David Templeton, Samuel Patton

2. 457 acres Burke County, NC on both sides of upper Muddy Creek and adjacent to land belonging to William Patton and John Joanes (Jones).
c.c. Samuel Patton, John Joanes.
Ent. 1778 Grant No. 844 Iss. 1784 Book 57, p. 35.

CENSUS LOCTIONS

1790 Burke County, NC 1st Co.

REFERENCES

Huggins, Edith W. Burke County Records Vol I & II 1977
AIS 1790 Census North Carolina
Pittman, Betsy D., "Burke County NC 1815 Tax Lists" Valdese, NC 1990.
Swink, Daniel D. "Minutes of the Court of Pleas and Quarter Sessions" (1791 - 1795 & 1795 - 1798) 1986, 1987 Lawndale NC

LOCK, JAMES

SUMMARY OF EARLY LIFE

James Lock, one of the older veterans, was also a veteran of the French and Indian War. He was born in Pennsylvania ca. 1732 and at a young age served in General Braddock's force as a wagoner.

SUMMARY OF PARTISAN ACTIVITY

During the Revolutionary War, Lock served under Gen. Rutherford, most likely the Cherokee Expedition of 1776, though this is not clearly documented. Later, Lock participated in the Kings Mountain Campaign and Battle in September and October of 1780.

SUMMARY OF LATER LIFE

James Lock settled in Burke County and became a thrify and industrious farmer. He lived to be a ripe old age and died at age 99 on January 19, 1832.

REFERENCES

Rouse, J.K. <u>Another Revolutionary War Hero Dies</u> Salisbury 1978 page 127.

McCALL, ROBERT

SUMMARY OF EARLY LIFE

Robert McCall was born in County Antrim, Northern Ireland in 1752. He was the son of John and Helen Moore McCall. Prior to the Revolution, in 1773, he was married to Elizabeth Aiken.

SUMMARY OF PARTISAN ACTIVITY

A strong anti-British partisan in Ireland, McCall was charged by the Crown with treason. He escaped to America in 1775 along with his wife and six month old child. According to family records he fought with Gen. Daniel Morgan at Saratoga and at Yorktown. At this time he was a resident of Pennsylvania. He later served as a colonel of a North Carolina regiment (another source stated that he was a private and served on the Carolina frontier.)

SUMMARY OF LATER LIFE

Moving south after the war, McCall and his family lived briefly in Henry County, VA, and in 1793 moved to Burke County, N.C. near the present Burke-Caldwell line. McCall was a Methodist and a follower of John Wesley. Children of Robert and Elizabeth McCall were as follows.

b. 1774 Margaret m. John Shell
b. 1777 William m. Mildred Holland
b. 1778 Samuel m. Sarah Shell
b. 1780 John m. Phoebe Smith
b. 1782 James m. Katie Kincaid
b. 1784 Elizabeth m. Andrew Hall Tuttle
b. 1789 Robert m. Lydia Gillespie
b. 1790 Jessie m. Benedict Bristol
       Nancy not married
b. 1792 Henry m. Jane Rector
b. 1794 Alexander m. Mary Cryder

Robert McCall was a large land owner and possessed many slaves. He died in 1820 and is buried at Littlejohn's Church in Caldwell County, NC.

LAND HOLDINGS AND TRANSACTIONS

Burke Co., NC 1815 tax lists show Robert McCall with 300 acres of land on north side of Catawba River.

REFERENCES

McCall, James L. Morganton. NC "The McCall Family in Ireland and America"
McCall, Michael, M.D. Personal communications to the Author
Pittman, Betsy D., Burke County, N.C. 1815 Tax Lists 1990 p.65

McCall, Mrs.Howard Roster of Revolutionary Soldiers of Georgia
GPC 1968 Vol II p.16

McDANIELS, JAMES

SUMMARY OF EARLY LIFE

James McDaniels was born in Cumberland County, NC. His stated age was 76 years when applying for pension in May 1834. He liv[ed] in Burke County, NC during the Revolutionary War.

SUMMARY OF PARTISAN ACTIVITY

James McDaniels first entered Revolutionary War military servic[e] in 1776 as a militia volunteer in Col. Charles McDowell's Burke Regiment. His commanding officers were Major Daniel McKissock, Capt. Reuben White and Lt. Samuel Simpson. They marched to the western frontier in order to counter recent raids by the Cherok[ee] Indians. His Company met with an ambush on the north fork of t[he] Catawba River. In this skirmish, Captain White was killed. Th[e] Company then joined in Rutherford's Cherokee expedition of August-September 1776. They marched to the big Tellico Towns a[nd] back, taking some prisoners and destroying property.

His next tour of duty was in the spring of 1779 as a volunteer [in] the Company commanded by Captain LeRoy Taylor. Col. Charles McDowell commanded the Regiment. Under McDowell, they marched [to] Stono Ferry near Charleston, S.C. There McDaniels took part in the battle of Stono Ferry on June 20, 1779. McDaniels, in his pension statements, mentioned that the battle began early and lasted until about twelve. He also stated that the dead were n[ot] buried until two or three days later. McDaniels next volunteer[ed] as a mounted horseman in the Company commanded by Maj. Francis Locke and Col. William Murray. They proceeded to the outskirts of Charleston, then under siege by the British, in early 1780. Here they joined the forces of Gen. Isaac Huger. On April 14, 1780, in a predawn attack, the entire group was defeated and scattered by the British (Commanded by Webster and Tarleton). McDaniels lost his horse and his clothing, except that which he wore. His Unit then marched back to Ramsour's Mill in Lincoln County, NC joining General Rutherford's troops. They took part in the battle of Ramsour's Mill on June 20, 1780. McDaniels continued on with General Rutherford's Brigade. They marched t[o] Charlotte, NC and joined the army of General Horatio Gates. On August 16, 1780 he fought in the battle of Camden, S. C. This battle was a disastrous defeat for the American forces. His immediate Commanding Officer, Col. Isaacs, was captured along with Gen. Rutherford. McDaniels makes note that the battle commenced early in the morning and lasted until ten.

McDaniel then stated that he took part in a short excursion int[o] SC under Major Joseph McDowell of Burke County in December 1780 They rendovoused at Lawson's Iron Works, at which place they to[ok] part in a small skirmish. In early 1781, McDaniels volunteere[d] in a Horse Company commanded by Maj. Joseph McDowell of Burke County (he also mentions Maj. Daniel McKissock. McKissock was severely wounded at Ramsour's seven months earlier and probably

186

was unable to participate actively). McDaniels, under McDowell, marched into South Carolina to near Ninety Six and then retreated to Cowpens, having joined the Brigade of Gen. Daniel Morgan. On January 17, 1781 he participated in the Battle of Cowpens, SC, a great American victory. He mentioned the taking of many prisoners and he assisted in escorting the prisoners into Burke County, NC.

McDaniels last tour of duty was in the Spring of 1781. He served under Col. Hampton, Major Richard Lewis and Capt. Robert Bell. They rendovoused at Blackstocks, S.C. and proceeded to Ninety Six, taking part in the unsuccessful siege operations in June 1781, commanded by Gen. Nathaniel Greene. After the siege was lifted they marched to Savannah River at Golphin's Bluff. There he was discharged in August 1781. McDaniels had served a total of about a year and nine months in Revolutionary service.

SUMMARY OF LATER LIFE

James McDaniels applied for federal pension in Morgan County, TN on May 31, 1834. At that time he was married to Ann Rodgers.

REFERENCES

US National Archives, Pension Statements as "James McDonald" #W7424
DAR Patriot Index, page 452
AIS Census Indices
McDonald, Stephen, Okla. City, OK, Personal communication, including data given by W.D. Bennett of Wendell, N.C.

McDOWELL, JOHN (Q,M,)

SUMMARY OF EARLY LIFE

John McDowell was born in Rockbridge County Va. in 1751, the son of pioneer settler Joseph McDowell of Quaker Meadows and his wife Margaret O'Neill McDowell. He was a brother to Hugh, Charles and Joseph McDowell.

The McDowells moved to their Quaker Meadows home from Virginia ca. 1765.

SUMMARY OF PARTISAN ACTIVITY

John McDowell served first as a junior officer in his brother Charles' Burke Militia Regiment. Military activities were directed against the hostile Cherokee Indians and against local Loyalists.

In September and October of 1780, John McDowell served in the Kings Mountain campaign. He took part in the victorious strugg of October 7, 1780.

In the latter part of the war he joined in with the Wilmington Expedition of 1781, under Brig.Gen. Griffith Rutherford. Durir 1782, he was active in campaigns against the Cherokees. Towarc the end of he war, he had obtained field officer status with the rank of Major. After the war he was known as "Major John McDowell" so as to distinguish him from his well known kinsman, "Hunting John" McDowell of Pleasant Gardens.

SUMMARY OF LATER LIFE

John McDowell married ca. 1775 Hannah Keller of Winchester, Va. (1755-1832). Children: three sons died in a fire at the home on October 30, 1812 (all young men at the time). Daughter Margaret 1782-1854 married Robert McElrath. Daughter Elizabeth (Betsy) 1786-1870 married John McElrath.

John McDowell died 24 March 1822. He is buried at McDowell Presbyterian Church Cemetery near Cathy Road, Burke County, NC and about nine miles from Morganton, N.C. near Silver Creek.

McDowells home was in close proximity to the church.

LAND HOLDINGS AND TRANSACTIONS

1. Burke Co., NC 640 acres on both sides Silver Creek, adjacent to his own improvements and those of William Causby. Grant #93 Iss. 1779 Ent. 1778 Book 28 p. 93

2, Burke County, NC 640 acres north side of Catawba River

"Swan Ponds" survey previously occupied by William McBride and
James Lapsley. Original Granville grant by John Watkins.
cc. Joseph McDowell, Henry Highland. *
Grant #198, Iss. March 1780, Ent. 1778 Book 28 p.197
*There is some question as to whether this is Major John McDowell
or Hunting John McDowell.

3. Burke County, NC 300 acres west side Silver Creek.
Grant #500, Iss.,28 October 1782, Ent. 1778 Book 44 p. 227

4. Burke County, NC 640 acres Caney River above great Cane
Break.
Grant #1020, Iss. August 1787, Book 65, p. 90

1815 tax lists show John McDowell with 1100 acres on Silver
Creek in three tracts.

CENSUS LOCATIONS

1790 Burke Co., NC 6th Company
1800
1810
1820

REFERENCES

Pittman, Betsy D.,1815 Burke County Tax Lists
Pittman, Betsy D., Genealogical data in vertical files
  Morganton-Burke Library, Morganton, NC
McElrath, Charles, personal communication and data.
Land Grant data from Morganton-Burke Library, Morganton, NC
Huntsman, Maude, data in vertical files Morganton-Burke Library,
  Morganton, NC
US National Archives, Revolutionary War pension declarations of
Isaac Grant (R 4196), Samuel Lusk (W 8092), William Morrison (W
1455). Edward Poteat (W 110853).

McDOWELL, JOSEPH (Pleasant Gardens)

SUMMARY OF EARLY LIFE

Joseph McDowell of Pleasant Gardens was the son of Hunting" John" McDowell and Anna Edmisten McDowell. He was born inRockbridge County, VA in 1758, though his father at that time was establishing his residence in western North Carolina. They settled first in Mecklenburg County on a creek still known as McDowell's Creek, but later they pushed on farther westward, eventually establishing their permanent residence on a beautiful tract of land known as "Pleasant Gardens" (now McDowell County, N.C.)

Joseph McDowell grew to maturity on the harsh western North Carolina frontier. Joseph McDowell's sister Rachel was married to John Carson. Another sister Anna was married to William Whitson.

SUMMARY OF PARTISAN ACTIVITY

While only a teenager, Joseph McDowell took part in the early campaign against the hostile Cherokee Indians, including the large Cherokee Expedition of Gen. Griffith Rutherford. This took place in the late summer and early autumn of 1776. After this campaign and prior to the Kings Mountain campaign, activity on the western frontier was centered mainly around several strongly fortified forts. Some of the better known forts included Davidson's Fort, Cathey's Fort, Fort Charles and White's Fort. Joseph McDowell at this time was serving as a company grade officer with the rank of Captain. Captain McDowell took an active role in the Kings Mountain Campaign of August September and October 1780. At the great battle of October,7, 1780, he commanded the Burke Militia. After the battle, he came in possession of Major Ferguson's valued china dishes.

In January of 1781, the battle of Cowpens was fought, resulting in another American victory. It is not clear as to whether or not Capt. McDowell was present. There is some evidence that he was not there. The Burke troops at Cowpens were headed by his cousin, Maj. Joseph McDowell of Quaker Meadows.

In the summer of 1781, Capt. McDowell commanded his company on the Wilmington Expedition, under the overall command of Brig. Gen. Griffith Rutherford. On his return from the Wilmington Expedition, Capt. McDowell sat in on the Court Martial proceedings of Col. Charles McDowell. The Court Martial was brought about by the complaints of frontier fort officers, saying that Col. McDowell showed partiality toward certain Loyalists and had used illegal strong arm type tactics. He was convicted and relieved of command but later restored. The records do not indicate how Capt. McDowell felt about the issues. His final military service during the Revolutionary War was in 1782 participating in the spring raid against the Cherokee Indians, headed by Maj. Joseph McDowell of Quaker Meadows (who had taken over his brother's duties after his command was relinquished).

SUMMARY OF LATER LIFE

Joseph McDowell P.G. was married to Mary Moffett of Rockbridge Co., VA, the daughter of Col. George Moffett and Sarah McDowell Moffett. Her sister was married to Joseph McDowell of Quaker Meadows. Joseph and Mary McDowell had the following children:
1. John m. Mary Mansfield Lewis of Rutherford Co., N.C.
2. Annie m. Capt. Charles McDowell of Quaker Meadows, son of Col. Charles McDowell.
3. James Moffett McDowell m. Margaret Erwin, daughter of W.W. Erwin and Matilda Sharpe Erwin.

After the close of the American Revolution, Joseph McDowell P.G. rose to prominence as one of western North Carolina's most outstanding public servants.

He was highly educated and gifted individual. Professionally he practiced the art and science of medicine in his area. The late noted Burke historian, Edward Phifer, Jr., seemed to think that Joseph McDowell, though lacking a formal training in medicine, "rode the circuit" with the well known, highly trained physician of his region, Dr. Joseph Dobson, Sr. He probably inherited Dobson's practice after Dobson's accidental death in the early 1790's. Besides medicine there were many other contributions by McDowell. In 1788 and again in 1789 he was one of western North Carolina's Representatives to the Constitutional conventions at Hillsboro and Fayetteville. In the first convention held at Hillsboro in 1788, McDowell, along with the majority, voted against adoption of the proposed Constitution. At the second convention at Fayetteville in 1789, and after the Bill of Rights addition, he, with the majority, voted for adoption.

McDowell represented Burke County both in the House and in the Senate.

McDowell served as one of the early Trustees of the newly created University of North Carolina at Chapel Hill.

Militarily McDowell became Commanding Officer of Burke Militia with the rank of Colonel. One of the most controversial subjects about the life of Joseph McDowell P.G. is concerning whether or not he served in the U.S. Congress. There is no question that a great deal of confusion has arisen concerning the exploits of the two Joseph McDowells --- both were of the same approximate age, both served in the Revolutionary War under similar circumstances, they married sisters and so on.

In the Author's opinion, and for more than a decade of research, it is apparent that only Joseph McDowell of Quaker Meadows served in the U.S. Congress. The evidence is simply too overwhelming to conclude otherwise. More will be written on this subject.

Joseph McDowell P.G. represented Burke County in the N.C. House of Representatives from 1787 through 1792. Thereafter he served in the N.C. Senate. In the Author's opinion, it was in the N.C. Legislature that he received the appellation of "Joseph McDowell Jr." so as to distinguish him from Joseph McDowell of Quaker Meadows who was his senior in the Legislature (and in age.) When only one was in the Legislature the name "Joseph McDowell" was used. About the only way to distinguish them was to know the number of miles placed in travel expense declarations.

Joseph McDowell of Pleasant Gardens died prematurely in 1795, the cause and circumstances of his death not definitely known. The exact date of his death is unknown though the historian and chronicler Heitman lists February 27, 1795. Administrative functions are given in the April Burke County Court minutes. None are given in the January 1795 minutes indicating that his death probably occurred between January and April 1795.

His widow, Mary Moffett McDowell, later married John Carson who was earlier married to Joseph McDowell's sister Rachel.

CENSUS LOCATIONS

1790 Burke Co., NC 1st Co.

LAND HOLDINGS AND TRANSACTIONS

1. Burke Co., NC 400 acres E. Side of French Broad River, above mouth of Swannanoa River. Ent. 6 Oct 1783 Ent. No. 131 Grant issued 8 Dec 1787 Grant No. 1081. CC Jas Chambers, Wm. Whitson.

2. Burke Co. NC 26 ac on both sides of Nick's Creek, adjacent to upper portion of John Carson's tract. Ent. 1 Sep 1788 Ent. No. 123, Grant issued 16 Nov 1790. Grant No. 1390. CC John Carson, Thos. Wilson.

3. Burke Co NC 700 ac on both sides of the first large creek that empties into the Pigeon River. Ent. 1 Aug 1783 Ent. No. 65, Grant issued 4 Jan 1792. Grant No. 1400. CC Robert Reed, James Dunn.

REFERENCES

AIS Census Indices North Carolina 1790
US National Archives; R.W. pension declarations of Arthur McFalls, David McPeters, Andrew Neill, Jacob Grindstaff, John Penland, George Hodge.
McDowell, John Hugh McDowell Erwins and their Connections 1918
Green, T.M. Historic Families of Kentucky 1889
DAR Patriot Index National Soc. DAR Washington 1966 p. 453
Phifer, Edward W. Jr. Burke 1977

Biography of the American Congress   Washington 1971
McDowell, Col. Charles, Court Martial Records. Facsimile
 presented to Author by the late Miss Eunice Ervin of
   Morganton, NC
For detailed bibliography of the McDowell family, see Vol.I
of this work under Col. Charles McDowell and Major Joseph
McDowell of Quaker Meadows.

McKISSOCK, DANIEL

SUMMARY OF EARLY LIFE

Daniel McKissock was born ca 1755. During the Revolutionary period he was residing in southeastern Burke County, (later Lincoln and then Catawba County.)

SUMMARY OF PARTISAN ACTIVITY

Daniel McKissock was one of the ranking officers of Col. Charles McDowell's Burke Regiment. McKissock, while a member of the 2nd Rowan Regiment, participated in the Cross Creek Expedition of March 1776. This was the cleanup operation following the battle of Moore's Creek Bridge in February. In the summer of 1776, McKissock was in company with Col. McDowell on the western frontier fighting against the sudden bloody raid of the Cherokee Indians. Holding their own at Catheys Fort, they were relieved by the large expeditionary force of Gen. Griffith Rutherford. McKissock then took part in the Cherokee Expedition of August and September of that year.

On his return to Burke County he was active against local Loyalist activity. He also served as high sheriff of Burke County in 1778 and 1779. He was appointed a field officer of Burke Militia serving under Lt. Col. Hugh Brevard, with the rank of Major.

In June 1780, McKissock and Brevard along with Capt. John Hardin, Maj. Joseph McDowell, Capt. John Bowman, Capt. John Dobson and others joined forces with the Rowan Militia in suppressing Tory forces in Lincoln County. They won a major victory at the battle of Ramsour's Mill on June 20, 1780. Unfortunately the toll paid was high. Capts. Dobson and Bowman were killed, Maj. McKissock was critically wounded in the left arm. He recovered but was permanently disabled.

Afterwards he participated in some of the administrative duties but did not do any active fighting. In early 1782 he, as senior officer, provided over the Court Martial proceedings of Col. Charles McDowell.

SUMMARY OF LATER LIFE

After the war, Maj. McKissock became one of the military auditors of Morgan District.

Daniel McKissock was married to Jane Wilson in about 1776 or 1777. They were the parents of the following children. (Jane Wilson was age 80 in 1839.)

Margaret b. 1777   John b. 1784   Joseph b. 1791

Mary b. 1779   David b. 1786   Wilson b. 1794
James b. 1782   Daniel b. 1789   Elizabeth b.? 1797

In 1782 McKissock was one of the Commissioners chosen to select the new County seat of Lincoln County.

McKissock applied for and received a pension from the State of North Carolina, because of his disabling wounds received at Ramsours.

Daniel McKissock was active in Lincoln County Court affairs well into the first decade of the 1800's. In 1807 he moved to Tennessee, Shelbyville area in Bedford County. He died in Shelbyville, TN March 18, 1818. His widow lived in Bedford County until 1836, moving then to Benton County, Arkansas.

LAND HOLDINGS AND TRANSACTIONS

Burke County, N.C. 324 acres on Allen's Creek and Maiden Creek at fork, tributaries of south fork of Catawba River (now Catawba County, NC) adjacent to land of John Allen and which contained a part of McKissock's improvements. cc John Boyd, John Boreland.
Ent. 8 Jan 1779 #861 Grant No. 217 Iss. March 14, 1780 Book 28 p. 216.

CENSUS LOCATIONS

1790 Lincoln Co. NC 2nd Co.
1800 Lincoln Co. NC
1810 Bedford Co., TN (1812 tax list)

REFERENCES

Burke Co. Land Grant Data, Morganton Burke Library, Morganton, NC
Pruitt, Dr. A.B., Abstracts of Land Entries Lincoln Co., N.C. 1987
Huggins, Edith, Burke Co. Records Vols I-IV
Swink, Dan D., Burke County Minutes of Court Pleas and Quarter Session 1791-1795 and 1795-1798.
AIS Census Indices
Sisler, Byron & Barbara, Early Tennessee Tax Lists 1977 Evanston Ill. p. 136
Whitley, Edythe, Tennessee DAR Records, p.1190
<u>DAR Patriot Index</u> National Society DAR, Washington, DC 1966
Phifer, Edward <u>Burke</u> 1977 Morganton, NC pp. 54,308
U.S. National Archives, Pension declarations of Richard Crabtree, Thomas Craig, Arthur McFalls.
White, Emmett R., <u>Revolutionary War Soldiers of Western N.C.</u>, Vol I. (articles on McDowell family and statement of pensioners.)
U.S. National Archives (application of widow, Jane McKissock, 1839) # W26251.

McPETERS, JONATHAN

SUMMARY OF EARLY LIFE

Jonathan McPeters was born in Mecklenburg County, NC on January 14, 1756. At the beginning of the Revolution, he was living in Western Burke County, NC. He was a member of a family that possessed strong Loyalist sympathies. Other family members included Charles and Joseph McPeters. (See Vol. I).

SUMMARY OF PARTISAN ACTIVITY

Jonathan McPeters first entered military service in Burke County NC (then Rowan County) in March of 1776. He served in Capt. William Moore's Company of Col. Christopher Beekman's 2nd Rowan Regiment. Under Beekman he participated in the Cross Creek Expedition, in early 1776. In the summer of 1776 he served in Capt. Reuben White's Company, of McDowell's Burke Regiment. This Company was later commanded by Capt. Moore after White's death at the North Fork of the Catawba.

His next tour of duty was for a six month period of time in the Spring of 1777 under Col. Charles McDowell. He served as an Indian spy or scout. In 1778 he served a term of three months under Col. (Francis) Cunningham. Their activities were directed against the Tories of Lincoln County, NC. In early 1780, he enlisted in Capt. Robert Patton's Company of Col. Charles McDowell's Burke Militia, mounted. They marched through Charlotte to the outskirts of Charleston, SC, then under siege by the British. There on April 14, 1780, they were overwhelmed by the British and were scattered. Later they regrouped and returned to near Ramsour's Mill, Lincoln Co., NC arriving there shortly after the battle of June 20, 1780. His next duty tour was in the Spring of 1781. He participated in the unsuccessful siege of Ninety Six, SC. During this period of time he served i Capt. Joshua Inman's Company. Other officers were Lt. Elias Alexander and Ensign William Snoddy. High ranking officers included Gen. Nathaniel Greene and Col. Howard of the Maryland Line. In his pension application McPeters (about the Ninety Six siege) stated that "...was aiding Capt. Campbell when he was killed storming the sand bags the day after they were compelled to raise the siege".

In the fall of 1781 McPeters took part in the Wilmington expedition of General Griffith Rutherford. He served in a Company commanded by Capt. Joseph McDowell of Pleasant Gardens. At Wilmington they heard of Cornwallis' surrender at Yorktown.

NOTE: In November 1782, Jonathan McPeters was cited in Burke County Court, for being disloyal to the American Cause. Joseph and Charles McPeters were also listed.

SUMMARY OF LATER LIFE

After the Revolution, McPeters lived in North Carolina, then Tennessee and finally back to Buncombe County, NC and Yancey County, NC. He applied for Federal Pension on October 18, 1832 while residing in Buncombe County, NC, age 76. He was awarded a pension of $80.00 per annum. Jonathan McPeters died in Yancey County, NC on March 16, 1846 at age 90. Apparently he had moved to Yancey County some time before 1838.

LAND HOLDINGS AND TRANSACTIONS

1. 200 acres, Burke County, NC on both sides of the First Creek north of Richland Creek. This land lay near the lands of John McDonald.
Ent. Jan 28, 1779, #1489, Grant No. 1088, Iss Dec 8 1787, Book 67, p. 225.

2. 200 acres Prices Creek, Buncombe County, NC, State Land Grant No. 144, 19 Jan 1795, Book 51-2, p. 142.

3. 640 acres French Broad River, Buncombe County, N.C. State Land Grant No. 783, 2 Apr 1800, Book 51-6, p. 25.

CENSUS LOCATIONS

1790 Burke County, NC, 1st Company
1800
1810 Haywood County, NC
1820
1830 Buncombe County, NC
1840 Yancey County, NC

REFERENCES

Marriage and death motices from extant Asheville, NC newspapers 18040-1870 index edited by Robert M. Topkins, NC Genealogical Society, Raleigh, NC 1977, page 101.
US National Archives, Pension Declarations
AIS Census Indices

INSERT

The Case involving the McPeters brothers demonstrates the very reason Loyalists are included in these volumes as well as Patriots. Johnathan McPeters (and his brothers, and many other Loyalists) fought actively and bravely for the Patriot Causes before and after Kings Mountain. They defected, probably on seeing the aftermath of the bloody Ramsour's battle of June 1780. Their participation in the Kings Mountain campaign as Loyalists is verified by the still extant Court Martial documents involving Col. Charles McDowell. After Kings Mountain, they were made to obey McDowell's Mandata...."good" Tories went to the nearly quiescent Frontier outposts for easy duties close to home. The "bad" Tories, who fought at Ramsour's and Kings Mountain, were sent to South Carolina. The military duties there involved hard fighting and tough campaigning...and far away from home. Remember, they were still under parole obligations from their capture, but, most of all, they were under the direct hard-line scrutiny of Col. McDowell and his colleagues. (Most notably, Capt. Mordecai Clark of McDowell's command. Others were placed in varoious South Carolina units of Sumter's brigade.)

For genealogists and historians, the pension declaration of Jonathan McPeters demonstrates the typical "Loyalist Hiatus of 1780". In other words, the declaration relates in detail military activities throughout the conflict, except for those events occuring in those hard fought, tough days of 1780. One had to choose sides. There was no compromise, no wishy-washy. If they told of these activities, their pension would be promptly denied..as was the case with the truthful, but unfortunate, John Franklin, Jr. (See Vol. I)

McPETERS, JOSEPH

SUMMARY OF EARLY LIFE

Joseph McPeters was living in Western Burke County, NC at the beginning of the Revolutionary period.

SUMMARY OF MILITARY SERVICE

Joseph McPeters entered military service as a volunteer militiaman in Burke County, N.C. (then Rowan County) in February 1776. He was assigned to Capt. William Moore's Company. Other officers were Lt. Robert Patton and Lt. Col. Charles McDowell. Their Regimental Commander was Col. Christopher Beekman. Under Brigade Commander, Gen. Griffith Rutherford, they took part in the Cross Creek expedition of February and March 1776, a sequel to the battle of Moore's Creek Bridge which had been fought earlier. On returning home to Burke County, the Indians were becoming very hostile. McPeters entered again in Capt. Reuben White's Company of Charles McDowell's second Rowan Regimant (Subaltern Officer, Lt. Samuel Simpson). He was stationed at the frontier forts (Davidsons Fort, Cathey's Fort). They were in a skirmish with the Indians on the North Fork of the Catawba River. His Commanding officer Capt. Reuben White was killed. The Indians were dispersed. The troops then retreated to McDowells Fort, remaining there until re-inforcements arrived under the command of Gen Rutherford. McPeters took part in Rutherford's Cherokee expedition of August-October 1776. They marched from Davidson's Fort to the Tellico and Cowee Towns, destroying property and taking a few prisoners.

In May 1777 he served a short term of duty at the frontier outpost without seeing any appreciable action. In late 1778 McPeters entered service as a nine months enlistee in the North Carolina Continental Line. He served under Capt. LeRoy Taylor, Maj. Daniel Mckissock and Col. Charles McDowell. In 1779 they advanced to the Cherokee Ford of the Broad River joining with Virginia Militia. Marching to Stono Ferry, SC they took part in the battle of Stono on June 20, 1779. Afterwards McPeters was verbally discharged and returned home. In March 1780 he volunteered as a Light Horseman in Capt. William Murray's Company. Other officers were Lt. James Richardson, and Col. Francis Locke. They marched to the outskirts of Charleston then being assaulted by the British. At Monck's Corner, SC their Units were totally defeated by the British under Webster and Tarlton (Apr 14, 1780). Eventually they made their way back to General Rutherford's camp in Mecklenburg County. McPeters was sent home in order to recruit more militiamen. On returning back to Gen. Rutherford's camp they met with the Tories at Ramsour's Mill. McPeters took part in the battle of June 20, 1780 in which the Tories were defeated. Staying with Gen. Rutherford he marched into South Carolina joining with Gen. Gates Army. Rutherford, with his troops, took part in the American disaster at Camden, S.C. on August 16, 1780. Rutherford was captured along with Col. Isaacs. McPeters was also captured but later escaped by swimming the Santee River. McPeters next tour was a Mounted Rifleman under Maj. Joseph McDowell of Burke County. They conducted a scouting party to the vicinity of Ninety Six, S.C. Returning, they joined up with Daniel Morgan and participated in the great American victory at Cowpens on Januar 17, 1781. Marching with prisoners back to Wilkes County, NC he was verbally discharged near his home. His final tour of duty was in April or May of 1781 as a member of Capt. William Bell's Company. They were in the unsuccessful siege operations at the Fortress of Ninety Six, SC in June 1781. Later they were stationed at Golphin's Fort on the Savannah River.

SUMMARY OF LATER LIFE

Joseph McPeters was married to Nancy Cross. She was age 64 in 1852. Josepy McPeters applied for Revolutionary War pension in morgan County, TN on October 15, 1832, age 71. Joseph McPeters died on Feb 15, 1846. His widow applied for a Bounty Land Warrant in 1855.

CENSUS LOCATIONS

1790
1800
1810
1820
1840 Morgan Co., TN

REFERENCES

US National Archives, Pension Statement # W 1303

Note: In late 1782 Joseph McPeters, along with his brothers, we cited to Burke County Court to show cause why their property should not be confiscated, for being disloyal to the American Cause.

MACKEY, JAMES

SUMMARY OF EARLY LIFE

James Mackey was a resident of Burke County, North Carolina on entering military service during the Revolutionary War.

SUMMARY OF MILITARY SERVICE

James Mackey entered military service in 1778. He enlisted for a term of nine months in the NC Continental Line. He served in the Company commanded by Captain John Armstrong of the 4th North Carolina Regiment, or Battalion. The Regiment was commanded by Lt. Col. James Thackston. They marched to South Carolina, joining the army of General Benjamin Lincoln. On June 20, 1779, Mackey took part in the battle of Stono Ferry, S. C. He was discharged in August 1779. Later, Mackey became a Captain in the Burke County Militia (13th Company). In 1792 Mackey (as a Captain of Militia) testified to the service of fellow soldiers, William T. Lewis of Surry County, North Carolina, John Lions, David Eberhart. Alexander Erwin, Clerk of Burke County Court in an Affidavit, stated that Mackey "is an officer of the Militia, duly Commissioned, and a respected citizen in the County of Burke".

LAND HOLDINGS AND TRANSACTIONS

1. 200 acres Burke County, NC adjoining his own land and next to the County line. Ent. May 20, 1780, No. 106.
2. 100 acres Burke County, NC on the east side of Schoolhouse Branch and adjacent to the land of James Lock.
Ent. June 15, 1790, No. 64, Grant No. 1580, issued on Nov. 27, 1792, Book 80, p. 49.
3. 84 acres Burke County, NC on a small branch of Silver Creek. The land lay adjacent to that of Alexander Bailey, Joseph Scott, and to his own land.
Ent. April 23, 1793, No. 398, Grant No. 1699, iss. July 7, 1794 Book 85, p. 62.
4. 50 acres Burke County, NC on Silver Creek, at the head of Sandy Run. The land was adjacent to his own land and to that of the Widow Alexander and Joseph Scott.

SUMMARY OF LATER LIFE

As a resident of Burke County, NC, Mackey made application for final Revolutionary War Settlement on September 24, 1792.

James Mackey was married to Rebecca Scott. Mackey, in the late 90's served as a Juryman, as jury foreman, and as a militia captain and county patroller. Ca 1804 he was appointed a Justice of the Burke County Court of Pleas and Quarter Sessions.

CENSUS LOCATIONS

1790 Burke Co., NC 13th Co.
1800 Burke Co., NC
1810 Burke Co., NC ("James McKee") ??

REFERENCES

Revolutionary War Final Settlements, Burke County, NC
NC Department of Archives, Comptroller Account, Boxes 14-20 as quoted in Huggins, Vol. II, pages 159-60.
DAR Patriot Index (1966) Page 432
AIS Census Indices
Burke, by Phifer, Edward W. Jr., 1977 ed. P. 419
Burke County, NC Minutes of Court of Pleas and Quarter Sessions 1791-1795 and 1795-1798)1986 & 1987, Swink, Daniel D.)
Roster of Soldiers from North Carolina in the American Revolution
NCDAR Reprint issue p. 197.
Revolutionary Army Accounts Vol II Boof 22 Voucher No 311.

MARSHALL, JESSE

SUMMARY OF EARLY LIFE

Jesse Marshall was born in Brunswick County, VA. in November 1765. He was living in Brunswick County at the commencement of the Revolutionary War.

SUMMARY OF PARTISAN ACTIVITY

Jesse Marshall entered Revolutionary service as a private in Capt. James Marshall's company of Virginia militia (Capt. Marshall was a cousin). He entered in April 1781.

Under Capt. Marshall, he took part in the siege operation in and around Yorktown in the fall of 1781. He was present at the surrender of Cornwallis. During this tour of duty, he was wounded, receiving a musket-ball wound of the thigh.

SUMMARY OF LATER LIFE

After the Revolution, Marshall lived in Brunswick County, Va., and in Caswell,Rowan,Mecklenburg and Rutherford Counties North Carolina. He then moved to Burke County, NC and remained there until 1833. He moved last to Franklin County, Ga.

Jesse Marshall applied for Revolutionary War pension in Burke County, NC on January 28, 1833. He was awarded a pension of $20.00 per annum.

Jesse Marshall died in Franklin County, Ga. on February 28,1840. His wife, Nancy Marshall, survived him and later received a pension. She was age 78 in 1843.

CENSUS LOCATIONS

1790
1800 Rowan Co., NC
1810 Mecklenburg Co., NC
1820 Burke Co., NC
1830 Burke Co., NC

REFERENCES

US National Archives, Pension Data, #W5350
AIS Census Indices

MARTIN, HENRY

SUMMARY OF EARLY LIFE

Henry Martin was a resident of Burke County, North Carolina at the time of his military service during the Revolutionary War. In a statement in 1792, Alexander Erwin stated that Henry and Francis Martin "have lived in Burke County sometime, nothing against their character".

SUMMARY OF PARTISAN ACTIVITY

Henry Martin entered military service in late 1778 as a Private in the North Carolina Continental Line. He enlisted for a tour of nine months. He served in Captain John Lick's Company in a Regiment commanded by Col. John Armstrong (4th N.C. Regiment). They marched to South Carolina, joining the Army of Gen. Benjam Lincoln. The 4th North Carolina Regiment (or Battalion) took part in the battle of Stono Ferry on June 20, 1779. The North Carolina troops were commanded by Gen. Jethro Sumner. The Nine Month Continentals of which Henry Martin was a member, were discharged in August 1779.

SUMMARY OF LATER LIFE

As a resident of Burke County, Martin applied for final Revolutionary War Settlement on July 16, 1792. Court records indicate that he appeared as a defendant in a civil court case Burke County, NC in 1791-92.

LAND HOLDINGS AND TRANSACTIONS

1. Burke Co., NC Oct. 8, 1796 Deed from Henry Martin to Jas. Be 300 acres, location not specified.

CENSUS LOCATIONS

1790 Burke Co., NC, 6th Company
1800 Burke Co., NC

REFERENCES

Final Revolutionary War Settlements in NC Department of Archives, Comptrollers Account, Boxes 14-20 as quoted in Huggin Vol. II , pages 159-60.
AIS Census Data
Burke Co.,NC Minutes of the Court of Pleas and Quarter Sessions 1791-1795 and 1795-1798 Complied by Swink, D.D. 1986, 1987.
Roster of Soldiers from NC in the American Revolution
NCDAR Reprint issue p. 197. (Soldier not to be confused with another of the same name, a member of the 2nd NC Regiment.. A 3 year Continental).
Revolutionary Army Accounts, Vol.X Book 22, Voucher #312.

MILLER, ROBERT JOHNSTONE

SUMMARY OF EARLY LIFE

Robert J. Miller was born in Baldovie, near Dundee, Scotland July 11, 1758. He came to America in 1774 and lived in Boston, Mass.

SUMMARY OF PARTISAN ACTIVITY

Robert Miller, from family records, served in the northern campaigns under Gen. George Washington. He entered the American army at about age 18 and saw service at the battles of Long Island and White Plains (July 1776) and at Yorktown (October 1781).

At White Plains, he received a saber wound across the nose. He did not apply for Revolutionary War pension when it became available in 1833.

SUMMARY OF LATER LIFE

Robert J. Miller married Mary Perkins, daughter of "Gentleman John" Perkins, on March 12, 1787. They were given land on Lower Creek, now Caldwell County, by his father in law. It was called "Mary's Grove" after his wife. Miller became an Episcopal Priest and preached in the Catawba valley and Yadkin valley as well as in Virginia and Tennessee. He was called "Parson Miller".

Children by Robert and Mary Miller were as follows:

John Wesley b. 1787
George Osman b. 7/8/1809
Catherine Lourance b. 11/15/1790 m. Godfrey Dresher
Margaret Bothier b. 8/5/1792 m. John Suddreth
Sarah Amelia b. 7/23/1794 m. (1) Col Sumter of S.C. (2) Joseph Puett
Elisha Perkins b. 7/21/1795 m. Sidney Caldwell
Robert Johnstone, Jr. b. 6/1/1798
William Sidney 3/18/1802
Eli Washington b. 1802
Horatio Nelson b. 1805

Miller was active in his endeavors for a period of about 40 years. He died in his home in 1834, Age 76 years. Census records indicated that he may have lived for a short while in Lincoln County.

LAND HOLDINGS AND TRANSACTIONS

1795 and 1798 Burke County NC tax Lists show Robert Johnston Miller with 300 acres, Capt. Highland's Company

CENSUS LOCATIONS

1790 Burke County, NC 9th Co.
1800 Lincoln County, NC
1810 Burke County, NC
1820 Burke County, NC
1830 Burke County, NC

REFERENCES

Rouse, J.K. Another Revolutionary War Hero Dies Salisbury 1978 p. 145-6
AIS Census Indices
Loose records concerning life of John Perkins, copies in vertical files, Morganton-Burke Library, Morganton, NC.

MONTGOMERY, DAVID

SUMMARY OF EARLY LIFE

David Montgomery was born in Lancaster County, Pa. In "1754 or 1755". He gave his age as 77 years in 1832 when applying for pension. At the time of the beginning of the American Revolution, he wa living in Mecklenburg County, NC.

SUMMARY OF MILITARY SERVICE

Davis Montgomery first entered Revolutionary military service in 1776 (or late 1775?). He enlisted in a Militia Company in Mecklenburg County, NC under Capt. James Alexander, Col. Thomas Polk's Regiment. They served in upper SC against local Tories (Snow Campaign?). In March of 1776, in the same outfit, he participated in the Cross Creek Expedition under Gen. Rutherford. This was the latter part of the Moore's Creek Bridge Campaign (the Western Militia arrived at Cross Creek after the battle, but did assist in "mop up" activities).

After having been discharged, in a company commanded by Capt. William Alexander he served against Lincoln County Tories.

In early 1780, Montgomery was drafted for a three months tour in Capt. James Osborne's Company of Col. Lillington's N.C. Regiment. His Company marched to the defense of Charleston, then under siege by the British in early 1780. The American forces were commanded by Maj. Gen. Benjamin Lincoln. On May 12, 1780 Montgomery surrendered along with the remainder of the American troops enclosed within the siege lines. Later he was paroled. Following his parole Montgomery served a few short periods of duty against the Tories in and about Mecklenburg County.

SUMMARY OF LATER LIFE

David Montgomery lived for about twenty years after the war in Mecklenburg County. At about the turn of the century, he moved to Burke County, NC and remained there for the remainder of his life.

In 1783 or 1784, Montgomery married Margaret Allen in Mecklenburg County. There were at least seven children, five of which are listed below:

Jane
Anne m. William Bradshaw
Martha b. December 30, 1789, M. England
Polly, b. January 21, 1797, m. Westmoreland
Allen, b. February 28, 1794

In October 1832 he had applied for Revolutionary War Pension in Burke County, N.C. and was awarded $24.63 per annum.

David Montgomery died at his residence in Burke County in April 1834.

Montgomery's wife, Margaret Allen Montgomery, was born on December 30, 1754 and died in Cherokee County, NC July 25, 1845

LAND HOLDINGS AND TRANSACTIONS

"A David Thomas Montgomery" received a Burke County, NC Land Grant for 200 acres of land lying on the west fork of Turkey Creek. The land was adjacent to that belonging to William Whitson and Arch Neill.
Ent. 6 September 1787, No. 93, Grant No. 1194, Iss. May 18, 1789
Book 71, page 56.

CENSUS LOCATIONS

1790 Mecklenburg Co., NC
1800 Burke County, NC
1810 Burke County, NC
1820 Burke County, NC
1830 Burke County, NC

MOORE, WILLIAM

SUMMARY OF EARLY LIFE

According to DAR records, William Moore was born in Northern Ireland in 1726. He was married twice, first to Ann Cathey and second to Margaret Patton. He was living in western Burke County, now McDowell County, at the beginning of the Revolution.

SUMMARY OF PARTISAN ACTIVITY

William Moore received his Captain's commission of militia in 1775. In early 1776, he commanded a Company in the 2nd Rowan Regiment under Col. Christopher Beekman. This Regiment took part in the Moore's Creek Bridge Campaign (known to local militia as the "Cross Creek Expedition") of February and March 1776.

Returning from Cross Creek, Moore then became a frontier fort Commander, guarding against the hostile incursions of the pro British Cherokee Indians. The fort he commanded was called Fort Moore. It was located in western Burke County, now McDowell County. The Cherokees conducted a major thrust against the western frontier in July 1776. During this period Lt.Col. Charles McDowell was in command. Moore assumed command of Capt. Reuben White's company, upon the death of Capt. White at North Cove of the Catawba.

In August and September of 1776 Moore joined in with the huge Cherokee Expedition headed up by Brig. Gen. Griffith Rutherford. During this campaign, Moore played a major role in suppressing the Cheorkees.

Moore gave a written report of his actions during the Cherokee Campaign. He tells of the killing and scalping of several braves and how they plundered and destroyed their villages. Moore also related some insubordination within his group concerning the selling of prisoners as slaves for easy money. Moore objected to this practice but was powerless to do anything about it. He made recommendations to his superiors concerning a unified chain of command.

SUMMARY OF LATER LIFE

From land records, it appears that Moore had entered the western Catawba Valley along with fellow settlers George Cathey and Hunting John McDowell. At this time he was married to Ann Cathey, the daughter of George Cathey. Shortly before the Revolution on August 4, 1774, he was married to Margaret Patton, daughter of Charity Patton. Children of William Moore were as follows:

William
Thomas

Robert
Mary   m. Robert Penland
Alice m. John Penland
Ann m. John Rutherford
Margaret m. Benjamin Tutt
Charles Augustus m. Margaret Penland
Samuel

William Moore continued to live in Burke County until the early 1790's. During this period he served in a variety of public positions, including Sheriff.

Moore had taken up substantial quantities of land on HominyCreek of the French Broad Valley. He removed to this ca. 1794 and lived there until his death in 1812. He is buried in a private cemetery near Hominy Creek.

LAND HOLDINGS AND TRANSACTIONS

1. Burke Co. NC 640 acres Shadrick's Creek and both sides of main Catawba River adjacent to Thomas Young, Abraham Denton, Charles McPeters. Ent. 1778 Grant Issued 1779 Book 28 p.70.

2. Burke Co., NC 220 acres on Mill Fork of Muddy Creek. Ent. 1778 Grant #1232 Iss. Dec 1795 Book 89 p.320

3. Burke Co., NC 100 on Muddy Creek
Ent. 1798 Grant #2308 Iss. Dec. 1798.
4. Buncombe Co., 75 acres Hominy Creek on path leading from French Broad to Cherokee Nation.
Ent. 1783 Grant #961 Iss. 1787.

5. Buncombe Co., 450 acres both sides Hominy Creek on main path between French Broad River Ford and Cherokee Nation. Grant #1031 Iss. 1787.

6. Buncombe Co., 250 acres on west side French Broad River and on both sides of Hominy Creek on path to Cherokee Nation. Ent. 1783 Grant #1064 Iss. 1787.

7. Buncombe Co., 100 acres on both sides of Hominy Creek Grant #1170 Iss. 11 May 1789.

Note: Above Grants though lying in persent Buncombe County were in Burke County at time of Grant Issues.

CONSUS LOCATIONS

1790 Burke Co., NC
1800 Buncombe Co., NC
1810 Buncombe Co., NC

REFERENCES

AIS Census Indices
Lamb, Martha June, article in The Heritage of Old Buncombe County, Vol.I pp.282-283 Winston Salem, 1981
Holcomb, Brent, Marriages of Rowan County, GPC 1981 p.287
Wooley, J.E., Buncombe County, NC Index to Deeds, 1783-1850 SHP 1983
Huggins, Edith, Burke County Records Vol.I-IV SHP
Phifer, Edward, Burke 1977
Whitley, Edythe, Roster of Soldiers of American Revolution, Tenn. DAR Vol.II p. 580, 1970.
US National Archives Pension Declarations of the following soldiers: Richard Crabtree, John Dysart, John Carson, David McPeters, Patrick O'Neal, Arthur McFalls, John McPeters, Joseph McPeters.
DAR Patriot Index (National Society DAR, Washington, D.C. 1966). p. 478
Revolutionary Army Accounts, Vol.VII, p. 76 folio 1. (verification of service in Cherokee Expedition).

MORRIS, WILLIAM

SUMMARY OF EARLY LIFE

William Morris was living in Burke County, NC at the beginning the American Revolution. He was born in the year 1750.

SUMMARY OF MILITARY SERVICE

William Morris first entered military service in Burke County, N.C. in 1780, at age 28. He served a three month tour of duty Jonathan Kemp's Company of Charles McDowell's Burke Regiment. They marched from Burke County, NC to the North Carolina-South Carolina line at Edward Hampton's plantation. While encamped, they were attacked that night by British and Tories under Maj. Dunlap. Several Americans were taken prisoner. Morris, in his pension application, stated that Capt. Kemp and Capt. Kennedy's Company "done the hardest of the fighting". The skirmish took place in July 1780. Morris was one of the horsemen that was selected to give chase to the British the next morning. He stated that they caught up with them after riding about twelve miles. They defeated the British, took twenty prisoners and al freed twenty American prisoners. Morris received an early discharge from his tour because "of my wife whose situation required me to be home".

His next tour of duty was for three months in a Company command by Capt. Whitaker. Capt. Whitaker was killed and his place was taken by Lt. Boykin. Under Lt. Boykin they marched to South Carolina and were in several skirmishes with the Tories led by Capt. "Bloody Bill" Cunningham's men on the Pacolet River. In a skirmish with Tories led by Capt. Bright, Morris lost his brother-in-law, John Raburn, who was killed.

Morris's next tour of duty was for three months under Capt. George Walker of Burke County. He spent his tour at the upper Forts of the Catawba River (Davidson's Fort). There were no actions.

He next went on two separate raids against the Cherokee Indians The first was under Capt. Daniel Smith. On this raid Morris stated the "we killed a good many and took some prisoners and plunder. I killed on Indian warrior myself and took another prisoner...".

The second tour was a raid led by Joseph McDowell of Quaker Meadows. Again some Indians were killed and others were taken prisoners. This was probably the Spring Cherokee raid of 1782. This ended his military service.

NOTE: In November of 1782 a William Morris was cited to Burke County Court, for being disloyal to the American cause.

SUMMARY OF LATER LIFE

William Morris continued to live in Burke County for the remainder of his life. In 1832 he applied for Federal Pension in Burke County, NC at age 82 years. He was awarded an annual pension of $28.88.

LAND HOLDINGS AND TRANSACTIONS

1. 150 acres Clear Creek, Buncombe County, NC, from Adam Corn, 29 June 1818, Book 11, page 87.

2. 409 acres Buncombe County, NC, from Richard Allen, 3 Nov 1842, (?). Book 25, page 287. This is probably not William Morris, the soldier.

3. Burke Co., NC 90 acres on the East side of "his tract he dwells on". The land lay on the E. Side of Mumford's Cover..ch carr..Thos. Williams, Jno. Woods.
Ent. 1 Aug 1789 # 222 (15 Dec. 1784 ?) Grant # 1216 Iss. 18 May 1789 Book 71 p. 65.

4. Burke Co., NC 25 acres in Mumford's Cove, adjacent to property that he purchased from John Greer. Ent. 18 Jan 1792 # 127. Grant # 1664 Iss. 26 Nov 1793. Book 81 p. 232 cc Wm. And Thos. Morris.

CENSUS LOCATIONS

1790 Burke County, NC
1800 Burke County, NC
1810 Burke County, NC
1820 Burke County, NC
1830 Burke County, NC

MORRISON, JAMES

SUMMARY OF EARLY LIFE

The Morrisons were early settlers of Rowan County, NC, having moved there from Pennsylvania. Before the Revolution, several of the Morrison clan migrated to the Muddy Creek section of Burke County, now Burke and McDowell Counties. James Morrison came to Burke County along with brothers William Morrison, Sr., Andrew Morrison and Thomas Morrison. James Morrison was the son of James Morrison, Sr. and Mary Morrison of Rowan County, Third Creek area.

SUMMARY OF PARTISAN ACTIVITY

In 1776, James Morrison had obtained a Captain's commission in the 2nd Rowan Regiment, commanded by Col. Christopher Beekma In March of 1776, he led his company on the Cross Creek Expedition headed by Col., later General Griffith Rutherford. This action, which amounted to a mop-up procedure, was the sequ to the action at Moore's Creek Bridge in late February. This campaign suppressed Tory activity in south eastern North Carolina. Morrison's participation is verified by State auditor records.
Later he served in McDowells Burke Regiment, though not as acti a role as his brother William Morrison.

SUMMARY OF LATER LIFE

James Morrison and his wife Elizabeth lived on Muddy Creek afte their departure from Rowan County. James Morrisan's will was listed in 1790 names his wife Elizabeth and a minor son, Thomas Morrison. Daughters were mentioned but names were not given. His death was probably about this time as Elizabeth only was listed on the 1790 census. Mary and Rachel Morrison listed in probate records with Elizabeth Morrison in October 1828. *James Morrison, Sr. was listed on a condemnation jury list of January 1793. Huggins noted that his name was marked throug most likely due to his earlier demise. His death probably occurred ca. 1790-91.

LAND HOLDINGS AND TRANSACTIONS

1. Burke County, NC 500 acres on lower Little River "including his own improvements".
Grant #71 Iss. Sept. 20, 1779, Book 28 p. 71.
Two additional tracts were listed on lower Little River adjacen to his own land, Granted in 1783.

(The above may have been his property prior to his removal to the Muddy Creek area of Burke County).

CENSUS LOCATIONS

1790 Burke Co., NC 6th. Company ("Eliza. Morison")

REFERENCES

Philbeck, Miles & Turner, Grace "Burke Co., N.C. surviving Will
  and Probate abstracts 1777-1910". Chapel Hill 1983, #380,381.
Huggins, Edith, Burke County Land Records Vols. I-IV 1977
  Vol. IV p.4.
Burke County NC Land Grant Records, Morganton-Burke Library
  Morganton, NC
1790 NC Census by AIS Inc.
Haun, Weynette P., "N. C. Revolutionary Accounts..." 1775-1776
  1998 Durham, N.C. p. 5.

MULL, PETER

SUMMARY OF EARLY LIFE

Peter Mull was born in Montgomery County, PA in 1736, the son of Christopher or "Stoffel" Mull (often spelled "Moll"). Peter Mull, along with his kinsmen, was one of the earlier settlers of the South Fork valley of the Catawba River. Peter Mull received Crown Grants in what is now Burke County, but then listed as being in "Mecklenburgh". (Since Granville's line was indeterminate in the early sixties, many crown grants were issued in what was later to be Burke County). He was probably married at this time but name of first wife unknown.

SUMMARY OF PARTISAN ACTIVITY

Peter Mull was elected to the Rowan County Committee of Safety in 1775. The Committee of Safety was the governing organization in each county prior to the adoption of the New State Constitution in late 1776. The Committee supervised the court system, appointed military officers and dealt with local Tories. They confiscated military supplies and jailed active opponents to liberty.

In March of 1776, with a Captain's commission, Peter Mull took part in the Cross Creek Expedition. This was the latter phase of the Moore's Creek Bridge battle and campaign.

In August and September of 1776, Capt. Mull led his company on the Cherokee Expedition. His company was part of the large multi-county army under the leadership of General Griffith Rutherford of Rowan County. The Expedition was a punitive one, brought about by the raids and atrocities carried out by the Indians on the Catawba frontier.

Mull was to continue his Revolutionary War activity as a Captain of militia in Charles McDowell's Burke regiment.

SUMMARY OF LATER LIFE

After the conclusion of the Revolutionary War, Mull continued his role as a prominent civic servant of Burke County. He served as high Sheriff. He also served periodically as Magistrate, Constable, and as a Captain of a Judicial Military company. He remained a rather large land owner. Prior to his removal to Burke County, he disposed of at least 1,000 acres of land in Lincoln County. (later Catawba County, NC)

Most of the sell off occurred from 1785-88 and Mull appeared to have moved to the Hunting Creek area of Burke County on property formerly owned by Joseph Morgan. Mull also acquired property in the city of Morganton and had some land on Upper Creek from a previous acquisition from Conrad Mull.

Peter Mull was married to Barbara-? some sources give her name as Barbara Carpenter, others Barbara Klein. There is a possibility that he may have been married twice. Children of Peter Mull were as follows:
John b. 1760 d. Lincoln C., 1812 m. Catherine Weidner (Whitener)
Henry b. 1771 Rowan Co. d. 1850 m. 1-? (2) Susannah ?
Peter Jr., b. 1773 Rowan Co. d. Buncombe Co. 1856 m. Susannah?
Barbara b. 1779 Burke Co. d. 1861 m. Mark Brittain, both are buried at Mount Home Church.
Jacob b. 1783 Burke Co. d. 1843 in Burke Co. m. (1) Gemima Brittain (2) Mary Van Horn, both are buried at Salem Church cemetery.
Susanna b. ca.1789 m. Philip Pitts

Peter Mull died ca. 1805, the date of his administrative papers in Burke County Court. Barbara Mull died in Burke County 1836. Peter and Barbara Mull are probably buried at a Mull family cemetery and burying ground near present day Brookstone Church, Burke County, NC not far from the junction of Enola Road and Highway I40.

LAND HOLDINGS AND TRANSACTIONS

1. Peter Mull's first land acquisition was in 1763. He received a Crown grant of 300 acres in Rowan County (later Burke, Lincoln and finally Catawba County, NC). Date of Grant April 22, 1762. Mull later sold a portion of this land to Joseph Moyer on 13 Jan 1772.
2. Peter Mull received land from Conrad Mull (originally a 1756 Granville grant). 451 acres west side Catawba River on Elk Creek. Sold in 1771 to Wendle Wyant.
3. In 1771 he acquired land on Upper Creek (later Burke Co., NC) From Abraham Collett 320 acres (Linn- p.112).
4. In 1774 he sold 320 acres north side of Catawba River adjacent to Conrad Mull to Wendle Wyant. This may be the tract listed above.
5. Burke County, NC land grant 500 acres on Finley's Branch and containing a portion of the road that extended from Ramsours' Mill to Beatties' Ford. It lay adjacent to Casper Shell, George Wilfong and Martin Coulter. The entry stated "all improvements made by Mull and his mill for compliment...". Ent. #1176 Dec. 12, 1778 Grant #746 Iss. 11 Oct 1783. Book 50, p. 280. (Peter Mull had obtained a Crown grant earlier for this tract on April 28, 1768). It was re-entered via the State land grant system.
6. 560 acres Burke County, NC lying on both sides of the wagon road and on both sides of Horse Ford, including Edward Smith's former place, the house on the west side of the branch. Land crossed portions of "old" road and "new" road. This tract was the site of Burke County's first "Courthouse" ie. Edward Smith's house. The property ws sold to Daniel Smith by Mull in 1794.
7. 450 acres Henry's Fork Burke County, N.C., a tributary of

South Fork of Catawba River, containing lower end of a previous Grant issued to John Frohock of Rowan County. The land include earlier improvements of Jacob Beck. It lay adjacent to land belonging to John Butts.
Ent. Feb 29, 1778, Grant #588 Iss. Oct 11, 1783 Book 50 p. 210.

The above tracts as well as several smaller ones were sold by Peter Mull between 1785 and 1788. Recipients included Daniel Smith, Conrad Wagoner, Jacob and John Yount, John Shell, John Gross and John Deitz.

Mull continued to expand his Burke County land holdings with acquisitions from John Spears (376 acres 1793), Benjamin Britta (100 acres 1797), Joseph Morgan (200 acres 1798), David Barr (3 acres 1794).

1805 tax lists show Mull with 1560 acres in Burke County.

CENSUS LOCATIONS

1790 Burke County, NC 13th Co.
1800 Burke County, NC

REFERENCES

Mull, B. Rondall and Mabel 1994; personal data submitted to author, "Peter Moll (Johannis Peter' Sheriff Peter)".
N.C. Land Grant Data, Morganton-Burke Library, Morganton, N.C.
Revolutionary Army Accounts.
Hofmann, Margaret M. Colony of North Carolina Land Patents 1735-1764 Vols.I * II 1982.
AIS Census Indices
Heritage Books of Burke and Catawba Counties. Various articles on Mull family.
Wheeler, John H. Historical Sketches of North Carolina (originally 1851, Reprint 1964 edition by regional publishing company). Pp. 360-381 -- Rowan County Committee Safety minutes.

MURPHY, JAMES

SUMMARY OF EARLY LIFE

James Murphy was born on May 24, 1759. Earlier in life he had lived in Mecklenburg County, NC.

SUMMARY OF PARTISAN ACTIVITY

James Murphy, as a private soldier, took part in the military activities of 1780. He fought at Ramsours' Mill on June 20, 1780, receiving a hand wound. Later, on September 12, 1780, he played a conspicuous role in the skirmish at Cane Creek. This was a delaying action against the forces of Major Patrick Ferguson of the British Army, then advancing northward into Burke County. Still later he fought in the battle of Kings Mountain on October 7, 1780. In late 1781 Murphy joined up with the McDowell's and Gen. Rutherford, taking part in the Wilmington Expedition. This action freed Wilmington, and North Carolina, from British rule. An unrelated sidelight with Murphy occurred with the acquisition of a   gown for his bride to be and its later disappearance. (See Sarah Nicholson biography).

Toward the end of the war, he saw service on the frontiers, with duty at the forts that were constructed to oppose the incursion of the Cherokee Indians. He served under Maj. Joseph McDowell Capt. Thomas Kennedy, Capt. Robert Patton and Capt. George Cathey.

SUMMARY OF LATER LIFE

Toward the end of the Revolutionary War, James Murphy was married to (1) Margaret McDowell a daughter of Hugh McDowell. They had a son, John Murphy. Both John Murphy and Margaret Murphy died in 1827. James Murphy married (2) Jane Fleming.

James Murphy, after the war, became one of Burke County's most prominent citizens. He was founding member of Morganton Academy and Morganton Agricultural Society. He served in the N.C. Senate in 1797. He was on the planning commission responsible for erection of the Burke County Court House in 1830. Some of James Murphy's typical humor is found in the article in Burke Heritage by Joseph Moore Walton.

James Murphy died accidentally in 1831. His widow, Jane Murphy, applied for federal pension. James Murphy owned vast quantities of land and had many slaves. He is buried in Quaker Meadows Cemetery, Morganton, NC.

LAND HOLDINGS AND TRANSACTIONS

1. 200 acres south side Swannanoa River adjacent to John McDowell's survey and Joseph McKinney's survey.
Ent. 1 Aug 1783 Grant No. 1044 Iss. Aug 7, 1787 Book 65 p.397
2. 100 acres east side Canoe Creek on corner of his "Tramel"survey and adjacent to land of Patrick McKinney and Penland.
Ent. 3 Apr 1824 Grant No. 5256 Iss. 28 Dec 1827 Book 147 p.248
3. 300 acres Little Silver Creek, both sides including O'Neal's Saw Mills and adjacent to Tate Heins (Wm) Stansberry and McKey's old line.
Ent. 16 Jan 1824 Grant No. 5348 Iss. 2 Jan 1829 Book 138 p.105
4. 50 acres north side Catawba River adjacent to land of John Fox.
Ent. 21 Mar 1818 Grant No. 3879 Iss. 21 Nov 1818 Book 132 p.356.
5. 50 acres on Liville River on road from Morganton to North Cove adjacent to Joseph McGimpsey.
Ent. 4 Apr 1816 Grant No. 4039 Iss. 30 Nov 1820 Book 134 p.311
6. 250 acres both sides Mulberry Creek adjacent to Joseph White's old survey and Gabriel Lovings old line.
Ent. 14 Feb 1825 Grant No. 5224 Iss. 30 Jan 1827 Book 137 p.141
7.. 14 acres water of Will's Branch adjacent to his own land and that of Charles McDowell and William Miller.
Ent. 24 Jan 1802 Grant No. 3196 Iss. 12 Dec 1802 Book 110 p.74.
8. 250 acres Canoe Creek adjacent to his own land and that of Gen. Charles McDowell.
Ent. 7 Oct 1795 Grant No. 2210 Iss. 2 Dec 1797 Book 97 p.200.
9. File #1025 (absent data)
10. Received from James Richardson a deed for 300 acres on Silver Creek, previously owned by Thomas Kennedy Dec 10, 1782.
11. 100 acres Pea Vine Branch on north side Canoe Creek adjacer to Nathan Smith.
Ent. 23 Jan 1813 Grant No. 3002 Iss. 24 Nov 1813 Book 127 p.511.
12. 120 acres Linville River adjacent to Benjamin Moore and John Waggerly.
Ent. 12 Apr 1813 Grant No. 3603 Iss. 24 Nov 1813 Book 127 p.512.
13. 50 acres adjacent to David Tate's "Trammell Place".
Ent. 23 Jan 1813 Grant No. 3604 Iss. 24 Nov 1813 Book 127 p.512.
14. 50 acres adjacent to land Murphy bought from John Waggerly and adjacent to Waight Avery (on south side place he now lives on).
Ent. 23 Jan 1813 Grant No. 3605 Iss. 24 Nov 1813 Book 127 p.513.
15. 150 acres on both sides Linville River adjacent to John Waggerly and Henry Kesley.
Ent. 12 Apr 1813 Grant No. 3606 Iss. 24 Nov 1813 Book 127 p.513.

CENSUS LOCATIONS

1790 Burke Co., NC 7th Co.
1800 Burke Co., NC
1810 Burke Co., NC

1820 Burke Co., NC
1830 Burke Co., NC

REFERENCES

Walton, Joseph Moore, Article in Burke County, N.C. <u>Heritage</u>
Winston Salem 1981 p.324. (this article also shows a portrait
of James Murphy).
US National Archives Pension Declaration R7512
Burke County, NC Land Grant Data, Morganton-Burke Library
Morganton, NC
AIS Census Indices

MURRAY, JOHN B.

SUMMARY OF EARLY LIFE

John B. Murray, during the American Revolution, lived in that part of Burke County that eventually became Caldwell County. The Murrays were a well known family, mainly of Loyalist sentiments

SUMMARY OF PARTISAN ACTIVITY

John Murray, early in the Revolution, served on the western Carolina frontier, most likely during the Cherokee Wars of 1776 and perhaps later also.

In 1781 Murray joined with South Carolina State troops that were being recruited in North Carolina, frequently from Loyalist families. He served in a regiment commanded by Col. Charles Starke Myddleton. Family members list his participation in a battle near Orangeburg, S.C., most likely Eutaw Springs, SC. (Sept 1781).

South Carolina authorities (Comptrollers Office) list a John Murray who served in S.C. troops under Goodman and Col. Taylor. The family of John B. Murray received a pension verified by this data.

In 1782 a John Murray was cited to Burke County Court on charge of treason. (For being inimical to the American Cause). These persons, for the most part, were never tried because many, like John B. Murray, were then serving in the American Army.

It is noteworthy that the Murray family members were active Loyalist participants in the battle of Ramsour's Mill on June 20 1780. A Captain John Murray is mentioned frequently. (There were two other John Murrays in Burke County during this period)

SUMMARY OF LATER LIFE

John and Rosannah Murray were married in 1776. By this union the following children were born:

Ezekial b. 1777
Thomas b. 1779 d. 1781
Joseph b. 1781 d. 1786
Charity b. 1783
Dority or Dorothy b. 1788
Elizabeth b. 1788

Benjamin b. 1790 d. ?1809
David b. 1792 d. 1792
Jane d. 1794
Nancy b. 1797
Peggy? B. 1799

John B. Murray died January 31, 1828. His widow applied for federal pension via the Act of 1836 (appealed Nov. 9, 1836). She was awarded an annual pension of $22.20. Rosannah Murray, the time of the above application was residing in Union County NC??.

CENSUS LOCATIONS

1790 Burke Co., NC

REFERENCES

US National Archives Pension Data #W24025
AIS Census Indices NC 1790
Moss, Bobby G. <u>Roster of SC Patriots in the American Revolution</u>
GPC 1983 p. 713

MURRAY (MURRAH),JOSHUA

SUMMARY OF EARLY LIFE

Joshua Murray was born March 15, 1764 in Pittsylvania County, Va. At the time of the American Revolution, he was living in Burke County, NC, now Caldwell County.

SUMMARY OF PARTISAN ACTIVITY

Joshua Murray entered Revolutionary service in Burke County, N.C. in the opening of 1781. He was signed up for a ten months tour of duty with South Carolina State Troops. (South Carolina was actively recruiting in North Carolina particularly those persons from Loyalist families.) Under Capt. Godfrey Adams of South Carolina, he marched to Camden, SC. There he was placed in a company commanded by Capt. Francis Moore of Charles Myddleton's S. C. Regiment. They marched from Camden to Congar River and Brown;s Old Fields, joining the army of Gen. Nathanie Greene. In September 1781, he fought in the battle of Eutaw Springs, SC. Just prior to the battle, he was in a skirmish with Cunninghams Tories at Orangeburg, SC. His tour ended at Four-Hole Bridge near Charleston..

After returning home to Burke County, Murray took part in the spring 1782 raid directed against the Cherokee Indians. He served in a company commanded by Capt. Joseph McDowell of Pleasant Gardens. The regiment was commanded by Col. Joseph McDowell of Quaker Meadows. He remained mainly at John McDowel place at Pleasant
Gardens.

In the summer of 1782 he served again under the McDowells in a company commanded by Capt. Martin Davenport on the Catawba frontier.

His final tour of duty began in September 1782 for three months He served in a company commanded by Capt. George Blair, Col. Joseph McDowell and Capt. (now Major) Joseph McDowell of Pleasa Gardens.

This was a composite campaign under Gen. Charles McDowell, Lt. James Miller, Col. Benjamin Herndon et al. It was directed against
the Cherokee Nation and was one of the last, if not the last, action of the American Revolution. Murray was discharged near the head of the Catawba River.

Note; In November 1782 a Joshua Murray was on a list of Loyalists cited to Burke Co. Court. This was probably the subject of this sketch. There were others like him, Loyalist, but actively serving the American Cause.

Murray, Joshua   P.2

SUMMARY OF LATER LIFE

Joshua Murray was married to Lucy Suddreth (b.June 19, 1771) daughter of William Suddreth, Sr. and Margaret Suddreth. By this union were born the following children.

William b. 5 Sept 1787	Jane b. 19 Sept 1798
Nancy b. Feb 1788	Emanuel b. 14 March 1799
Margaret b. 9 Jan 1790	Joseph b. 28 Jan 1801
Sally b. 15 Dec 1791	Jeremiah b. 13 Feb 1803
Joshua b. 21 Sept 1793	John B. b. 24 April 1805
Ale b. Dec 1795	Abraham b. 30 March 1807
Lucy b. 29 March 1810	Robert b. 29 March 1812

Joshua Murray, after the Revolution, moved from Burke County, N.C. to Wilkes Co., N.C. (In Burke Co. 1790 census, Wilkes Co. 1800). He and his family moved to Logan Co., KY after having acquired land on Red River (grants in 1805, 1807).

Joshua Murray applied for Revolutionary War pension in Logan County, KY in 1833. There was a supporting affidavit by fellow soldier, Leonard West. Murray was awarded a pension in the amount of $63.33 per annum. His widow later applied for an received continuation of pension payments. She filed from Robertson Co., TN

Joshua Murray died in Logan Co., KY on July 12, 1836.

CENSUS LOCATIONS

1790 Burke Co., NC 9th Co.
1800 Wilkes Co., NC
1810 Logan Co., KY
1820 Logan Co., KY
1830 Logan Co., KY

LAND HOLDINGS AND TRANSACTIONS

Wilkes Co., NC
From John Jones, South side Yadkin River 100 acres, tract where Thomas Fields lives, January 1792 Book B-1 p. 156.

Kentucky Land Grants (South of the Green River)
100 acres Logan Co., KY Red River 23 Jan 1805 Book 3, p.308
43½ acrs Logan Co., KY Red River 29 June 1807 Book 7, p.74

REFERENCES

US National Archives Pension Data # W1063
AIS Census Indices NC & KY (1810)

Absher, Mrs. W.O. Wilkes County Deed Abstracts SHP 1989 p.57
Moss, Bobby G. Roster of S.C. Patriots in the American Revolution GPC 1983 p.713
Wiggins, Edith W., Burke County N.C. Land Records etc. 1977. Vol. II p.154, 149.
Jillson, W.R. The Kentucky Land Grants Part. I GPC 1971 p.369.
Volkel Lowell 1820 Kentucky Census Index Vol. II.
Smith, Dora W. 1830 Kentucky Census Index Vol. II

MUSCANOOK, GEORGE (Moose)

SUMMARY OF EARLY LIFE

George Muscanook was living in eastern Burke County, now Catawba County, in 1779. He was residing on property obtained from Michael Grindstaff.

SUMMARY OF MILITARY SERVICE

George Muscanook was drafted into the Militia for a period of twelve months beginning in 1781. He, along with other Militiamen, rendezvoused at Frohock's Mill in Rowan County, was furloughed, but failed to return to duty. He was arrested as a deserter by Capt. Francis Cunningham and delivered into the Continental Service under Maj. (Reading) Blount at Charlotte. He was then sent to South Carolina, Santee area. Later, in July 1781, Muscanook was relieved of his duties, a substitute being hired in his place. Apparently this was arranged through his immediate superior, Capt. Mordecai Clarke of Burke County.

SUMMARY OF LATER LIFE

Following the Revolution, George Muscanook continued to live in the Lincoln County area (now Catawba Co.) Until at least to the turn of the century. Another person in close proximity, with same name, Anthony Muscanook appears in the records.

LAND HOLDINGS AND TRANSACTIONS

1. George Muscanook entered 400 acres in eastern Burke County NC adjacent to land belonging to Matthias Barringer, William Craig, and Whisnant. It included "improvement whereon he lives". Entry No. 1787, 1 Dec 1779. Entered 200 acres on Bullinger's Mill Creek adjacent to land belonging to Conrad Tippong, John Smyors, and David Howell. 1 April 1780, not paid.

2. Lincoln Co., NC Deed from John Dawsey 150 acres on south side Maclin's Creek (now Catawba Co.) adjacent to Wm Sloan, Richard Harris. Originally a grant to Wm. Craig, 1782. Nov 3, 1792 Book 16; p. 337. (From Abstract by Pruitt).

3. Lincoln Co. NC Court records show deed from Philip Horse to George Muscanook 24 Jan 1799, 200 acres.

4. Lincoln Co., NC Court Records show deed from John Dorsey (or "Dawsey") Nov 20, 1792, 175 acres. Also Deed from Henry Barlow Baker Dec 18, 1793, 150 acres.

5. Lincoln Co., NC two entries, later granted as follows: 300 acres on Clark's Creek, adjacent to Conrad Tips, Falls, Matthew Barringer, Wissanat (Whisnant). May 21, 1795. 200 acres Clark's Creek adjacent to Nancy Harbinson, John Smire, and Conrad Tipps (Tippong) Aug 22, 1796.

CENSUS LOCATIONS

1790 Burke Co., NC

REFERENCES

Lincoln County., NC Abstracts of Land entries and Deeds. Pruit A.B. in multiple volumes 1987-1988.
Lincoln Co. Court of Pleas and Quarter Sessions 1789-1796 and 1796-1805. Anne W. McAllister and Kathy G. Sullivan 1987-1088 Vol.
AIS Cemsus Indices
Revolutionary War Service: Pierce's Register #90469. 10th N.C. Regiment Continental Line. Ent, June 5, 1781, out June 6, 1782.
Revolutionary Army Accounts Vol. X#408, Vol II pp 46-73 Book ZZ #408
Burke Co., NC Court Martial Records of Col. Charles McDowell 1782. Facsimile given to Emmett R. White by the late Miss Eunice Ervin of Morganton, N.C.

NEILL, JOHN

SUMMARY OF EARLY LIFE

John Neill was born in Rowan Co., NC c. 1758/59. John Neill (pronounced, and often spelled, "Nail") was the son of William Neill and was a brother to William Neill Jr., Andrew Neill, and James Neill. There were other brothers and sisters.

SUMMARY OF MILITARY SERVICE

John Neill entered military service in the spring of 1780 in Charles McDowell's Burke Regiment. With the Burke troops, Neill fought in the battle of Ramsour's Mill on June 20, 1780. His brother Lt. William Neill was killed in this engagement. (He had just returned from Continental Line duties, taking part in the northern campaigns.) Neill continued to serve under McDowell and on October 7, 1780 was in the battle of Kings Mountain. In early 1781 Neill was serving in Joseph McDowell's mounted troops and took part in the battle of Cowpens fought on January 17, 1781. Following this campaign he continued to serve and was with the American troops under General Nathaniel Greene. On March 15, 1781 he participated in the battle of Guilford Courthouse. (The above information supplied by his widow and family members).

SUMMARY OF LATER LIFE

John Neill married Cynthia Forgy, daughter of Capt. James Forgy and Rebecca Forgy, on October 30, 1799. The following children were born:

William Neill b. November 15, 1800   Mariah b.c. 1807
James Neill b. February 2, 1803   Gilbreath b.c. 1812-1815
Elizabeth b. C. 1801   Hiram b.c. 1818
John b.c. 1807?

There may have had additional children. John Neill died May 3, 1828 in Logan County, KY. His widow applied for Federal pension in 1854, age 72. Rejected.

LAND HOLDINGS AND TRANSACTIONS

A John Neill was issued a North Carolina Land Grant on both sides of the main fork and Kennedy's Fork of Silver Creek. Exact relationship to the soldier John Neill not known. Previous Granville Grant 1763.
Ent. 10 sep 1778 No. 213 Grant No. 44, Iss. 20 Sep 1779, Book 28 p. 44.
State of Kentucky, Land Grants South of the Green River...Jno. Nail received two grants in Logan County, 200 acres on Spring Creek Oct. 23, 1804. Book 12; p. 402, 184 acres on Big Mud Creek, Oct. 30, 1807. Book 29; p.41.
Above from The Kentucky Land Grants, by Willard R. Jillson, 1925, Reprint

CENSUS LOCATIONS

1790 Burke County, NC 13th Company (Jno Neall)
1800
1810
1820 Logan County, KY ("John Nail")
1830 Logan County, KY ("Cynthia Neil")

REFERENCES

US National Archives Pension Data # R 7578
AIS Census Indices
N.C. Land Grant Data in Morganton-Burke Library, Morganton, NC.
The Kentucky Land Grants, Jillson ... see above.____
Trabur, James D., Judge (Ret) Bellville IL and Sun City West AZ
detailed historical and genealogical information on Neill famil
submitted to author 1992

NEILL, JOHN

SUMMARY OF EARLY LIFE

John Neill was born in Rowan Co., NC c. 1758/59. John Neill (pronounced, and often spelled, "Nail") was the son of William Neill and was a brother to William Neill Jr., Andrew Neill, and James Neill. There were other brothers and sisters.

SUMMARY OF MILITARY SERVICE

John Neill entered military service in the spring of 1780 in Charles McDowell's Burke Regiment. With the Burke troops, Neill fought in the battle of Ramsour's Mill on June 20, 1780. His brother Lt. William Neill was killed in this engagement. (He had just returned from Continental Line duties, taking part in the northern campaigns.) Neill continued to serve under McDowell and on October 7, 1780 was in the battle of Kings Mountain. In early 1781 Neill was serving in Joseph McDowell's mounted troops and took part in the battle of Cowpens fought on January 17, 1781. Following this campaign he continued to serve and was with the American troops under General Nathaniel Greene. On March 15, 1781 he participated in the battle of Guilford Courthouse. (The above information supplied by his widow and family members).

SUMMARY OF LATER LIFE

John Neill married Cynthia Forgy, daughter of Capt. James Forgy and Rebecca Forgy, on October 30, 1799. The following children were born:

William Neill b. November 15, 1800   Mariah b.c. 1807
James Neill b. February 2, 1803   Gilbreath b.c. 1812-1815
Elizabeth b. C. 1801   Hiram b.c. 1818
John b.c. 1807?

There may have had additional children. John Neill died May 3, 1828 in Logan County, KY. His widow applied for Federal pension in 1854, age 72. Rejected.

LAND HOLDINGS AND TRANSACTIONS

A John Neill was issued a North Carolina Land Grant on both sides of the main fork and Kennedy's Fork of Silver Creek. Exact relationship to the soldier John Neill not known. Previous Granville Grant 1763.
Ent. 10 sep 1778 No. 213 Grant No. 44, Iss. 20 Sep 1779, Book 28 p. 44.
State of Kentucky, Land Grants South of the Green River...Jno. Nail received two grants in Logan County, 200 acres on Spring Creek Oct. 23, 1804. Book 12; p. 402, 184 acres on Big Mud Creek, Oct. 30, 1807. Book 29; p.41.
Above from _The Kentucky Land Grants,_ by Willard R. Jillson, 1925, Reprint

CENSUS LOCATIONS

1790 Burke County, NC 13th Company (Jno Neall)
1800
1810
1820 Logan County, KY ("John Nail")
1830 Logan County, KY ("Cynthia Neil")

REFERENCES

US National Archives Pension Data # R 7578
AIS Census Indices
N.C. Land Grant Data in Morganton-Burke Library, Morganton, NC.
The Kentucky Land Grants, Jillson ... see above.____
Trabur, James D., Judge (Ret) Bellville IL and Sun City West AZ detailed historical and genealogical information on Neill famil submitted to author 1992

NEILL, WILLIAM, JR.

SUMMARY OF EARLY LIFE

William Neill was the son of Capt. William Neill of the Burke Militia and a brother of James, Samuel, Galbraith, Robert, Andrew and John Neill (often spelled and pronounced "Nail".) He was born and raised in Rowan County, N.C. (later Iredell County, near McDowell's Creek or Lambert's Mill Creek.) Trabue gives his birth date as c. 1751, unmarried.

SUMMARY OF PARTISAN ACTIVITY

William Neill Jr. was commissioned an officer of the N.C. Continental Line and served as a Lt. in Capt. Joel Brevard's Company of Col. John Williams' Ninth Regiment. He was commissioned in May 1777. The regiment spent several months in north east North Carolina near Halifax. They saw service in suppressing Tory activity near Cross Creek in the summer of 1777. Later that year, the regiment became a part of the North Carolina Brigade in the Northern Campaign of Gen. George Washington. The Ninth was at Valley Forge in the winter of 1777-1778. In 1778, the N.C. Continental Line underwent re-structuring and consolidation. Many supernumerary officers were discharged - to cooperate with militia units, particularly in recruiting.

In early 1780, William Neill joined in with the militia units gathering together so as to oppose the Tory gathering at Ramsours'Mill. While taking part in that epic struggle of June 20, 1780, Lt. William Neill was mortally wounded. He was one of only two Continental Line officers from Burke County (along with Lt. David Vance.)

SUMMARY OF LATER EVENTS

On October 20, 1784 "William Neil and eldest son James of Burke County, N.C. sold to Alexander Brevard whole amount of account due Lt. William Neil for service in Ninth N.C. Regiment". David Falls Brevard papers I, p.27 as quoted by Huggins, Vol.II Burke records.
* Lt. William Neill is being listed as a Burke Co., resident in view of the family move from Rowan to Burke Co. Neill apparently associated himself with western Rowan officers - Alex & Joel Brevard, Galbraith Falls (near S. Iredell Co., N.C).

LAND HOLDINGS AND TRANSACTIONS

Rowan Co., N.C. 1778 tax lists give Wm Neill Jr. as a land owner in Capt. (Galbraith)Falls District (as well as Wm. Neill, Sr., James Neill, Alexander Neill, Samuel Neill and Galbraith Neill.)

REFERENCES

NC DAR (Reprint ed.) Roster of North Carolina Soldiers in the American Revolution pp. 43,102,546.
Linn, Jo White 1983, "Abstracts of Deeds of Rowan Co. NC 1753-1758"
Rankin, Hugh F., Chapel Hill 1971.pp. 87,126,127
The North Carolina Continentals
Huggins, Edith W., Burke Records Vol I&II
Pension Statements of Andrew Neill, John Neill, George Hodge.
Trabue, James D. Judge (Ret.) Belleville,IL and Sun City West AZ Historical and Genealogical information submitted to author 1992 1995.
Linn, Jo White, "Abstracts of Wills and Estates Records of Rowan Co. NC 1753-1805 and Tax Lists of 1759 and 1778", Salisbury, NC 1980 pp. 135-6.

NEILL, WILLIAM SR.

SUMMARY OF EARLY LIFE

The Neill brothers, Andrew, James and William came to North Carolina via Maryland, Chester Co., PA and possibly the Shenandoah Valley of Virginia.

William Neill (or Nail) Sr. was one of Rowan Counties earlier settlers. In 1758 he had acquired land east of the Catawba River in what is now Iredell Co., then Rowan Co. He purchased his land from John McCullough and John McDowell. (566 acres and 640 acres). Another tract of 100 acres was acquired from James McDowell. At this time his wife's name was listed - Mary Neill. During the French and Indian War, William Neill commanded a company of militia. The sale of the 100 acre tract in 1779 definitely links the William Neill who received land from McDowell in 1758 to the William Neill who later moved to Burke County. William Neill and at least three of his sons were Revolutionary war veterans.

SUMMARY OF PARTISAN ACTIVITY

In 1775, William Neill, Galbraith Falls, John Work, and John Oliphant had to appear before the Rowan County Committee of Safety because of a dispute involving Loyalists. Later John Oliphant was cited as being a Tory. Neill and Falls were ardent participants. In 1776 William Neill was appointed a Lieutenant of militia in a company commanded by Capt. John Work.

Most of the early activity of the Rowan Militia was directed against Loyalist activity - and also against the Indian menace on the western frontier. It may be that Neill was favorably impressed by the frontier way of life by the Davidsons and McDowells during the Cherokee Expedition of 1776. For whatever reason,** Neill, in 1778 or so, decided to dispose of his land in Rowan and move to the North Fork (Cherokee region of Burke County, present day McDowell County near Marion). His neighbors included the Pathfinder himself, "Hunting John" McDowell - who had sold land to Neill earlier and the Catheys and Davidsons from old Rowan.

In his new location, he became a Captain of Militia in Charles McDowell's Burke Regiment and subsequently participated in the Kings Mountain Campaign. During this period, his son William Neill, Jr. was killed at Ramsours Mill, after having served a tour in the N.C. Continental Line.

For the remainder of the war, Neill served in the frontier forts of the western Catawba. He served under the senior officer, Col. William Wofford.

In late 1781 Neill, along with James Davidson, a fellow militia

Neill, William Sr.   P.2

officer, brought formal charges against their regimental
commander, Col. Charles McDowell. There were a multitude of
charges, but mainly centered around McDowells partial treatment
of Loyalists and his heavy handed policies. The minutes of
the subsequent court martial are extant. The data contains
information about militia affairs during the period and relates
much about loyalist activities in North and South Carolina.

McDowell was found guilty, relieved of his command, only to
be reinstated several months later, mainly through the efforts
of his friend Gen. Griffith Rutherford. Not only was McDowell
reinstated, but promoted to Brig. General and became Commandant
of the newly formed Morgan Military-Judicial District.

Neill's military activity during 1781-1783 is verified by the
Auditor's records and Revolutionary army accounts. There are
multiple listings giving compensation to Neill and his company
of militiamen.

SUMMARY OF LATER LIFE

William Neill continued to live in Burke County for remainder
of his life. In the 1790's he served as Captain of a military
tax district, as a constable and gave security for Sheriff Thoma
McEntire. He served on jury duty intermittently. His security
bond was given in July 1798. The previous year he had made
his will listing his wife Sarah, sons Andrew, Samuel, Robert
and Galbraith, son in law John Webster, Jacob Haws and daughters
Catherine Arthurs, Jane ??.

William Neill's will was probated in the January 1800 court
session of Burke County, indicating his death in 1799 or possibl
later 1798. His land was divided between three of his sons
Samuel, Robert and Galbraith ("Gilly"). Andrew was left a sum
of money. Another William Neill appears on 1800 census records
and on 1815 tax lists (Silver Creek), possibly the son of John
Neill. William Neill Sr. married (1) Mary Clinton, in 1750, of
Chester Co. PA. Children by this marriage were as follows:
William b.c. 1751 k. Ramsour;s June 1780

James c. 1753	Robert b.c. 1765
Andrew b.c. 1753	Hannah b. 1768
John b. 1758/59	Gilbreath b. 1770
Archibald b.c. 1758	Samuel b. C. 1772
Sarah b. C. 1760	Mary b.c. 1774
Alexander b.c. 1762	Elizabeth b.c. 1776

William Neill Sr. married (2) Sarah (Allen) Arthurs, a widow.

LAND HOLDINGS AND TRANSACTIONS

1. Rowan Co., NC Deed from John McCullough 566 acres, 18 Jan
1758. Originally a Granville Grant to McCullough 6 May 1756.

Deeded to Galbraith Falls 1 Jan 1758. (By William Neill and wife, Mary).
2. Rowan Co., NC deed from John McDowell 640 acres on McDowell's Creek 20 Nov 1754, proved Jan 1758. (Originally Granville Grant to McDowell 25 March 1752). Deeded to William Simanton 14 Jan 1778.
3. Granville Grant, Rowan Co., NC to William Neill 630 acres on North Fork Beaver Creek 10 May 1762.
4. William Neill of Burke County to Galbraith Falls of Rowan 100 acres on North Fork Lamberth's Creek granted by Granville to John McDowell, who sold it to Neill. Proved Nov. 1779.
5. Burke Co., NC 125 acres north side of Catawba near the mouth of the north Fork of Catawba and old improvements of William Rickey, adjacent to McPeters, Collett (old heirs), John Neill. Ent. 6 Feb 1778 #143 Grant No. 820 Iss. 9 Nov 1784 Book 57, p. 24.
6. Burke County, NC 440 acres adjacent to his upper survey, John McPeters, and to Collett's old line. The land includes both sides of North Fork Catawba River, just above juncture with main Catawba River, but including bank of north side of Catawba River. Ent. 28 July 1778 #1456, Grant No. 794, Iss. Nov 9, 1784, Book 57 p. 11.
7. Burke County, NC 60 acres on east side of Stillhouse Creek on branch (on which William Richey's still once stood) adjacent to John McPeters.
Ent. 12 Nov 1783 #1433 Grant No. 785, Iss. Nov 9, 1784, Book 57, p. 6.

CENSUS LOCATIONS

1790 Burke Co., NC 1st Co.

REFERENCES

Huggins, Edith W., Burke County NC Land Records, Southern Historical Press
Linn, Jo White, Rowan County NC Deed Abstracts, 1983
Swink, Dan D., 1986,87, Burke County Court Minutes 1791-1795 1795-1798
Burke Co. Land Grant Data, Morganton Burke Library, Morganton NC.
Burke Co., NC Surviving Will and Probate Records 1777-1910
Revolutionary Army Accounts
AIS Census Indices
Roster of Soldiers from North Carolina in the American Revolution
NC DAR Reprint p.43
US National Archives Pension Statements of Joseph Starnes, Philip Burns, George Hodge, Nicholas Houck, Richard Matlock, Andrew Neill, John Neill, Thomas Patton.
Trabue, James D. Judge (Ret) Belleville, IL and Sun City West AZ. Historical and Genealogical information submitted to the author 1992-1995.

NORTHERN, SOLOMAN

SUMMARY OF EARLY LIFE

The early domicile of Soloman Northern not definitely determine There were persons by that name in nearby Wilkes and Rowan Counties, N.C. Northern was age 73 in the year 1821, as shown his pension records.

SUMMARY OF MILITARY SERVICE

Soloman Northern entered military service in 1779. He enlisted for a tour of eighteen months in the North Carolina Continental Line. He served in Capt. Alexander Brevard's Company. In his pension application he stated that he served in General Gates' Army but does not mention any engagements including Camden. He does mention subsequent militia service, possibly post-war. Du Roster shows him as a Private in the 10th Reg. N.C. Continental Line. Entered 15 May 1781; discharged 8 Apr 1782.

SUMMARY OF LATER LIFE

After the Revolution Northern was living in Burke County, N.C. indicated by land and census records. After the turn of the century he moved to Wayne County, KY and then to Blount County, TN, In his 1818 pension statements he stated that he had a wife age 60 and that she was "...very frail and is rather a burden than a help to this applicant...". He gave his livelihood as a farmer.

He was awarded a pension of $8.00 per month. He gave his age a 73 in 1821 when submitting a second pension declaration. (1818 in Wayne Co., Ky; 1821 in Blount County TN). There was also affidavit filed in Monroe County, TN September 1821.

CENSUS LOCATIONS

1790
1800 Burke Co., NC
1810 Burke Co., NC (? Soloman Northcut)

REFERENCES

AIS Census Indices
US National Archives Pension Data # s 38965
<u>Roster of Soldiers from N.C. in the American Revolution</u>
NCDAR Reprint Edition

Pierces's Register # 90368
Revolutionary Army Accounts Vol. II, Book ZZ and Vol. X #308

PAINTER, JOSEPH

SUMMARY OF EARLY LIFE

Burke County, NC Land records indicate a Joseph Painter living in the vicinity of McLin's Creek, now Catawba County. Also living in the same general area were John Painter (Sr.?) and Jacob Painter.

SUMMARY OF PARTISAN ACTIVITY

Joseph Painter first entered Revolutionary service in Burke County, NC (Then Rowan County) in early 1776 in Capt. William Beekman's Company of Col. Christopher Beekman's Rowan Regiment. They marched from Rowan County to Cross Creek, arriving there shortly after the battle of Moore's Creek Bridge. (February-March 1776).

Painter next served a term of six months as a private militiaman in Capt. John Turnbull's Company of Lt. Col. Hugh Brevard's Regiment, Col. Rutherford's Brigade. He took part in Rutherford's Cherokee Expedition in the late summer and fall of 1776.

Painter, in his pension statements, said that he "killed two Indians just before their arrival at the Overhill Towns". Painter later served two short terms against the Indians. He served in Capt. James Robinson's Company. In June of 1780 he was in the battle of Ramsour's Mill and served under Capt. Galbreath Falls ("Gilly Falls"). Painters last tour of duty was in the Continental Line in Col. (John) Armstrong's Regiment. He was marched to Eutaw Springs, SC, arriving there a day after the battle of September 8, 1781.

SUMMARY OF LATER LIFE

After the Revolutionary War, Painter lived for about five years in Georgia. He then moved to Kentucky, living there about twenty years and then to Illinois Territory.

He applied for Revolutionary War pension in Coles County, Illinois on October 10, 1833 at age 89 years. He was awarded a pension in the amount of $53.33 per annum. Painter stated that he was born in NJ in the year 1744. Joseph Painter died after 1840 and is probably buried at Hutton, Coles County, Illinois. (See reference).

CENSUS LOCATIONS

1820 Grayson County, KY ?
1830 Clark County, IL

REFERENCES

US National Archives Pension Data # S 32403

Revolutionary Soldiers buried in the State of Illinois;
Springfield 1976 (Illinois State Genealogical Society) p. 180
AIS Census Indices
Burke County NC Land Entries # 1251 as quoted in Huggins, E.W.
Vol II p. 1

PAINTER, JOHN

SUMMARY OF EARLY LIFE

John Painter was born in Lincoln County, NC in 1754.

SUMMARY OF PARTISAM ACTIVITY

John Painter first entered Revolutionary service as a private militiaman in 1779 (probably 1780). He served under Col. Joseph McDowell and Brig. Gen. William Davidson. Painter was in the skirmish at Cowans' Ford on February 2, 1781 in which Gen Davidson was killed. His Company Commander was Capt. John Robinson.

He later described his tour with the American army under Gen. Nathaniel Greene and Capt. John Culbertson. He describes action at Guilford Courthouse (March 15, 1781), the advance to Ramsay's on Deep River (March 1781) and his march to South Carolina and the battle of Hobkirk's Hill (April 1781). From Hobkirk's, they were marched to the British held fort at Ninety Six, S. C. He described the hard fought unsuccessful American seige operation of June 1781.

His last action was in the battle of Eutaw Springs on September 8, 1781, again serving under Capt. Culbertson.

Painter apparently was somewhat confused in his dates and details and there were some problems in getting his pension. In an earlier declaration he stated ther he entered service in 1776 and was at the battle of Ramsour's Mill (June 20, 1780) and Camden (August 16, 1780).

SUMMARY OF LATER LIFE

John Painter applied for Revolutionary War pension in Greene Co., Illinois on Sept. 6, 1836, age 82 years. He was awarded a pension in the amount of $20.00 per annum. John Painter died in 1851 and is buried in the Willson Cemetery, Cambria, Williamson County, Illinois.

LAND HOLDINGS AND TRANSACTIONS

1. 100 acres in Burke County NC on Bottle Run, west side of Catawba River, and a tributary of Mountain Creek. The land lay adjacent to that of Jacob Painter, Charles Ward and John Salings. Ent. Nov. 28, 1778, No. 698, Grant # 234, Iss. March 14, 1780, Book 28, p. 233.
2. 150 acres Burke County, NC both sides of the long glade near Bottle Run, a tributary of Mountain Creek. The land was adjacent to that of Charles Ward and across the "Wagon Road".
3. 100 acres Burke County, NC on north side of Linville River, formerly owned by Charles Wakefield. It lay next to Wakefield's land and was near the "old schoolhouse".

Ent. Sept. 26, 1778, NO. 792, Grant # 105, Iss. Aug. 7, 1787, Book 65. P. 400.

**Note: The land descried in NOS. 1 & 2 above, probably represen the John Painter who died in Lincoln Co., N.C. ca 1792. No 3 possibly the soldier (son of the older John Painter?). This woul correspond with the location in 3rd Co. 1790 Census, Burke County.

CENSUS LOCATIONS

1790 Burke County, NC 3rd. Co.
1800 Burke Co., NC
1810 Wayne Co., KY (a son?)
1820 Grayson County, KY ?
1830 Greene County, IL

REFERENCES

Burke Co., NC Land Grant Data; Morganton-Burke, Morganton, N.C.
US National Achives and Pension Data, S32432
Soldiers of the American Revolution buried in IL, Springfield 1976, p. 180 (Illinois State Genealogical Society).
AIS Census Indices

PARKS, GEORGE

SUMMARY OF EARLY LIFE

George Parks was born in Amherst County, VA on August 5, 1759. He was a brother of Samuel Parks, also a Revolutionary War soldier. "When a boy" he came with his father and family to Wilkes County, NC and lived on the Yadkin River. Parks was still living in Wilkes County at the beginning of the Revolutionary War.

SUMMARY OF MILITARY SERVICE

George Parks first entered military service in Wilkes County in 1775 in William Lenoir's company of the Wilkes Militia. He entered as a substitute. He was assigned to the upper Yadkin and assisted in the erection of fortifications at Fort Defiance. He was stationed there three months.

In the summer of 1776, he served again in the militia in a company commanded by Capt. Samuel Johnston of Col. Benjamin Cleveland's Wilkes Regiment. In this Regiment he participated in the Cherokee Expedition of 1776, serving in what is now East Tennessee. He assisted in the building Fort Carter, on the north side of the Watauga River. Parks' third tour of duty was in Capt. William Lenoir's Company beginning in 1779. This was a mounted rifle Company of Cleveland's Wilkes Regiment. Their activities were directed against local Loyalists. Parks specifically mentions a raid against the Tories of the New River section. He stated In his pension declaration that the "mountains near the New River were full of them --ie. Tories."

He described the taking of many prisoners. Later they were on the trail of about thirty Tories who had come from the "hollows of the Yadkin River", had crossed at Parks Ford and were headed toward South Carolina "plundering, stealing and doing other mischief". Parks and his comrades surprised them and chased them back across the Yadkin. A little while later they surprised another group in camp and hanged two of them (William Cool and Sam Jones) and "whipping the rest nearly to death". Parks also tells of the taking of the celebrated Tory, Old Solomon Sparks. They decoyed him away from his horse "without his gun" and captured him. He put up a good fight and "considerably injured this applicant by kicking him". They tied old Sparks hand and foot, on his back, and sent him down the Yadkin in a canoe. As he was being sent away he "repeatedly hollowed --- Hurrah for King George!".

Parks also mentioned the taking of another Tory, Peter Holt. Parks later took part in the Kings Mountain Campaign. He was assigned to the foot soldiers and consequently did not participate in the battle of October 7, 1780. He assisted in caring for a wounded nephew, Henry Parks.

Parks recalls another short duty assignment to Ramsour's Mill after the battle of June 20, 1780 and later to Salem, Deep River and Guilford Courthouse, after the battle of March 15, 1781. Altogether he served a total of about eighteen months.

SUMMARY OF LATER LIFE

After staying in Wilkes County for five or six more years Parks moved to Burke County, NC, living that for almost eighteen year He then moved to Monroe County, IN, living there for the rest o his life. He applied for Revolutionary War pension in Monroe County, IN and was awarded $40.00 per annum. George Parks married (1) Millie Davidson, (2) he married Catherine Reed in Surry County, N.C. in July 1796. The children of George Parks were as follows:

Elizabeth   Hannah b. 1797 m. Wm. Pue
James (later a State Legislator)   Meredith
Samuel   Alfred
Polly   Curtis
Benjamin   Sarah
Pleasant (later a Col. Of Militia   Rebecca
Nancy   And State Legislator)   Carlton
Millie

George Parks died December 7, 1837 in Monroe County, IN. His widow, Catherine Parks, was allowed a warrant for 160 acres of bounty land in 1856, Dallas County, Texas.

LAND HOLDINGS AND TRANSACTIONS

1. Wilkes Co., NC Deed from George Parks to John Parks 300 acre on Little Elkin Creek, near Cattail Marsh, including both sides of creek "whereon George parks now Lives". March 16, 1796.

2. Burke Co., NC Deeds from Thomas White, Sr., to George Parks, tracts, 125 acres and 112 acres, Sept.2 and 22, 1796.

3. Burke Co., NC 1815 Tax Lists show George Parks with 237 acr in Capt. John Fox's Company.

CENSUS LOCATIONS

1790 Wilkes County, NC 7th Co.
1800 Burke County, NC
1810 Burke County, NC
1820
1830 Monroe County, IN

REFERENCES

DAR Patriot Index 1966 Washington D.C. p. 514 (1st marriage)
US National Archives Pension Data # W 27457
AIS Census Indices

Wilkes Co., NC Deed Abstracts, by Absher, Mrs. W.O. Book D/348 Southern Historical Press 1990.
Burke Co., NC Minutes of Court of Pleas and Quarter Sessions by Swink, Dan D. 1987.
1795-1798 Sessions p. 56

PARKS, SAMUEL

SUMMARY OF EARLY LIFE

Samuel Parks was born in Amherst Co., VA November 28, 1757. At the beginning of the Revolutionary War, he was living in Wilkes Co., NC.

SUMMARY OF PARTISAN ACTIVITY

Samuel Parks first entered military service in Wilkes Co., NC under Capt. William Lenoir and Col. Benjamin Cleveland. He also served under Capt. (Later Major) Micajah Lewis.

Parks participated in Rutherford's Cherokee Expedition of 1776, directed against the Overhills Cherokee Indians.

Samuel Parks continued to serve in the Wilkes Militia for a total of two years. Most of their activities were against local Loyalists.

SUMMARY OF LATER LIFE

Parks was still living in Wilkes Co. At the time of the 1790 census. (P.I. lists him, but not his wife). By 1800 he had moved to Burke Co., NC and remained there for the duration of his life. His wife predeceased him. Children included the following:

William Parks   Ransome Parks
George Parks   Martin Parks
Benjamin Parks   Mary (Polly) Alexander
Gabriel Parks   Elizabeth Penland
John S. Parks

Samuel Parks was a brother to George Parks, also a Revolutionary War soldier.

SUMMARY OF LATER LIFE

Samuel Parks died in Burke County, NC On October 23, 1844. His son, John S. Parks, and other heirs, applied for Revolutionary War benefits due their father, then deceased. (1851) An award of $80.00 per annum was given. His will was presented for probate January 1845, Burke Co, NC. Executors John S. Parks and John Parks - proved.

LAND HOLDINGS AND TRANSACTIONS

1. 100 acres on west fork Warrior Creek, including improvements made by Thomas Wadkins. Ent. Sept. 4, 1804, # 5048, Grant No. 3409, Iss. Nov. 29, 1806, Book 122, p. 193. Chain carriers, Benjamin Parks, George Parks.

2. A Samuel Parks received several tracts of land in Buncombe County, NC between 1803 and 1808. Total 625 acres in six tracts on Beaverdam Creek, French Broad River, Ream's Creek. Books A,B,3,7 & 8. Acquired from James McNabb, Davy Smith, Will Forester, and State of NC.

3. Wilkes Co., NC Deed from Samuel Parks to James Downey 270 acres and 49 acres N. Side of Yadkin River adjacent to Gabriel Loveing and Hughes. 27 Jan 1796. Deed from Samuel Parks to James Sheppard 50 acres north side of Yadkin River, 31 Jam 1798. Parks listed as being from Burke Co., NC on 1798 Deed.

4. Burke Co., NC Deed from Thomas White to Samuel Parks 200 acres Sep 22, 1796.

5. Burke County Tax Lists in 1797 list Samuel Parks with 360 acres, Capt. John Fox's Company. 1815 Tax Lists show 200 acres Marler's Co. 1817.

CENSUS LOCATIONS

1790 Wilkes Co., NC 7th Co.
1800 Burke County, NC
1810 Burke County, NC
1820 Burke County, NC
1830 Burke County, NC
1840 Burke County, NC

REFERENCES

DAR Patriot Index (1466) p. 515
US National Archives Pension Data # S 8937
Absher, Mrs. W.O., Wilkes County, NC Deed Abstracts, Book C1/98-99
Southern Historical Press 1989 p. 101. Book D pp. 159, 160, 171, 341. 1990.
Burke County Land Grant Data; Morganton-Burke Library, Morganton, NC.
AIS Census Indices
Pittman, Betsy, Dodd, Burke Co., NC 1815 Tax Lists, p. 115, 1990.
Swink, Dan D. 1987. Burke County Minutes of the Court of Pleas and Quarter Sessions 1795-1798.
Turner, Grace and Philbeck, Miles, Chapel Hill 1983, No. 407, Burke County NC. Surviving Will & Probate Abstracts 1777-1910
Huggins, E.W., Southern Historical press; 1987 p. 119; Burke County, NC Records Vol. IV.

PATTON, THOMAS (PATTEN)

SUMMARY OF EARLY LIFE

Thomas Patton was born in Marlborough, Pa., April 25, 1735. At the time of the American Revolution, he was living in Rowan County (that part which later became Burke County). The names Patton and Patten are used in his pension application.

SUMMARY OF PARTISAN ACTIVITY

Thomas Patton, in his pension application, stated that he served for about three years in the Revolutionary Army, but (because of age) could only remember two or three distinct tours of duty.

In June of 1780, he served in Maj. Joseph McDowell's Burke Militia under Capt. John Hardin (called "Hardy" by Patton) and Lt. Thomas Kennedy. He took part in the battle of Ramsour's Mill on June 20, 1780 and in the subsequent pursuit of Tories. He was discharged afterwards.

In the fall of 1780, he again was in Capt. Hardin's Company and fought in the Battle of Kings Mountain on October 7, 1780.

He was transferred over to Capt. William NeiLL's Company of Maj. Joseph McDowell's Mounted Battalion and took part in the Cowpen's battle of January 17, 1781. Later, he was in the pursuit of Cornwallis through central North Carolina. On March 15, 1781, participated in the battle of Guilford Courthouse.

SUMMARY OF LATER LIFE

Thomas Patton applied for Revolutionary War Pension in 1832 at age 97, at that time a resident of Crawford, IL. He was awarded a Federal pension of $40.00 per annum. He is buried in Palestine Township, Crawford, IL.

NOTE; The soldier Thomas Patton or Patten, in his pension statements, gives Rowan County as his place of residence during and after the Revolution. The author has listed his residence Burke County, based on census data as well as from the names of his military superiors, (all Burke County Officers). Because of his age, he probably had lived in Rowan County a considerable number of years, thus associating the name, though it later became Burke County in 1777.

LAND HOLDINGS AND TRANSACTIONS

Thomas Patton received the following Grants:

1. 345 acres on Silver Creek in Burke County, N.C. adjacent to land belonging to George Hipps, Richard Bailey, William Bailey and John Berger. Chain carriers, John Berger and Ezekial Stringfield. Ent. May 30, 1778, Grant No. 327, Iss. Oct. 28, 178

Book 44, p. 118.

2. 100 acres on Silver Creek adjacent to land belonging to John Cooper. Ent. Oct. 17, 1778, Grant No. 392, Iss. Oct. 28, 1782, Book 44, p. 155. c.c. Ezekial Stringfield, James Stringfield.

3. 50 acres east side French Broad River, joining the land "he now lives on". Ent. June 22, 1800, Grant No. 929, iss. Dec. 7, 1801, Buncombe Co., NC Book 114, p. 104.

4. 60 acres, 50 acres, 50 acres French Broad River as land grants from State of NC. On April 13, 1803 and November 24, 1808. Grant No. 956 and 929. Buncombe County Deeds.

5. 460 acres Swannonoa River, Buncombe County, NC from James McNabb. Ent. July 21, 1795, Book 3, p. 91.

6. 400 acres French Broad River, Buncome County, NC from William Davidson. Ent July 19, 1803, Book 9, p. 7.

CENSUS LOCATIONS

1790 Burke Co,, NC 13th Co., Landholder with tracts 1 & 2 above
     Burke Co., NC 11th Co. Landholder in western Burke, later Buncombe Co.
1800 Buncombe Co., NC most likely person in 11th Co. above. Tracts 3-6 above correspond with census location in Buncombe County.

REFERENCES

US National Archives Pension Data. # S32429
Soldiers of the American Revolution Buried in IL - Springfield 1976 (Il. State Genealogical Society) p. 182.

PENLAND, GEORGE

SUMMARY OF EARLY LIFE

George Penland was born c. 1753, probably Newcastle County Delaware. He, along with his brothers William Penland and Robe Penland moved into Burke County, NC, then Rowan County c. 1765. All three signed the petition urging the Legislature to form a new county west of Rowan. (1771-1773).

SUMMARY OF PARTISAN ACTIVITY

George Penland, along with his brothers served with the McDowells during the Revolutionary war. Later George Penland received a Captains commission of militia. His rank and servic is verified by the official North Carolina Revolutionary Army Accounts, Book A.

SUMMARY OF LATER LIFE

George Penland was married to Ann Alexander. They first lived on Upper Creek, Burke County but later in 1798 moved to Reems Creek, Buncombe County. Their children were: Robert, Chris, Rachel, Alexander, William, Jane.

George Penland died in 1829.

LAND HOLDINGS AND TRANSACTIONS

1. 200 acres, middle fork of Upper Creek including "his improvements" adjacent to James Alexander.
Ent. #790, Grant No. 666 Iss. Oct. 11, 1783 Burke County,NC

2. 200 acres on the middle fork of Upper Creek adjacent to John Simpson. Ent. #1780, Grant No. 697 Burke County, NC

3. 200 acres on Warrior Fork of Upper Creek adjacent to John McMullens and John Dobson. Ent. #631, Grant 710, Iss. Oct. 11, 1783, Burke County, NC

4. 50 acres Burke County on School House branch of Upper Creek adjacent to his own land including the Schoolhouse and the cabi where "Thomas McKee now lives". Ent. 1780, Grant #1864, Iss. July 7, 1794, Burke County, NC

5. 100 acres Reams Creek Buncombe County, NC Land Grant #133, Jan. 19, 1795.

6. 100 acres Sandy Mush Creek, Buncombe County, NC, NC Land Grant No. 736, December 6, 1799.

7. 150 acres Reems Creek, Buncombe County September 24, 1801. An additional 700 acres is listed on Reems Creek and Bull Creek

from 1801 through 1811.

CENSUS LOCATIONS

1790 Burke County, NC, 3rd Co.
1800 Buncombe County, NC
1810 Buncombe County, NC
1820 Buncombe County, NC
1830 Buncombe County, NC (?)

REFERENCES

Burke County, NC Land Grant Data, Morganton Burke Library, Morganton, NC.
AIS Census Indices
Wooley, James E., Buncombe County, NC **Index To Deeds** 1783-1850. SHP 1983 pages 389-91.
Phifer, Edward W., **Burke** 1977 Edition p. 361
Browder, Blanche Penland **The Penland Family** of North Carolina 1975.
NC State Treasurers and Comptrollers Accounts. Book "A" p. 227 Acct. No. 7072

PENLAND, JOHN

SUMMARY OF EARLY LIFE

John Penland was born in Newcastle Co., PA November 27, 1764. was the son of William Penland and Anna Dorral. At the beginni of the Revolutionary War, he and his family were living on Uppe Creek in Burke County, NC.

SUMMARY OF MILITARY SERVICE

John Penland entered military service in Burke County, NC in th early summer of 1781 (or 1780 ?). He was a substitute militiaman, serving in the place of Robert Penland. His regimental Commander was Col. Charles McDowell. His company Commander was Capt. (Jonathan) Kemp or Camp. In his pension application, he stated that, "...he marched into South Carolina, Spartanburg District, where he continued marching from one poin to another, not remaining long at any one place...", until his month tour was completed.

His second tour of duty was in the fall and winter of 1781. Penland served in the Wilmington Expedition. He served in a Company commanded by Capt. Joseph McDowell of Col. Charles McDowell's Regiment. Before reaching their destination, Penland became ill and had to be left behind. He was provided a horse ride home by his Col. (McDowell ?).

He also stated that he served an additional six months against the Indians and Tories.

SUMMARY OF LATER LIFE

John Penland continued to live in Burke County until the year 1811. At this time he moved to Buncombe County, NC, remaining there the remainder of his life.

John Penland married (1) Alice Moore, daughter of Capt. William Moore. Their children were as follows:

Abraham b. 1791 m. Elizabeth Jones
William b. 1797 M. Nancy Stephens
Elizabeth b. 1800 m. James Cathey
John Harvey b. Ca. 1800 m. Evaline Nichols
Charles Davidson b. 1804 m. (1) Elizabeth (2) Mary Smith
George Newton b. Ca. 1812 M. Nancy Jones

John Penland applied for Revolutionary War pension in July 1837 His widow applied for benefits in 1855, Buncombe County. John Penland died in 1855 at age 88 years (?). He was buried near Enka High School, Enka, Buncombe County, NC.

LAND HOLDINGS AND TRANSACTIONS

1. 50 acres on Shadrick's Creek, including a shoal. It lay adjacent to land belonging to Abraham Denton and Thomas Young. Burke Co., NC, Ent. March 29, 1793, No. 367, Grant No. 1360, Iss. August 22, 1795.

2, 75 acres , Hominy Creek, Buncombe County, acquired from William Moore, December 4, 1805 (rec. 3/28/07) Book "A" p. 137

3. 125 acres Hominy Creek, Buncombe County, acquired from Thomas Moore, 20 July 1811 (rec. 3 Feb. 1813) Book "D" p. 227.

4. 100 acres on Little Fork of Shadrick's Creek, Burke Co., NC adjacent to land of Isaiah Bradshaw, Tilman Walton and Abraham Denton.
Ent.Sept. 25, 1810 No. 5799, Grant No. 3687, Iss. Dec. 15, 1815, Book 129, p. 345.

CENSUS LOCATIONS

1790 Burke Co., NC ?? A Jno. "Pennly listed in 1st Company
1800
1810 Burke Co., NC again, a John "Penly" listed. A separate Burke Co. Name
1820 Buncombe Co., NC
1830

REFERENCES

US National Archives Pension Data # R 8093
N. C. Land Grant data, copies in Morganton-Burke Library, Morganton, NC.
Buncombe County, NC Index to Deeds 1783-1850
Wooley, James E. 1983, Southern Historical Press, Easley, SC p. 390.
DAR Patriot Index (1966) p. 526

PENLAND, ROBERT

SUMMARY OF EARLY LIFE

Robert Penland was born in Chester Co., PA (?) Ca. 1744. He was one of the earlier settlers of Burke Co., having migrated there from New Castle County, Delaware, along with his brothers George and William Penland. All three were living in Burke County, N.C. (Then Rowan) in 1771 and signed a petition calling for the Assembly to form a new county.

SUMMARY OF PARTISAN ACTIVITY

Robert Penland, along with his brothers George and William Penland and his nephew John Penland, served during the Revolutionary War under the McDowells.

Robert Penland took part in the bloody conflict at Ramsour's Mill on June 20, 1780. Later he served under the McDowells in the Kings Mountain campaign, culminating in the great American victory on October 7, 1780. Robert Penland also served in several campaigns against the Cherokee Indians. (1776 and 1782

SUMMARY OF LATER LIFE

Robert Penland married Elizabeth Brank. After the Revolutionary War Robert Penland lived on Canoe Creek in Burke County, NC. He was an Elder in the Quaker Meadows Presbyterian Church, near Morganton, N.C. The children of Robert and Elizabeth Penland were as follows:

Jane (or Jean) b. 1771 m. Samuel Alexander
George b. 1778 m. Rachel Moore
Robert b. 1779 m. Mary (Polly) Moore
Peter b. 1782 m. Rachel Henry
Leah b. C. 1783 m. John Saulman
Harry (Henry) b. C. 1786 m. Elizabeth Parks
Eleanor (Nellis m. Nathan Gibson
Pricilla m. _____Wakefield
Ruth m. _____Alexander
Rachel b. 1795 m. William A. Erwin

Robert Penland's will registered in Burke County Court on Feb. 25, 1828. No probate date given.

LAND HOLDINGS AND TRANSACTIONS

1. 150 acres Quaker Meadows on both sides of Canoe Creek, bordering lands of James Greenlee, George Bates and "Just above his improvement whereon the said Penland now Lives". Burke County, N, C.
Ent. 3 June 1778; No. 119; Grant No. 52, Iss. Sept. 20, 1799 Book 18 p. 52.

2. 100 acres both sides Canoe Creek. Ent. May 12, 1778; No, 427; Grant No. 612, Iss. Oct 11, 1783, Book 50 p. 221, Burke County, NC.

3. 175 acres on East side of Canoe Creek and both sides of Falling Branch, Burke County, NC adjacent to his "old" survey and to land of James Greenlee. Burke Co., NC Ent. Jan 25, 1779, No. 1503, Grant No. 734, Iss. Oct. 11, 1783, Book 50 p.274.

4. 150 acres on a branch that enters French Broad River, east side and above mouth of Newfound Creek. Iss. Nov. 16, 1790, Grant No. 1367, Book 77 p. 146. Ent. Jan 15, 1789 No. 16. Burke (Buncombe) Co., NC.

5. 100 acres on the Jumping Branch of Canoe Creek. Ent. Jan 25, 1795 No. 1111, Grant No. 2546, Iss. Jan 7, 1799, Book 101, p.82. Burke County, NC.

The records below could be those of Robert Penland, Jr. as well as Sr.

400 acres Bald Mountain, Buncombe County, NC acquired from Thomas Houston. Book "B" p. 20. April 8, 1808.

150 acres Turkey Creek, Buncombe County, NC acquired from Wm. Davidson; Book 1, p. 206.

225 acres S. Fork Mills River, Buncombe Co., NC acquired form George Penland. Book S 102, p.11.

225 acres S. Fork Mills River, Buncombe County, NC acquired from George Penland. Book S 2-2, p.11.

282 acres Pigeon River, Buncombe Co., NC acquired from Jos. Daleson. Book 5, p. 42.

225 acres Mills River, Buncombe Co., NC acquired from Geo. Penland, Book 7, p. 660.

CENSUS LOCATIONS

1790 Burke Co., NC. 3rd Co.
1800 Burke Co., NC
1810 Burke Co., NC (Pinland)
1820 Haywood Co., NC (Robert Jr.?)
1820 Burke Co., NC ?? "John Penyan"?

REFERENCES

Avery, A.C., Notes concerning Quaker Meadows Presbyterian Church Land Grant Data, copies in Morganton Burke Library, Morganton, NC.
<u>Revolutionary Army Accounts:</u> Vol. I - XII "O-Z" Vol. 1 p. 91 Folio 2.

Will of Robert Penland, Burke County, NC, probably 1828
"The Penland Family of North Carolina", Blanche Penland Browder, Raleigh 1986
Buncombe Co., NC Index to Deeds 1783 - 1850 Wooley, Jas. E. Southern Historical Press, Easley SC 1983 p. 390-391
DAR Patriot Index (1966) p. 526
Burke Co., North Carolina Surviving Will and Probate Abstracts 1777-1910, by Grace Turner and Miles Philbeck, 1983 No. 434.

PENLAND, WILLIAM

SUMMARY OF EARLY LIFE:

William Penland was born in Newcastle County, Delaware in 1742. William Penland was the oldest of three brothers who came to Burke County (then Rowan) in the 1760's. All three were signers of the 1771-1773 petition to create a new county west of Rowan. He was married to Anna (Annis) Donnal in 1762. He was married in Chester County, PA. In Burke County, they lived on Upper Creek.

SUMMARY OF PARTISAN ACTIVITY

In November 1775 William Penland was appointed a Lt. of militia by the Rowan County Committee of Safety. This appointment was verified by the North Carolina Provincial Assembly. Penland served in Capt. Charles McDowell'a Company of Col. Christopher Beekman's 2nd Rowan Regiment. Later as a Captain he participated in the Cross Creek Expedition of Gen. Griffith Rutherford (sequel to the Moore's Creek Bridge campaign). In the summer and fall of 1776 he was in the Cherokee Expedition of Gen. Rutherford.

Penland continued to serve under Col. Charles McDowell for the duration. Capt. Penland was compensated for his military duties and also for attending to wounded soldiers.

An interesting account of Capt. Penland's service on the frontier was given by Henry Wakefield, a pensioned soldier of the Revolution (see Vol. I, page 290).

SUMMARY OF LATER LIFE

William and Anna Donnal Penland lived on Upper Creek, Burke County. Browder gives a tentative list of children as follows:

John b. 1764
James b. 1765
William
George b. ca. 1780
Peter
Alexander b. 1782
Census of 1790 lists three females, presumably wife and two daughters in addition to sons.

William Penland served at various times on Jury duty in Burke County and was a Justice of the Peace. Near the turn of the century he began to sell off his Burke land and later began to acquire property in Buncombe County on Reems Creek, where other Penlands had settled. He was still listed in the Burke County census in 1800 and 1810. He died in 1815.

LAND HOLDINGS AND TRANSACTIONS   Penland, William

1. 300 acres on Upper Creek adjacent to land of Thomas Scott and James Alexander.
Ent. 1778 No. 136 Grant 138, Iss. March 1780, Burke County, NC

2. 100 acres on the Big Branch of Linville River and above the land of Henry Wakefield.
Ent. 1779, No. 788, Grant No. 1177, Iss. May 15, 1789, Burke County, NC.

3. 160 acres on south fork of Upper Creek adjacent to his own land and that of James Alexander.
Ent. 1778, No. 945 Grant No. 1838, Iss. July 7, 1794, Burke County, NC.

4. 100 acres on a branch of Canoe Creek and adjacent to Robert Penland,s plantation.
Ent. 1793, No. 336 Grant No. 1365, Iss. August 22, 1795, Burke County, NC.

5. William Penland obtained several tracts of land in Buncombe County as follows: Five tracts of land of 100 acres each on Reems Creek in 1807. An additional 50 acres on Ivy Creek obtained in 1808.

REFERENCES

Burke Land Grant Date, Morganton Burke Library, Morganton, N.C.
AIS Census Indices
Wooley, James E., Buncombe County, N.C. Index to Deeds 1783-1850 SHP 1983 p. 389-391.
Swink, Dan D., Abstract of Burke County Court Minutes 1795-1798 (1987)
Wheeler, John H., Historical Sketches of North Carolina (1851)- Reprint. This book contains minutes of the Rowan County Committee of Safety, p. 374
Revolutionary Army Accounts, Book "A" p. 227, Book 1-6 pp. 9-10; Book "A" p. 185 Vols. I-XII, multiple listings.
US National Archives Pension Statements of Henry Wakefield. #W35
Phifer, Edward W., Burke 1977 Ed.p. 361
Browder, Blanche Penland, The Penland Family of North Carolina Revised edition 1975 (copy in Morganton-Burke Library, Morganton NC.

PEPPER, ROBERT

SUMMARY OF EARLY LIFE

Robert Pepper appears to have been living near the North Fork of the Catawba River at the time of the American Revolution.

SUMMARY OF PARTISAN ACTIVITY

Robert Pepper was cited to Burke County Court in November 1782 to show cause as to why his property should not be confiscated, for being disloyal to the American Cause.

A witness in his case included Joseph Dobson, Jr. who lived in the same neighborhood.

SUMMARY OF LATER LIFE

Robert Pepper apparently died either near the conclusion of the Revolution or shortly afterwards. Administrative papers were filed in Burke County Court by Catherine Pepper (wife ?). Samuel Bright and William Wofford were listed.

LAND HOLDINGS AND TRANSACTIONS

Robert Pepper entered 320 acres of land in North Cove of the North Fork of the Catawba (now McDowell County, NC), including "improvement he now lives on ....".
Ent. 29 October 1778.
Transferred to James Ainsworth, also a resident of North Cove-
- on 7 August 1788.

REFERENCES

Huggins, Edith W., Burke County North Carolina Land Records Vols. I & II 1977. SHP

PIERCY, BLAKE

SUMMARY OF EARLY LIFE

Blake Piercy was a resident of Burke County, NC at the time of his first enlistment in the Revolutionary War.

SUMMARY OF MILITARY SERVICE

Blake Piercy served two consecutive three month terms of duty in the Burke County, NC Militia in 1779, Col. Charles McDowell commanding the Regiment. Capt. (Joseph) White was Company Commander on the first tour, Capts. Kennedy (Thomas) and Camp (Jonathan) on the second tour. Their activities were mainly directed against Tories.

In late 1780, he enlisted again in McDowell's Regiment for a six month tour, His Battalion Commander was Maj. Joseph McDowell of Quaker Meadows.

Under Joseph McDowell, they marched to near Charlotte, joining u with the troops headed by Brig. Gen Daniel Morgan. Piercy, under Morgan and McDowell, participated in the great American victory at Cowpens, S.C. on January 17, 1781. During the battle Piercy was "dangerously wounded and left behind". He remained in the area with some Continental soldiers until he was brought home by his Mother and relatives. His wife later stated that the long term effects of his battle wounds led to his death.

Note: Blake Piercy was cited by subpoena to Burke County Court, January session 1783, on suspicion of being a Tory.

SUMMARY OF LATER LIFE

Blake Piercy married Mary _____ on October 15, 1791. They were married in Warren County GA. By this union were the following children:

Ephraim b. Apr 12, 1794
William b. Oct 20 1796
Sebon b. March 13, 1799
Willis b. Dec 26, 1807 d. 1809
Mary b. June 15, 1810
Wilbourn b. June 2, 1813

Piercy was embroiled in a law suit against Reuben White of Burke Co., in 1796-98. Blake Piercy died (Jan. Or Dec.?) 1837. His widow was living in Indian Creek in Yancy County, NC when applying for pension in 1850.

LAND HOLDINGS AND TRANSACTIONS

Blake Piercy received the following NC Land Grants in Burke County.

1. 50 acres located on the east side of Upper Creek. The land was adjacent to property belonging to Widow (Elizabeth) Piercy and to WilliamPenley.
Ent. March 4, 1799, Grant No. 2046, Iss. Dec 6, 1799, Book 107, p.37.

100 acres, by Deed from Elizabeth Piercy, 23 Jan 1798. Registered in January session, Burke County Court.

Blake Piercy acquired several tracts of land in Buncombe County, NC as follows:

150 acres from William Lawson, on Bald Mountain Creek, Ent. March 11, 1808, Book 7, p. 630

50 acres from William Moore, Bald Mountain Creek, Ent. March 8, 1808 Book "A" p.536.

75 acres from William Lawson, Ent. March 13, 1808, Book 7, p.635.

25 acres from Edward Carter on Lindsy Creek, Ent. June 22, 1818, Book 11, p.34.

150 acres from John Strother, et al, on Caney River, Ent. Sept. 22, 1819, Book 11, p. 465.

750 acres from John Hooper, John Ogle, et al, Big Ivy Creek, Ent. July 2, 1818, Book 11, p. 118

237 acres from John McDowell on Cane Creek, Ent. Spet 13, 1814, Book "G", p. 237.

650 acres from Robert Scott, Penland, et al, on Cane Creek, Ent. 1819 and 1830, Book No.

CENSUS LOCATIONS

1790 Columbia Co., GA (Probably part to become Warren Co.)
1800
1810 Buncombe Co., NC
1820 Buncome Co,., NC

REFERENCES

Huggins, E.W., Subpoena Docket, Jan. 1783 Session Burke County Court, Vol. OO, pp 153-154. Burke County, N.C. Land Records.
Swink, Dan D., Munites of the (Burke County Court) Pleas and Quarter Sessions, 1795-1798, 1987, pp 79,12,67,92,40.
AIS Census Indices
The Reconstruction 1790 Census of Georgia, DeLamar and Rothstein General Publishing Co., Baltimore 1983, p. 56.

POTEAT, EDWARD (Poteet, Pateete)

SUMMARY OF EARLY LIFE

Edward Poteat was born in Bedford County, VA. He was about 70 years old in 1834 when applying for Federal pension. During the Revolutionary period, he was living in the South Mountain area of Burke County, near the Rutherford line.

SUMMARY OF PARTISAN ACTIVITY

Edward Poteat first entered military service in 1781 as a private soldier of Charles McDowell's Burke County militia regiment. He served a short tour of duty under Capt. Thomas Kennedy. Their activities were directed mainly against Loyalist activities in western North Carolina and adjacent South Carolina. His next tour of duty was served under Capt. James McFarland. Poteat was stationed at the head of the Catawba River, guarding against the incursions of the hostile Cherokee Indians.

His final tour of duty was served in Capt. John McDowell's company in a regiment commanded by Maj. (then Col.) Joseph McDowell of Quaker Meadows. They were engaged in a short punitive raid against the Cherokees in the spring of 1782.

SUMMARY OF LATER LIFE

Edward Poteat was married to Martha _____ on March 22, 1786 (she died May 22, 1842). They had the following children:
Samuel D. of Lauderdale Co., AL
James
Nancy m. John Horne, Lawrence Co., TN
Elizabeth m. Thomas Horne, Lawrence Co., TN
William Poteat, Giles Co., TN
Jinsy m. Jesse Lindsay, Marion Co., AL
Sarah, died in infancy.

Edward Poteat appears to have left Burke County ca. 1794, the date of the sale of his property to Richard Ozgathorpe. Subsequently he lived at various times in South Carolina, Tennessee, Kentucky and finally in Alabama. Edward Poteat applied for Revolutionary War pension in Lauderdale County, AL on October 9, 1834, age about 70 years. He received a pension in the amount of $24.66 per annum. Edward Poteat died in Lauderdale County, AL on October 19, 1836. Pension records state that he lived in Alabama for about twenty years prior to his death and prior to then, in Giles Co., TN.

LAND HOLDINGS AND TRANSACTIONS

Burke Co., NC 200 acres at Walker's Gap including the head of Long Creek, South Mountain area of Burke County. Ent. 12 May 1778, Grant #1344, Iss. 16 Nov. 1790,

Poteat, Edward   P.2

Book 77, p. 141, cc. Elijah Walker, West Walker.

Burke Co., NC court records show sale of land, 200 acres from Edward Poteat to Richard Ozgathorpe Sept. 16, 1794 most likely the tract in number one above.

CENSUS LOCATIONS

1790 Burke Co., NC 13th Co. ("Boteat").
1830 Lauderdale Co., AL

REFERENCES

US National Archives Pension Declarations #W10853
Land Grant Records, Morganton-Burke Library, Morganton, NC.
Huggins, Edith, Burke County, NC Records Vol IV SHP 1987 p.24
AIS Census Indices

POWELL, ELIAS

SUMMARY OF EARLY LIFE

Elias Powell was born September 26, 1754 in North Carolina. He was the son of Elias Powell, Sr. of Virginia. Before and during the American Revolution, he was living on Lower Creek in Burke, now Caldwell County, NC.

SUMMARY OF PARTISAN ACTIVITY

Elias Powell was perhaps the best known Loyalist of old Burke County. An extensive description of Powell and his activities are related in Drapers book on the battle of Kings Mountain. it appears that Powell was very closely attached to his leader, Major Patrick Ferguson. After the Tory defeat at Kings Mountain on October 7, 1780 Powell assisted in the burial of Ferguson and also came in possession of his silver whistle. After his capture, Powell, along with other prisoners were marched to Salem and later to Hillsboro where he was paroled. The silver whistle remained in the Powell family for several generations.

In 1782 Elias Powell was indited at Burke Court on charges of being a Tory and for being disloyal to the American cause.

SUMMARY OF LATER LIFE

Elias Powell married Anne Barbara Albright (born 1 June 1754). They were the parents of the following children.

1. Benjamin b. Sept. 28, 1778 m. Nancy Harris
2. Mary b. Feb 23, 1787
3. George b. Feb 26, 1789 m.1. Mary Smith, 2. Lucinda Rowe
4. Elizabeth b. Mar 24, 1797 m Issac Harshaw
5. Philip b. Apr 18, 1793   m. Elizabeth Herman
6. Catherine b. Feb 20, 1795   m Stephen Tilley

Elias and Anna Powell lived near present day Lenoir, NC. Elias Powell died May 5, 1832 and was buried at Lower Creek Baptist Church.

LAND HOLDINGS AND TRANSACTIONS

1. 500 acres Burke County, NC on both sides of Muddy Fork of Lower Creek including improvements made by John Davis. The land lay adjacent to that belonging to Colbert Blair, James Blair, James Powell and John Powell.
cc. James Blair, James Powell
Ent. 4 Oct 1778 #422 Grant No. 843, Iss. 9 Nov 1784
Book 57, p. 34.

2. 200 acres Burke County, NC on middle fork of Lower Creek, that empties into Zack,s Fork, including the improvements made

QUEEN, THOMAS

SUMMARY OF EARLY LIFE

Thomas Queen was living in Burke County, NC at the time of his service in the Revolutionary War. He was age 80 in 1832.

SUMMARY OF PARTISAN ACTIVITY

Thomas Queen entered military service in Burke County, NC in March 1780. He was placed in a Company commanded by Catp. John McKenzie and Lt. Humphrey Barnett. Field officers included Major Bluford and Col. (William) Hill. They marched into South Carolina, joining the forces of Gen. Thomas Sumter at Brown's Old Fields, on the Congaree River. He was marched to several places in North Carolina, South Carolina and Georgia. He took part in an expedition to St. Augustine, Fla., directed against hostile Creek Indians. At one time he was with the troops of Gen. Anthony Wayne in Georgia. On September 8, 1781 he participated in the battle of Eutaw Springs, SC, losing his horse during the battle. Queen's total enlistment was for a period of fifteen months.

(One notices that Queen served entirely under South Carolina officers. It was common practice in 1780 and 1781 for South Carolina officers to enter North Carolina and recruit. This was done with the approval of local militia officers, including Col. Charles McDowell of Burke County).

SUMMARY OF LATER LIFE

Thomas Queen married Elizabeth _____. Their children ware as follows:

Margaret m. Michael Butler
Nancy   M. Andrew Bain
John
Elizabeth
Eliott
James

Thomas Queen applied for Revolutionary War pension in Morgan County, Alabama (his place of residence) on September 1, 1832. He was granted a pension of $55.00 per annum.

Thomas Queen died on March 15, 1845. His widow died shortly afterwards, in the same year.

CENSUS LOCATIONS

1790 Union Co., SC ?
1800 Union Co., SC ?
1810
1820

Powell, Elias

earlier by James Roddy. The land lay adjacent to that belonging
to John Morgan, Ambrose Powell, Colbert Blair, Elias Powell.
Ent. 11 Sept 1778 #763 Grant No. 782 Iss. 2 Nov 1784
Book 57 p. 5
cc Ambrose Powell, Robert Powell.

CENSUS LOCATIONS

1790 Burke Co., NC
1800 Burke Co., NC
1810 Burke Co., NC
1820 Burke Co., NC
1830 Burke Co., NC

REFERENCES

Land Grant Records in Morganton-Burke Library, Morganton, NC.
AIS Census Indices
Jarett, Sandra, Biography in Caldwell County Heritage
(Winston Salem 1983) pp. 466-Kings Mountain 67
Draper, L.C. Kings Mountain and It's Heroes Reprint Edition
Genealogical Publishing Co.,1967 (from original edition 1881)
p. 291
Thomas, I.W., "The Powell Family" Vertical Files, Caldwell County
Library, Lenoir, NC (from 1913 newspaper article).

REED, RICHARD (REID)

SUMMARY OF EARLY LIFE

Richard Reed (or Reid) was born in Baltimore County, Maryland ca. 1762. His father and family had just emigrated from Northern Ireland. He, along with is family, moved to Burke County, NC Reed was living in Burke County at the time of his initial enlistment. He was a brother of Robert Reed, also a Revolutionary War veteran.

SUMMARY OF PARTISAN ACTIVITY

Reed entered military service in 1781 or 1782 in a Company commanded by Capt. Thomas Lytle of Col. Charles McDowell's Burke Regiment. They embarked on a campaign directed against the Cherokee Indians. This tour lasted three months. Later he served another three month tour against the Cherokees. On this enlistment, he served in Capt. George Cathey's Company of McDowell's Regiment.

In mid 1781, Reed enlisted in Capt. Francis Cunningham's Company of McDowell's Regiment and was marched to South Carolina, becoming a part of Gen. Nathaniel Greenes Army. Shortly before the Battle of Eutaw Springs, SC (Sept. 8, 1781). Reed, in his pension statements, said, "...his Captain (see note*) deserted two days before the battle..." . His company was then attached to Col. Malmedy's Regiment (under Capt. James Little). Reed fought in the battle of Eutaw Springs. Afterwards, his unit marched back into North Carolina. Later he acted as a prison guard for those soldiers captured at Eutaw Springs.
*Probably not Capt. Cunningham, but Mordecai Clarke. See statements by Robert Reed, this volume.

SUMMARY OF LATER LIFE

After the Revolutionary War, Reed moved from Burke County, NC to Pendleton District, SC. In February 1788, in Abbeville District, SC, he was married to Jane Caven. They lived in Pendleton district, later that part which became Anderson District, SC.

Richard Reed applied for Revolutionary War pension on March 6, 1833. He was awarded an annual pension of $33.33.

Richard Reed died in Anderson District SC on May 25, 1835. His Widow applied for an received a federal pension in 1845, age 82.

CENSUS LOCATIONS

1790 Pendleton Co., SC
1800 Pendleton, Co., SC
1810 Pendleton, Co., SC
1820
1830

1830 Morgan Co., Ala.

REFERENCES

US National Archives Pension Data # S 32280
AIS Census Indices
Moss, Bobby G., <u>Roster of South Carolina Patriots in the American Revolution</u> General Publishing Company, Baltimore 1983 p. 795

REED, ROBERT

SUMMARY OF EARLY LIFE

Robert Reed was born in Northern Ireland and ws brought to America as an infant. His father died while Reed was a youth. They lived in that part of Rowan County which was Burke County during the Revolution, later Lincoln and then Catawba County, Reed was age 75 years in 1832. He was a brother of Richard Reed.

SUMMARY OF PARTISAIN ACTIVITY

Robert Reed first entered Revolutionary service in early 1779 under Capt. Benjamin Osborne. Other officers included Major David Watson, Col. Hugh Brevard and Ensign Bennett Osborne. Under Gen. Griffith Rutherford, they marched into South Carolina, joining the Army under Gen. Benjamin Lincoln and Gen. John Ashe. Reed's unit was bent to Purysburg and later to Sister's Ferry, where they erected breastworks. Reed, in his pension declaration, also mentions Capt. (Daniel?) Smith, Robert Brown, and Capt. (Francis) Cunningham. Reed served a total of five months on this tour.

Reeds next tour was in late 1779 and early 1780, for three months. He served in Capt. Robert Holmes' Company of Col. Andrew Hampton's Regiment. Other officers were Lt. Col. Frederick Hambright and Lt. Thomas Lytle. His unit was marched to the outskirts of Charleston, remaining there until shortly before the surrender in May 1780, when their time expired. All of those troops that came to relieve them were subsequently captured. Reed, during this tour, served in a quartermaster regiment.

His next tour of duty was in Capt. Jonathan Camp's Company of Charles McDowell's Burke Regiment. He participated in McDowells SC actions preceding the Kings Mountain Campaign. Reed was in the skirmish at Ned Hampton's place on the N. Pacolet River. He describes the death of Captain Chew of Georgia and the wounding of Col. (Jonathan) Jones. Reed then accompanied McDowell on his campaign along the Upper Broad River. (Summer 1780).

Reed next volunteered in August 1781 and served in a company commanded by Capt. Mordecai Clarke of McDowell's Regiment. Later, Clarke was Court Martialed (and convicted). He was succeeded by Capt. James Little. Under Little and Col. Malmedy (French Officer), they took part in the battle of Eutaw Springs, S.C. on September 8, 1781. Col. Francis Locke took command of this unit after the battle.

Reeds last two tours were in the Burke County area. He served as a mounted horseman under Capt. Francis Cunningham, for a period of nine months. Their activities were directed against local Tories. Reed then served a two month tour under Capt. David Falls on the Western Carolina frontier, guarding against the hostile Cherokee Indians.

REFERENCES;

US National Archives Pension Data # W 22054
AIS Census Data
Reed, Robert, Pension Statements # S 32471

RICHARDSON, AMOS

SUMMARY OF EARLY LIFE

Amos Richardson was born in 1762 (another source says May 2, 1760) in Bedford County, VA. At the beginning of the American Revolution, he was living in Burke County, NC on the Catawba River.

SUMMARY OF PARTISAN ACTIVITY

Richardson first entered military service in Burke County, NC in Col. Locke's Regiment (Rowan Co.), Capt. Shoky's Company. He volunteered in late 1780 for a three month tour of duty. His unit was marched to the Catawba River south of Charlotte, joining Col. William Washington's troops of Gen Nathaniel Greene's Army. He mentioned in his pension statements that his unit was on one side of a swamp and that Gen. Daniel Morgan's troops were on the other side. Other officers mentioned were Col. Phifer and Major Reid. They later marched to the Continental encampment at Cheraw, S.C. There, he was placed in a detachment going back to Salisbury, N.C. to guard prisoners. He was discharged at Salisbury on June 21, 1781.

He served a second three month tour in 1782 in Col. Isaacs militia regiment. In this duty tour they were marched from Hamblin's Old Store (Wilkes Co.) To Guilford, Randolph and Chatham Counties, chasing after the partisans of Col. David Fanning, a noted Loyalist leader. He recounts the capture of two of Fanning's men, Elrod and Still, and their subsequent execution. (They were shot).

SUMMARY OF LATER LIFE

In 1786, Amos Richardson moved from North Carolina to Tennessee, before Tennessee was granted statehood. Richardson was married to (2) Fannie Farmer. There were no children. She was age 65 when applying for pension rights in January 1854. Amos Richardson applied for Revolutionary War pension in Campbell Co., TN on September 11, 1832, age 70 years. He was granted an annual pension of $25.00.

Amos Richardson died in Campbell County, TN on May 2, 1853.

CENSUS LOCATIONS

1819 Campbell Co., TN (tax list)
1823 Campbell Co., TN (tax list)
1830 Campbell Co., TN

REFERENCES

US National Archives Pension Data #W 8552
AIS Census Data

SUMMARY OF LATER LIFE

Reed lived until after the turn of the century in Burke County, NC. The then moved to Missouri and finally to Alabama. He applied for Revolutionary War pension in St. Clair County, Ala. age 75 years. He had lived in Alabama for 22 years at the time of pension application. He was awarded a pension of $65.00 per annum. Robert Reed died January 16, 1842. One survivor was listed - a daughter, Elizabeth Langford. His wife predeceased him.

LAND HOLDINGS AND TRANSACTIONS

1. 320 acres Buncombe County, NC, Occondytee River, from Joseph Dobson. Ent. 15 Jan 1806, Book 9, p. 328.

2. 320 acres Buncombe Co., NC, Occondytee River, from Joseph Dobson. Ent. 18 Oct 1803, Book 9, p. 22.

3. 200 acres, Buncombe Co., NC, Pigeon River, from John Patton. Ent. 20 March 1804, Book 10, p. 141.

4. 200 acres, Buncombe Co., NC, Pigeon River, State of N.C. Grant No. 1395, Ent. 15 Dec 1804, Book 10, p. 142.

CENSUS LOCATIONS

1790 Burke Co., NC 1st Co
1800 Buncombe Co., NC?
1810 Haywood Co., NC?
1820
1830 Jefferson Co., AL
1840

REFERENCES

US Nation Archives Pension Data #S32471
AIS Census Data
Wooley, Jas.E., Buncombe Co., NC Index to Deeds, op.cit.

SCOTT, THOMAS

SUMMARY OF EARLY LIFE

Thomas Scott lived on Irish Creek in Burke County and was married to Anna Marie Dobson Scott (1750-1839). She was the daughter of Dr. Joseph Dobson and Ann Dobson. They were married 27 Feb. 1772.

SUMMARY OF PARTISAN ACTIVITY

Thomas Scott was militiaman in Charles McDowell's Burke regiment. In July and August of 1780, he took part in McDowell's advance into South Carolina, so as to oppose the western wing of the British force.

During the skirmishing in and around the Peach Orchard in upper South Carolina, Thomas Scott was killed in action. Interestingly, his demise is described by the British Provincial officer, Anthony Allaire, in his diary, published following the conclusion of the Revolutionary War.

SUMMARY OF LATER LIFE (Widow)

The widow of Thomas Scott, Anna Marie Dobson Scott, lived to a late age. She died at age 89 on Irish Creek in Burke County. She is buried in the Parks-Jaynes cemetery. There were five children, three male and two female. The following may have been their children:
Joseph 1774-1862
Nancy
John m. Nancy -
Thomas m. Mary Parks

REFERENCES

Vertical files, Morganton-Burke Library, Morganton, N.C.
Foothills Historical Society, Flyer, in Verical files.
Daper, L.C., <u>Kings Mountain and It's Heroes</u>
(The Diary of Lt. Anthony Allaire is appended to the back section of the book).

SCOTT, THOMAS (Two soldiers by this name)

SUMMARY OF EARLY LIFE

Thomas Scott was born in Maryland July 19, 1755. At the beginning of the Revolutionary War he was living in Wilkes County, NC. In1777 or 1778 he moved to Burke County. From lan records, it appears that he lived on Clark's River. (Upper Little River).

SUMMARY OF PARTISAN ACTIVITY

Thomas Scott first entered military service in the summer of 1777. He served a three month tour of duty in Capt. James Morrow's Company of Col. Benjamin Cleveland's Wilkes Militia. Their activities were directed against the Cherokee Indians.

In Burke County he enlisted in Capt. Charles Forester's Company, serving for about six months. Later he joined Capt. (John) Barton's company of Cleveland's Regiment. Scott, under Clevelan took part in the Kings Mountain battle of October 7, 1780. Lat he assisted in tending to the wounded. Following this action, was discharged home.

SUMMARY OF LATER LIFE

Thomas Scott married in Burke County Lettice Russell, the marriage taking place about 1775; Burke County, NC.

From this union were the following children:

Mary m. West
Samuel B. June 19, 1777
Nancy m. Davis
Lettice m. Long
Richard

Gemmia M. Blair
Jane m. Brashear
Elizabeth m. Beaty
?Martin

Thomas and Lettice Scott moved from Burke County, NC to Cumberland County, KY between 1800 and 1810.

Thomas Scott applied for Revolutionary War pension in nearby Fentress County, TN on December 25, 1833. He died a few months later on March 1, 1834, Cumberland County, KY. He was awarded $33.33 per annum, later transferred to his widow. Lettice Scot died January 31, 1837,Cumberland County, KY. (Later Clinton Co

LAND HOLDINGS AND TRANSACTIONS

Burke Co., NC Land Grant data shows a 100 acre tract on Clark's Little River, acquired by John Biggerstaff, which included "Thomas Scott's improvement".
Ent. De 29 1778. Warrant ordered. (From Huggins)

Wilkes Co., NC Deed from Thos. Scott to Isaac Davis, received b

Scott as N.C. Land Grant # 2453 Dec 10, 1803, conveyed to Davis on Nov 25, 1805. 80 acres Randolph Creek on waters of Little River, adjacent to Hodges' Knob. (From Absher)

CENSUS LOCATIONS

1790 Burke County, NC 8th Co.
1800 Burke County, NC
1810 Cumberland County, KY
1820 Cumberland County, KY
1830 Cumberland County, KY

REFERENCES

DAR Patriot Index (1966p. 599
AIS Census Indices
US National Archives Pension Data # W 5997
Huggins, Edith W. 1977, Burke County NC Land Records 1778 Vol.I p. 126.
Absher, Mrs. W. C., Wilkes Co., NC Deed Books D,F1, G-H 1795-1815. Southern Historical press 1990 p. 293. Abstracts.

SHARPE, HORATIO

SUMMARY OF EARLY LIFE

From Burke County, NC land entry records, it appears that Horatio Sharpe was living in the vicinity of Wilson's Creek, a tributary of Johns River, during the Revolutionary period. He was probably related to a John Sharpe and possibly to Jeremi Sharpe of Wilkes County, NC and Matthew Sharpe of Burke County.

SUMMARY OF PARTISAN ACTIVITY

Horatio Sharpe was a well known loyalist during the early and mid Revolutionary War. His name was mentioned in the Court Martial trial minutes of Col. Charles McDowell of Burke County (1782). In the trial James Blair was describing the bad character of both Benjamin Whitson and Horatio Sharpe. He related how they took his guns and later robbed him of several articles. It appears that Whitson and Sharpe were active loyalists at Ramsours and Kings Mountain. Both were captured a Kings Mountain. In the pension declarations of Joseph Roger James, he describes the Trial at Bickerstaff's, and was an eye witness. In his statements he says "...where one Race Sharpe a many others of the Tories who had been taken prisoners were hanged...". He also stated that "Sharpe and others who were hun lived prior to that time, in the neighborhood of their applicant...".

The noted historian Lyman C. Draper, in his work of the Kings Mountain campaign and battle, described in detail the celebrate Tory Trial at Bickerstaff's Plantation, in Rutherford County, NC. At the trial, which attracted world wide attention, Tories were condemned to death. Of these several were hanged o the spot, the remainder reprieved. Of those that were hanged, Draper names nine of them.

According to the diary of the British Provincial officer, Anthony Allaire, also captured at Kings Mountain, the date of the hangings was October 14, 1780.

LAND HOLDINGS AND TRANSACTIONS

Horatio Sharpe entered 150 acres on the right hand fork of Wilson's Fork of Johns River...including a cane break on said fork and some rich bottom land for complement.
Ent. 22 Dec 1778. Burke Co., NC

REFERENCES

Court Martial minutes of the Trial of Col. Charles McDowell
of Burke County, NC, facsimile copies presented to author
by the late Miss Eunice Ervin of Morganton, NC.
US National Archives; Pension Declaration of Joseph R. James
S32340
Huggins, Edith, Reprint of above, Burke County Land Records
Vol. II op.cit.
US National Archives Pension Statement of Joseph Rogers James
#S32340
Draper, L.C. **Kings Mountain and Its Heroes** Reprint Edition

SHERRILL, UTE (URIAH)

SUMMARY OF EARLY LIFE

During the Revolutionary period, Ute Sherrill appears to have been living on the upper Catawba River, now McDowell County, NC Most of the Sherrills originated from an earlier settlement on the Catawba River, now known as Sherrill's Ford Community.

SUMMARY OF MILITARY SERVICE

According to a pension statement made by his widow, Elizabeth Sherrill, in 1878, Ute Sherrill was a veteran of the battle of Kings Mountain, Oct. 7, 1780. He served under Col. John Sevier

SUMMARY OF LATER LIFE

Ute Sherrill married (1) Frances Dobson, (daughter of Joseph Dobson, Sr.) (2) Elizabeth Thompson. Elizabeth Thompson and Ut Sherrill were married by W. Keener, a Methodist Minister. Ute Sherrill died in Macon County, NC.

LAND HOLDINGS AND TRANSACTIONS

Uriah "Ute" Sherrill received the following North Carolina land grants.

1. 100 acres in Burke County on the north side of Catawba River and adjacent to land belonging to Joseph Dobson and John Mays. Entry states "including the place he now lives on". The notary taker (Charles McDowell erased the name Uriah and substituted "Ute". Entered November 16, 1778, Grant N0. 1014, Iss. August 7 1787. Book 65, p. 388.

2. 100 acres north side Catawba River adjacent to land of Josep Dobson and John Mayes. Chain carriers, Caleb Hobbs, George Sherrill. Ent. February 26, 1779, Grant No. 1146, Iss. May 18, 1789. Book 71, p. 39.

3. 100 acres north side Catawba River adjacent to John Mayes an his own land. Ent. January 31, 1801. Grant No. 3099, Iss. Nov 27, 1802. Book 110, p. 38. Chain carriers Joseph Sherrill, Jo Sherrill, Burke County.

4. Two grants of 50 acres and 145 acres on Cherokee land (Sect. 62 and 64 in Dist. 8) on north side of Chumckeskee's Creek. Grant Nos. 680, 681.
Iss. November 30, 1844, Book 149 p. 353. Macon County, N.C.

CENSUS LOCATIONS

1790 Burke Co., NC 3 rd Co.
1800 Burke Co., NC.
1810 Burke Co., NC

1820
1830 Macon County, NC

REFERENCES

US National Archives, Pension Statements No. R 17811
Burke Co., NC Land Grant Data; Morganton-Burke Library, Morganton, NC
AIS Census Indices

SHERRILL, GEORGE

SUMMARY OF EARLY LIFE

George Sherrill was born in Rowan County, NC September or October 1762, in that part which later became Burke, then Lincoln and finally, Catawba County. At the time of his enlistment, he lived in Burke County.

SUMMARY OF PARTISAN ACTIVITY

George Sherrill first entered Revolutionary service in March 1779 as a mounted militiaman in Capt. Robert Patton's Company of Col Charles McDowell's Burke Regiment. Their Company proceded to the outskirts of Charleston, then under siege by the British. At Monck's Corner, S.C., their forces, then under the command of Gen. Huger, were surprised and defeated by the British commanded by Tarleton and Webster on April 14, 1780.

Retreating to Eutaw Springs, they were joined by Virginia Continentals under Gen. Woodford. Later, Sherrill and his fellow soldiers from Burke County advanced to Camden, then to Cross Creek. From Cross Creek they marched to Salisbury and then to Ramsour's Mill, arriving there just after the battle of June 20, 1780. It is interesting that Sherrill, in his pension declaration, stated that "...Col. Joseph McDowell commanded the Whigs and Col. John Moore commanded the Tories...".

Sherrill was discharged at Burke Court House. Shortly afterwards, he moved to East Tennessee and enlisted in Samuel Williams Company of John Sevier's Regiment. Sherrill, under Sevier, then took part in the epic Kings Mountain Campaign, culminating in the victory of October 7, 1780.

After returning to east Tennessee, now Greene County, Sherrill enlisted in Sevier's Regiment under Major Jonathan Tipton. He was in a skirmish with the Indians at Buckingham Island. Later after being joined by Col. Arthur Campbell and his Virginians, he took part in a raid directed against the Overhills Cherokees. (Hiwassee).

SUMMARY OF LATER LIFE

After residing in East Tennessee, Sherrill moved to Franklin County Tennessee and remained there for the rest of his life. Apparently he lived in that area that eventually became Coffee County, TN. (Formed from Franklin in 1836).

George Sherrill applied for Revolutionary War pension in Frankl County, TN on August 30, 1832. He was awarded a pension of $25.00 per annum.

George Sherrill married Elizabeth Hunt. Their children were"

Uriah m. Nancy (Sherrill)
Samuel m. Penina (Sherrill)

LAND HOLDINGS AND TRANSACTIONS

George D. Sherrill received the following Tennessee Land Grants.

1. Franklin Co. Grant # 446 Jun 17, 1828, 350 ac. Book A/368
2. Franklin Co. Grant # 547 Jun 17, 1828, 400 ac. Book A/368-9
3. Franklin Co. Grant # 5626 Mar 27, 1827, 100 ac. Book 1 p. 777
4. Franklin Co. Grant # 5627 Mar 27, 1827, 80 ac. Book 1 p. 778

CENSUS LOCATIONS

1812 Franklin, County, TN (tax List)
1820 Franklin, County, TN (George D. Sherrill)
1830 Franklin, County, TN (George D. Sherrill)
1840 Coffee County, TN (George D. Sherrill)

REFERENCES

"Soldiers and Patriots of the American Revolution buried in Tennessee", (Bates and Marsh) 1979 p. 157
AIS Census Indices
US National Archives pension Data # S 3902
Tennessee State Archives and Library Nashville Land Grant Records

PRICHARD, JAMES (Pritchard)

SUMMARY OF EARLY LIFE

James Prichard was living in Burke County, NC. at and during the Revolutionary War. He was a tailor by profession.

SUMMARY OF MILITARY SERVICE

Even though he lived until 1838, James Prichard did not apply fo Revolutionary War pension. Application was made on behalf of hi heirs in 1853. In their statement, they mention that James Prichard was a soldier of the Revolution. Statements were made by Sidney S. Harshaw of Union County, GA and Linesfield Parks of Union County, GA. Both stated that they were acquainted with James Prichard and recognized him as being a Revolutionary soldier. No service description was given (battles, campaigns, units, etc.) Parks further stated that his father, Capt. Benjamin Parks, also recognized Prichard as a Revolutionary War soldier.

SUMMARY OF LATER LIFE

James Prichard married Mary_____. From this union were the following children:

James C.   Alfred
Sarah   Lucinda
Susan   Thomas
Pheba   Elizabeth

According to old Burke County records, Prichard served as a Burk County Constable from 1783-1786 and again in 1796-98.

James Prichard died June 4, 1838. His widow, Mary Prichard died May 8, 1840. James C. Prichard stated that his parents lived in Burke County for "40 years".

LAND HOLDINGS AND TRANSACTIONS

James Prichard received the following NC Land Grants:

1. 172 acres Burke County on Johns River adjacent to land belonging to Martin Davenport (formerly to John Brevard), John Rudolph and Andrew Rudolph.
Ent. July 10, 1778, Grant No. 30, Iss. Dec 10, 1778. Book 28, p.30. Chair carriers, John Browning, John Rudolph.

2. 50 acres on south fork of Upper Creek, adjacent to John Dobson's old survey.
Ent. April 20, '786, Grant No. 1604, Iss. Nov 27, 1792. Book 80, p. 57.

3. Burke County Tax Lists 1794 Thos. White's Co. Shows Jas.

Prichard with 325 acres ("James Prichard").

CENSUS LOCATIONS

1790 Burke Co., NC 7th Co.
1800 Burke Co., NC
1810 Burke Co., NC
1820 Burke Co., NC
1830

REFERENCES

US National Archives; Pension Date; # R8490
NC Land Grant Data; Morganton-Burke Library; Morganton, NC
Huggins, E.W., Burke Co., NC Records 1755-1821, Southern
Historical Press p.111 1987.   Vol IV

SHARPE, HORATIO

SUMMARY OF EARLY LIFE

From Burke County, NC land entry records, it appears that Horatio Sharpe was living in the vicinity of Wilson's Creek, a tributary of Johns River, during the Revolutionary period. He was probably related to a John Sharpe and possibly to Jeremia Sharpe of Wilkes County, NC and Matthew Sharpe of Burke County.

SUMMARY OF PARTISAN ACTIVITY

Horatio Sharpe was a well known loyalist during the early and mid Revolutionary War. His name was mentioned in the Court Martial trial minutes of Col. Charles McDowell of Burke County (1782). In the trial James Blair was describing the bad character of both Benjamin Whitson and Horatio Sharpe. He related how they took his guns and later robbed him of several articles. It appears that Whitson and Sharpe were active loyalists at Ramsours and Kings Mountain. Both were captured at Kings Mountain. In the pension declarations of Joseph Roger James, he describes the Trial at Bickerstaff's, and was an eye witness. In his statements he says "...where one Race Sharpe an many others of the Tories who had been taken prisoners were hanged...". He also stated that "Sharpe and others who were hung lived prior to that time, in the neighborhood of their applicant...".

The noted historian Lyman C. Draper, in his work of the Kings Mountain campaign and battle, described in detail the celebrated Tory Trial at Bickerstaff's Plantation, in Rutherford County, N.C. At the trial, which attracted world wide attention, 21 Tories were condemned to death. Of these hanged on the spot, th remainder reprieved. Of these, nine were hanged. Their names were given, but did not include Sharpe's. Could he have been a tenth victim ??

In the pension declarations of Joseph Roger James, he describes the Trial at Bickerstaff's, and was an eye witness. In his statements he says "...where one Race Sharpe and many others of the Tories who had been taken prisoners were hanged...". He also stated that "Sharpe and others who were hung lived prior to that time, in the neighborhood of their applicant..."

According to the diary of the British Provincial officer, Anthony Allaire, also captured at Kings Mountain, the date of the hangings was October 14, 1780.

LAND HOLDINGS AND TRANSACTIONS

Horatio Sharpe entered 150 acres on the right hand fork of Wilson's Fork of Johns River...including a cane break on said fork and some rich bottom land for complement.

Ent. 22 Dec 1778. Burke Co., NC

REFERENCES

Court Martial minutes of the Trial of Col. Charles McDowell of Burke County, N.C., facsimile copies presented to author by the late Miss Eunice Ervin of Morganton, NC.
US National Archives; Pension Declaration of Joseph R. James # S32340
Huggins, Edith, Reprint of above, Burke County Land Records Vol. II op.cit.
US National Archives Pension Statement of Joseph Rogers James #S32340
Draper, L.C. **Kings Mountain and It's Heroes** Reprint Edition

SIGMON, GEORGE (Sigman)

SUMMARY OF EARLY LIFE

George Sigmon was born in Pennsylvania, Near Delaware River, in February 1756. At an early age, he moved with his family from Pennsylvania to North Carolina. He lived in Burke County; Eastern part, later Lincoln and Now Catawba County.

SUMMARY OF MILITARY SERVICE

George Sigmon first entered military service in October 1778. enlisted in a Company commanded by Capt. Lee (leRoy) Taylor, Co Francis Locke's Regiment. Under General Rutherford they marched through Charlotte to near Charleston and then to Purysburg on t Savannah River. In 1779 he, under Gen. John Ashe, took part in the battle of Brier Creek, GA. The Americans were routed. Shortly afterwards, he was discharged home (April 1779) after having served for six months.

In December 1780, he again volunteered as a light horseman in Capt. John Dellinger's Company of McDowell's Burke Regiment. After marching one day, Sigmon was taken ill with smallpox and was forced to discontinue his tour of duty.

His final duty tour was in a Company of Burke Militia commanded by Capt. Henry Whitener.

SUMMARY OF LATER LIFE

George Sigmon married Catherine _____. They were married in Pennsylvania shortly after the Revolution (1783 or 1784). F this marriage were the following children:

Elizabeth (Betsy)	Peggy
George	John
Sally	Polly
Henry	

George Sigmon lived for a while in Lincoln County and then move to Burke County and remained there until old age. In 1835 he moved to Rockcastle County, KY to be near his children.

George Sigmon applied for Revolutionary War pension on July 23, 1833 in Burke County, NC. He was awarded a pension of $30.00 p annum. He died in Kentucky on October 20, 1841. His widow applied for pension on November 1, 1843, age 88 years.

LAND HOLDINGS AND TRANSACTIONS

1. 100 acres of land in Burke County on Upper Creek, adjacent t his own land and to that belonging to Spainhower and Murphey. Ent. August 14, 1813, No. 6118, Grant No. 3644, Iss. Dec 2, 181 Book 128, p. 421

2. Lincoln Co,. NC 380 acres on Mull's Creek Processioned for George Sigmon, adjacent to Balser and Em. Sigmon. Nov 26, 1813.

3. Lincoln Co., NC Grant of 150 acres Lyles Creek, adjacent to his own land and that of Jacob Hafner and Bolick...Jan. 8, 1788.

4. Lincoln Co., NC Deed from John Fisher to George Sigmon, 150 acres . April 2, 1787. January Court 1799.

5. Lincoln Co., NC Deed from George Sigmon to Adam Lattimore, 229 acres. Oct 6, 1797. January Court 1799.

CENSUS LOCATIONS

1790 Lincoln County, NC (2)
1800 Lincoln County, NC
1810 Lincoln County, NC
1820 Burke County, NC
1830 Burke County, NC (George Sigmon, Jr.)

REFERENCES

US National Archives pension Data # W 2969
AIS Census Indices
Burke County NC Land Grant Date in Morganton-Burke Library, Morganton, NC
Pruitt, Dr. A.B., Lincoln Co., NC Abstracts of Land Entries 1783-1795 (1987) and Abstracts of Land Entries 1780, 1795-97 Land processions 1783-1834 and Lincolnton NC Deeds 1785-1834. (1988)
McAllister, Anne W., and Sullivan, Kathy G., Lincoln Co., NC Court of Pleas and Quarter Sessions, July 1796- Jan 1805 (1988).

SORRELS, JOHN

SUMMARY OF EARLY LIFE

John Sorrels was living in Burke County, N.C. during the Revolutionary period.

SUMMARY OF PARTISAN ACTIVITY

John Sorrels entered military service in late 1778 as a private in a North Carolina Continental Line. He joined for a term of nine months. Initially he was placed in John Hardn's Company an was marched to Moon's Creek in Caswell County. Their destinatio was the northern army. When British and American activities reached a stalemate in the north, his unit was furloughed. In 1779 he was called back to duty on orders of Gen. Jethro Sumner. He was placed in a company commanded by Capt. William Goodman ar Lt. Joel Lewis of James Thackston's 4th North Carolina regiment. The 4th regiment was marched to South Carolina joining the army of Gen. Benjamin Lincoln. They took part in the battle of Stone Ferry, South Carolina on June 20, 1779. Following this, Sorrels was discharged home. Affidavits affirming the service record of Sorrels were made by Edward Bell of Lincoln County, GA. An affidavit was given on his behalf by Capt. James Mackie of Burke County, NC (1792). Revolutionary Army accounts verify his service as a Private soldier in 1778-1779.

SUMMARY OF LATER LIFE

When making application for Revolutionary War settlement in 1792 Sorrels was a resident of Wilkes County, GA.

REFERENCES

Huggins, Edith, Revolutionary War Final Settlements, N.C. Dept. Of Archives Comptroller's Papers, Boxes 14-20, Vol II, p. 160.
US National Archives Pension Statement of Walter O'Neill.
Haun, Weynette P. "NC Revolutionary Army Accounts Secretary of State" p.281 (Vol II; Book 2; 22) p.51

STEELE, SAMUEL

SUMMARY OF EARLY LIFE

Samuel Steele was born in Pennsylvania in 1762. He was living in Burke County at the time of his first enlistment. He lived on the Middle Little River, in present day Alexander County. Andrew Steele lived nearby, possibly his father.

SUMMARY OF MILITARY SERVICE

Samuel Steele first volunteered for military service in Burke County, NC, probably in later 1781 or 1782. He enlisted first in a Company commanded by Capt. Robert Holmes. They marched first to Camden, SC and then to the Charleston, SC area. He was discharged after serving a three month tour.

Steele then served as a light horseman in a Company commanded by Capt. John Bickerstaff. Their duties were directed against local Tories. Apparently several short tours were served under Capt. Bickerstaff.

SUMMARY OF LATER LIFE

Samuel Steele lived in Burke County until after 1800. He then moved to Maury County, TN and was there when he applied for Revolutionary War pension in September 1832. He was awarded a pension of $44.50 pr annum.

Steele had moved to Green County, MO by 1841. Samuel Steele married _____. He had the following children:

Mary b. 1784 m. Caleb Headlee
Mararet b. 1793 mm. David Headlee
Jane b. 1798 m. Daniel Headlee
Martha b. 1800 m. Joseph Headlee
Rachel b. 1803 m. Elisha Judge Headlee

Samuel Steele is buried in Mount Comfort Cemetery, nine miles north east of Springfield, MO.

LAND HOLDINGS AND TRANSACTIONS

1. Burke Co., NC 1794 and 1795 Tax Lists show Samuel Steele with 100 acres land, Capt. Austins Co. (Little River area).

CENSUS LOCATIONS

1790 Burke County, NC 8th Co.
1800 Burke County, NC
1812 Giles County, TN (tax lists)
1820 Maury County, TN
1830 Maury County, TN

REFERENCES

Houts, Alice, <u>Revolutionary Soldiers Buried in Missouri</u> p. 223
(1966)
US National Archives Pension Data # S 17123
Huggins, Edith W., Burke County, NC Records 1755-1821, 1987
Southern Historical Press. pp. 110, 114.

SULLIVAN, DANIEL

SUMMARY OF EARLY LIFE

Daniel Sullivan was born in Pittsylvania County, VA on March 2, 1763. He stated that he was apprenticed when young. He entered military service while living in Pittsyulvania County.

SUMMARY OF PARTISAN ACTIVITY

Sullivan first entered military service as a private soldier in the fall of 1780. He served in Capt. Thomas Smith's Company in the regiment commanded by Col. Peter Perkins. Their unit joined in with the main army under Gen. Nathaniel Greene shortly before the battle of Guilford Court House in March 1781. Other units that they met included those commanded by Col. William Washington and Lt. Col. Henry "Lighthorse Harry" Lee. Sullivan did not participate in the battle of Guilford Court House, having been furloughed home shortly before. Later he rejoined his unit, joined briefly in the pursuit of Cornwallis and then progressed with Greene's forces as far as Camden, S.C. (then known as Log Town). His tour ended and a discharge was given by a Capt. Shaw.

His next tour was in a militia company commanded by Capt. Cloud and Col. Penn's regiment. They went against the Tories of the New River section of North Carolina and Virginia.

Sullivan served another short tour of duty under Maj. Marr, going against the Tories in the vicinity of Salem, in Stokes County, N.C. This ended his military service.

SUMMARY OF LATER LIFE

Sullivan lived for about five years in Pittsylvania and Henry Counties, VA and the moved to Burke County, N.C. He filed for Revolutionary pension on 29 Jan 1833 in Burke County. His pension was approved in the amount of $20.00 per annum. sworn testimony as to his service was given by Richard Reid and Joseph Pyatt and Richard Bird.

REFERENCES

US National Archives Pension Statements No. S7661

SUMTER, WILLIAM

SUMMARY OF EARLY LIFE

According to family records, Willaim Sumter was born in Hanover County, VA on 29 October 1731. In 1754 he was married, in Albemarle County, VA. Later, in Burke County he was married to Judith Randall.

SUMMARY OF PARTISAN ACTIVITY

During the first part of the Revolutionary War, William Sumter was living in Albemarle County, VA. About 1777, he came to Burke County, NC, Lower Creek (now Caldwell County). In 1778, his son Thomas Sumter served in his place on the Catawba frontier.

Commissioned a Captain in McDowell's Burke Regiment, Sumter led his company on forays into Wilkes County, directed against local Loyalist activities.

SUMMARY OF LATER LIFE

Children of William Sumter included the following:
John b. 1755 m. Ann Alexander
William b. 1757 m. Jane –
James b. 1759 m. Elizabeth –
Thomas b. 1761 m. Lydia Kirkpatrick
Elizabeth b. 1763 m. Edwmond Owens
Amelia b. 1766 m. Buckner
Fielding b. 1769 m. Sally –
Judith b. 1771
Livingston b. 1773 m. Charlotte Temple
William Sumter died in Burke County, N.C. 1819.

LAND HOLDINGS AND TRANSACTIONS

1. Burke County, NC 400 acres on Brumley's Branch of Lower Creek (now Caldwell County, N.C.). The entry stated "including the improvements that said Sumter lives on ...". The land lay adjacent to that of James Isbell, Ramsey and Sothard.
c.c. Simon Ramsey, John Powell.
Ent. 18 Dec 1778 No. 772 Grant No. 871 Iss. Nov 9, 1784
Book 57 p. 46.

REFERENCES

Quam, LaVina Sumter, vertical files Morganton Burke Library, Morganton, N.C.
US National Archives Pension Data, statements of Thomas Sumter
Land Grant data Morganton Burke Library, Morganton, N.C.

SWANSON, WILLIAM

SUMMARY OF EARLY LIFE

William Swanson was eighty five years old in 1846 on applying for federal pension. At the time he entered Revolutionary service, he stated that he was a "citizen of Burke County, NC".

SUMMARY OF PARTISAN ACTIVITY

William Swanson entered military service in Burke County, N.C. on August 5, 1781. He ws placed in a militia company commanded by Capt. Clarke, (Capt. Mordecai Clarke of Burke County). They marched first to Camden, SC and then to Congaree, joining the American Army under Gen. Nathaniel Greene. On September 8, 1781 Swanson participated in the battle of Eutaw Springs, SC. After the battle, he volunteered to serve as a guard, guarding one captured British soldier on a march from Eutaw Springs to the prison at Salisbury, N.C. There he was discharged by Col. Locke.

SUMMARY OF LATER LIFE

During the late 1700's and early 1800's William Swanson was living on Beaver Creek in Wilkes Co. In 1815, he is apparently living on Lower Creek, Burke County. 200 acre tract. William Swanson is listed on early census records of Wilkes County and the Burke County. In 1846, when applying for pension, he was living in Monroe County, TN. He mentions that he attempted to get a pension earlier through his member of Congress. Both efforts failed.

LAND HOLDINGS AND TRANSACTIONS

1. Wilkes Co., NC Deed from John Parker to William Swanson, 50 acres on Beaver Creek, October 10, 1794, from Absher.

2. Wilkes Co., NC Deed from Charles Henderson to William Swanson 100 acres, branch of Beaver Creek. Dec 2, 1797. From Absher.

3. Burke Co., NC 1815 Tax Lists, 200 acres on Lower Creek, Capt. Hartley's District.

CENSUS LOCATIONS

1790 Wilkes County, NC 9th Company
1800 Wilkes County, NC
1810
1820 Burke County, NC
1816
1820
1830
1830 Monroe County, TN
1840 Monroe County, TN

REFERENCES

US National Archives Pension Data # R 10339
Absher, Mrs. W.O., Wilkes County NC Deed Abstracts, Books A1,
 B1, C1 D, F1, G-H in 2 Vol., Southern Historical Press 1989-90.
Pittman, Betsy D., Burke County NC 1815 Tax Lists, 1990. P.81.

***Note: Tennessee Land and Census Records show a William Swanson
in Williamson and Giles Counties, relationship, if any, to
William Swanson of Burke County unknown.

TATE, JOHN

SUMMARY OF EARLY LIFE

John Tate was born in Northern Ireland in 1758. He and his family came to America in 1763. At the time of the beginning of the Revolutionary War, Tate was living in the vicinity of Shippensburg, PA.

SUMMARY OF PARTISAN ACTIVITY

John Tate first entered military service in December 1776 as a volunteer in a Pennsylvania militia company commanded by Capt. Robert Culbertson and a Major Davis. They were marched from Shippensburg to Philadelphia and placed under the command of General Mifflin. From Philadelphia they marched to Borderttown, New Jersey. They were engaged in a skirmish with Loyalists at Monmouth, N.J. Afterwards they returned to Bordertown. They then followed the regular army to Trenton and to Princeton. Later they were ordered to the heights of Middleton, remaining there until March 1777. Tates unit returned to Philadelphia where was discharged, after having served three months.

His next tour was as a hired substitute for a tour of two months. He served in a company commanded by Capt. Etsky; under the overall command of Col. Dunlap. They marched first to Carlisle and then to Lancaster, joining in with the Continental soldiers near Brandywine, PA.

On Sept. 11, 1777, Tate fought in the battle of Brandywine. In his pension statements he mentions Generals Washington, Wayne, Greene, Sullivan, Erwin, Armstrong and Pather.

After Brandywine, his unit retreated to Chester, PA and then to Philadelphia. From Philadelphia they marched on Lancaster Road to Warren Hill, Bull Town and Schuylkill River. They were in a skirmish while en route. Later, suffering from dysentery, Tate was in another skirmish. His unit was "scattered". He rejoined his company and was marched to the Continental encampment, and was posted as an "out guard". He described how he went without food for three days. He remained at the encampment while the Regulars went on to the battle at Germantown. (4 Oct 1777). From the encampment they were marched to Chester and then to Fox Chase Tavern, where he was discharged from his tour.

In August 1781, Tate volunteered as a Light Horseman under Capt. Johnson. He was marched from Shippensburg to New Town in Bucks County. He remained there until the expiration of his two months tour. Altogether he had served seven months.

SUMMARY OF LATER LIFE

Tate moved from Pennsylvania to Baltimore, MD shortly after the war. He remained there nine months and then moved to Burke

County, NC. He remained in Burke County until 1796 and then moved to Franklin County, GA. He applied for Revolutionary War pension in Franklin County on September 3, 1832. He was awarde an annual pension of $23.33. (DAR records list a John Tate (b. 5/4/1758) and (d. 12/24/1838) and who was married to Anne Oliphant)

LAND HOLDINGS AND TRANSACTIONS

1. 50 acres in North Cove on North Fork of Catawba River, Burke County, NC.
Ent. January 7, 1793, No. 252 Grant # 2722, Iss. Dec 20, 1799
Book 107, p. 83.
Additional 100 acres, same area.
Grants # 2723 and 2724, Iss. Dec 20, 1799.

CENSUS LOCATIONS

1790 Burke County, NC 13 th Company
1820 Elbert County, GA
1830 Franklin County, GA

REFERENCES

DAR Patriot Index, Washington 1966, p. 666
US National Archives, Pension Data # S 32007
Burke Co., NC Land Grant Data; Morganton-Burke Library, Morganton, NC
AIS Census Indices

THOMPSON, ALEXANDER

SUMMARY OF EARLY LIFE

Alexander Thompson was born in Pennsylvania in 1739. At the beginning of the American Revolution, he was living on Thompson's Branch, a tributary of Muddy Creek and western Burke County, NC.

SUMMARY OF PARTISAN ACTIVITY

During the Revolution Alexander Thompson was associated with the Burke County militia of Col. Charles McDowell.

During Ferguson's advance into North Carolina and Burke County in September 1781, a British officer noted in his diary "Monday 18th (September)-- marched to a rebel Alexander Thompson's plantation ... and halted".

Georgia records state that he received land in Georgia for military service in that state.

SUMMARY OF LATER LIFE

Alexander Thompson was married to Elizabeth Mary Hodge ca. 1760. Children as follows:
William m. Mary Tilman
Alexander m. Eunice Strickland
Ruth
James
Robert
John
Sarah
Esther

Alexander Thompson continued to live in Burke County following the Revolution but in January 1796 Burke County Court Records show a transfer via deed from Alexander Thompson to Thomas Young for 300 acres of land and two tracts. This may have represented approximate time of his departure from this state. Alexander Thompson died 1815 (or 1808?).

CENSUS LOCATIONS

1791-93 Elbert County, GA (Jury list

LAND HOLDINGS AND TRANSACTIONS

1. Burke County, NC 50 acres both sides of Thompson's Fork of Muddy Creek and adjacent to land of Charles Findley and to his own land.
Ent. 1778, Grant #181 Iss. 14 March 1780 Book 28 p.180.

2. Burke County, NC 100 acres on Catawba River adjacent to his own land and to that of Robert McCusick. Ent. 1778 Grant #204 Iss. 14 March 1780.

3. Burke County, NC 100 acres on both sides of Thompson's Fork of Muddy Creek, including Thompsons improvements. Ent. 1778 Grant #300 Iss. 15 March 1780 Book 28 p.299.

4. Burke County, NC 50 acres Thompson's Fork of Muddy Creek. Ent. 1779 Grant #317 Iss. 28 Oct 1782 Book 44 p.112.

REFERENCES

Draper, L.C. <u>Kings Mountain and ITS Heroes</u> Reprint GPC 1967 Original 1881. (Allaire's Diary p.508)
McCall Mrs. Howard H. <u>Roster of Revolutionary Soldiers in Georg</u> GPC 1968 p.166. Reprint Issue.
Swink, Dan D. "Minutes Burke County Court 1795-98, 1987 pp.16-17.
Burke County Land Grant records in Morganton-Burke Library, Morganton, NC
DAR <u>Patriot Index</u> National Society DAR, Washington, D.C. 1966 p.674.
DeLamar, M. and Rothstein, E. The Reconstructed 1790 census of Georgia GPC 1985 p.89.

TROSPER, NICHOLAS

SUMMARY OF EARLY LIFE

Nicholas Trosper was living in western Burke County, N.C. during and after the Revolution(now McDowell County). Earlier he may have lived in Rowan County.

He was a blacksmith by trade.

SUMMARY OF PARTISAN ACTIVITY

Minutes of the Court Martial proceedings of Col. Charles McDowell in early 1782 indicate that Nicholas Trosper was a Burke militiaman under the command of Col. McDowell and that he carried orders from McDowell to the Commanders of the frontier forts, relating to service time by Loyalists. Trosper also gave testimony concerning the exchange of confiscated property.

After the war he rendered testimony that William Bradshaw was a Tory.

SUMMARY OF LATER LIFE

Nicholas Trosper was active in Burke County affairs until at least 1803, appearing at times on jury duty and in 1803, as an Administrator of the estate of neighbor Elizabeth Birchfield. He moved ca. 1806 to Knox County, KY.

Nicholas Trosper was married to Sallye -. Children: Robert, James, Nicholas, John, Peter, William, Elijah, Leonard.

CENSUS LOCATIONS

1790 Burke Co. NC 1st Co.
1800 Burke Co., NC
1810 Knox Co., KY
1820 Knox Co., KY
1830 Knox Co., KY

LAND HOLDINGS AND TRANSACTIONS

1. Rowan County, NC John Henderson to Nicholas Trosper 212½acres east side of Catawba "now in his possession". 28 September 1784 -- on Norwood's Creek, originally a Granville Grant to David Black.

2. Nicholas Trosper is listed with having 100 acres of land in Capt. John Hawkins Company, Burke Co., NC 1795 and 1796.

3. Deed of gift from Nicholas Trosper to Elijah Trosper "for all the property and substance of Nicholas Trosper". 10 March 1793, Burke County Court minutes.

4. Kentucky Land Warrants Knox County, Richland Creek, Middle Fork 2/14/1816 100 acres.

5. Kentucky Land Warrants Knox County, Richland Creek, Middle Fork, 1828 and 1829, 100 acres.

REFERENCES

AIS Census Indices
Huggins, Edith, Burke County Records Vol II-IV
Clark, Wanda L., The Trosper Tree 1987 McAlester OK.
Linn, Jo White "Abstracts of Rowan County, NC Deeds 1753-1785" Salisbury 1983.
Ervin, Eunice copies of Court Martial Minutes of Col. Charles McDowell as presented to author.
Jillson, Willard, Kentucky Land Grants Part I
GPC Reprint 1971 p.749
Swink, Dan, Burke County, NC Court Minutes 1791-1795 and 1795-1798 (1986 and 1987)

TURNER, ROBERT

SUMMARY OF EARLY LIFE

Robert Turner was born in 1758 in Northern Ireland, Armagh County. In 1771 he came with his family to Pennsylvania. They lived in Lancaster County for about three years. Shortly prior to the Revolution they moved to Mecklenburg County, NC.

SUMMARY OF PARTISAN ACTIVITY

Robert Turner first entered the service in the summer of 1776 under Capt. James Harris and participated in the Cherokee Expedition under Gen. Griffith Rutherford and Col. Charles McDowell. The tour lasted about six weeks.

His next tour of duty was in mid 1779 when he joined Capt. James White's Company of Col. Henderson's Regiment. They were marched to Stono Ferry, SC, near Charleston, under the command of Gen. Benjamin Lincoln. Turner took part in the battle of Stono Ferry which was fought on June 20, 1779. This tour lasted three months.

His final tour of duty began in August 1781. He enlisted in Capt. Richard Simmons' Company of Col. Robert Smith's Regiment. This regiment was in the Wilmington Expedition under Gen. Rutherford. In his pension statements, Turner recounts how Wilmington was attacked twice with small arms before being taken. His unit then marched to Brunswick where they received word of Cornwallis' surrender. Shortly thereafter, he was discharged home.

SUMMARY OF LATER LIFE

Robert Turner lived in Mecklenburg County, NC during the war. After the war he lived in Burke County for a number of years. He later moved to Haywood County (then Buncombe Co.) And last to Habersham County, GA. Robert Turner was married to Agnes _____ on July 6, 1780. He applied for Revolutionary War pension on November 5, 1832. He was awarded a pension of $24.66 per annum.

LAND HOLDINGS AND TRANSACTIONS

200 acres Buncombe County, NC, Nantahala River from John Fergus. 22 March 1806, Book 10 p. 365.

CENSUS LOCATIONS

1790 Burke County, NC 10th Company
1800 Buncombe County, NC
1810 Haywood County, N.C.
1820
1830 Habersham County, GA

REFERENCES

US National Archives Pension Data # R 10749
AIS Census Indices
Wooly, Jas. E., 1983, Buncombe County Index to Deeds 1783-1850
Southern Historical Press, p. 390

Ent. Feb. 12, 1798, No. 3344, Grant # 2370, Book 100, p. 210, Iss., December 21, 1798.

2. Thomas Wakefield also received an NC Land Grant for 70 acres, Burke County, N.C., on waters of Linville River (also described in entry account as on "south fork of the Jumping Branch."). It lay adjacent to "my own land".
Ent. July 26, 1810, No. 5771, Grant # 3553 Book 126, p. 261 Iss. December 11, 1811.

CENSUS LOCATIONS

1790 Burke County, NC 5th Company
1800 Burke County, NC
1810 Burke County, NC
1820 Franklin County, TN
1830 Franklin County, TN
1840 Franklin County, TN

REFERENCES

DAR Patriot Index Washington 1966, p. 710
Texas Society DAR Roster of Revolutionary Ancestors
Vol. IV p. 2196, Texas 1976
US National Archives Pension Data # W 1107
AIS Census Indices
Burke County NC Land Grant Data, Morganton-Burke Library, Morganton, NC

WAKEFIELD, THOMAS

SUMMARY OF EARLY LIFE

Thomas Wakefield was born in Albermarle County, VA on October 5 1762. Thomas Wakefield, prior to the Revolution, was living in western Burke County, along with his father and brothers.

SUMMARY OF PARTISAN ACTIVITY

Wakefield first entered military service in December 1779 under Capt. (Peter) Ford (or Fore), of Burke County. His unit was marched to the vicinity of Charleston, SC and was placed under the command of Col. Andrew Hampton of Lillington's Brigade. He served for about three months, but saw no action. After his discharge, he returned home.

In the spring and summer of 1780, he served on two tours under Maj. Joseph McDowell against the hostile Cherokee Indians. He related several skirmishes.

In 1781, following the battle of Cowpens (Jan. 17, 1781), he served again under Maj. McDowell. They marched to Beatties For on the Catawba, but saw no action.

SUMMARY OF LATER LIFE

Wakefield lived in Burke County until about 1816, when he moved to Franklin County, TN. He remained there for the rest of his life. Thomas Wakefield married (1) Lucy Johnson, (2) Nancy Johnson and (3) Jemina Griffin (she was age 87 in 1853). There were the following children:

Nancy m. Geo. ?	Thomas
Martha	Joseph
Mary George	Flora m. Robert Parks
Hamilton	Christian m. George Mosely
Henry Nelson	Lucy M.
Jane m. Newton Goodwin	Peggy m. Joshua Smith

First nine children by his first wife.

Thomas Wakefield applied for Revolutionary War Pension on Octob 26, 1832, age 70 years. He made his application in Franklin County, TN and was awarded $26.66 per annum. Wakefield died September 17, 1849. His widow continued to receive his pension until her death. (Another source gives his death September 17, 1846).

LAND HOLDINGS AND TRANSACTIONS

1. Thomas Wakefield received an NC Land Grant in Burke County f 55 acres adjacent "to his own land" and to land belonging to Charles Wakefield and Benjamin Moore.

WEST, ALEXANDER

SUMMARY OF EARLY LIFE

Alexander West was born in Orange County, N.C. in 1751. At the time of his first enlistment, he was living in Wilkes County, NC.

SUMMARY OF PARTISAN ACTIVITY

Alexander West first entered military service in Wilkes County, N.C. in a company commanded by Capt. Francis Hartgraves and Ensign Allison. He served in a tour of duty directed against the Cherokee Indians in ? 1779. In 1780 he was drafted for a three month tour of duty. He served in a company commanded by Capt. Peter O"Neal. This company was part of a brigade of Col. Porterfield in Gen. Horatio Gates' Army. They were marched to Guilford County, NC near Col. (John) Paisley's residence and were engaged in "casting balls". Later they were sent to Salisbury under Gen. Rutherford. West then took part in the encounter at Colson's Place. West stated the Gen. (Wm.L.) Davidson received a "mortal wound". (actually Gen. Davidson was seriously wounded, but not mortally. He was later killed in action at Cowan's Ford, February 1, 1781). (Colson's at mouth of Rocky River; Cowan's Ford on main Catawba River).

From Rocky River, his unit was marched to the Cheraw Hills of S.C. Still later they were marched to Rugeleys Mill and thence to Camden. West took part in the disastrous battle of Camden August 16, 1780. After the battle, West became sick and was left in the Waxhaws Settlement to recuperate. A few weeks later, he returned to Guilford Court House and was discharged.

His last tour of duty was in 1782 in Col. Cleveland's Regiment in a company commanded by Capt. Pendleton Isbell. The acting regimental commander was Col. Elisha Isaacs. Their regiment advanced through Salem to Bell's Mill on Deep River. Their activities were directed against the noted Loyalist partisan, Col. David Fanning; however, no confrontations occurred. West mentions a fellow soldier, Thomas Carlton.

SUMMARY OF LATER LIFE

In 1777, Alexander West married Hannah Langley (b. Oct. 1749), in Orange County. They had the following children:

Bethiah b. Mar. 18, 1779   Margaret b. Mar. 8, 1781
Alexander b. Dec. 23, 1783   Elizabeth b. Mar. 8, 1786
Thomas b. Sept. 23, 1788   Mary b. June 18, 1791

Alexander West applied for Revolutionary War pension in Burke Co., NC on January 6, 1834. He died three months later on March 28, 1834. Hannah West died May 5, 1839.

LAND HOLDINGS AND TRANSACTIONS

1. Alexander West received a NC Land Grant for 50 acres of land in Wilkes County, N.C., lying on Gladey Fork. C.c. Isaac West, Bray Crisp.
Entry No. 596, Ent. Sept. 3, 1782, Grant #747, Book 64, p. 123.
50 acres Issued August 9, 1787.

Alexander West received also the following N.C. Land Grants, Burke County, NC.

1. 150 acres on west bank of Clark's Little River, adjacent to land belonging to Bullinger and James Greenlee.
Ent. Oct. 27, 1778, No. 973, Grant #2669, Book 107, p.62
Iss. December 6, 1799.

2. 25 acres on north side of Clark's Little River adjacent to his own land and to that of John Sudderth.
Ent. March 29, 1814, No. 6212, Grant #3728, Book 130, p. 151
Iss. September 7, 1816.

3. 25 acres on "Hather's Branch" of Little River, adjacent to land belonging to thomas West, Bracton Roberts, John Robinson, Matthe Cox, and James Blair.
Ent. March 28, 1828, No. 9573, Grant # 5462, Book 139, p. 90.
Iss. December 18, 1830.

CENSUS LOCATIONS

1790 Burke County, NC 8th Company
1800
1810 Burke County, NC
1820 Burke County, NC
1830 Burke County, NC

REFERENCES;

US National Archives Pension Data# W 18328
AIS Census Indices
Burke County Land Grant Data, Morganton-Burke Library, Morganton NC

WHITE, JAMES TAYLOR

SUMMARY OF EARLY LIFE

James Taylor White was the son of William and Sophia Davenport White. His family had lived earlier in Culpeper, VA and in Craven County, SC. James Taylor White was named for his grandfather of the same name. His father, William White had settled on Johns River, Burke County, NC just prior to the American Revolution (now near Collettsville, Caldwell County, NC). White's Fort, a frontier fort built to guard against the hostile Cherokees, was built on White property.

SUMMARY OF PARTISAN ACTIVITY

James Taylor White was an active participant in the frontier actions against the Cherokee Indians, then allied with the British.

Later in the war he was elected Captain of a militia company and took part in the Wilmington Expedition of late 1781.

North Carolina Revolutionary Army accounts verify his service as an officer.

In 1782 James Taylor White's name appears in the Burke County Court Docket minutes as a witness against suspected Tories Alexander Clark, Paschal Estes and Charles Smith.

SUMMARY OF LATER LIFE

James Taylor White continued as Captain of a Burke County Company, or a precinct, until about 1785. During this period his name appears several times in Burke County Court records. In 1787 the records list his Company as "Capt. Taylor White's old Company". That would indicate that he may have left the area between 1785 and 1787.

A James Taylor White appears on the 1790 South Carolina census, Spartanburg County. No further records at this time.

LAND HOLDINGS AND TRANSACTIONS

1. Burke County, NC 287 acres on Johns River including portions of Long Branch and William White's Branch. The land lay adjacent to John Brevards upper line. It included a mill seat.
c.c. Alexander Cole, John White.
Ent. 11 June 1778 #181 Grant No. 17 Iss. Dec. 10, 1778.
Book 28 p. 17.
(A grant was also issued on John's River, Mulberry Creek, to "James White". James Taylor White was a chain carrier.)

CENSUS LOCATIONS

1790 Spartanburg County, SC
1800 Spartanburg County, SC
1810 Spartanburg County, SC

REFERENCES

Burke County N.C. Land Grant Records, Morganton-Burke Library Morganton, NC
AIS Census Indices including Burke County, N.C. and Spartanburg County, S.C.
Huggins, Edith, Burke County Records, SHP 1987
Revolutionary Army accounts
White, Gifford "James Taylor White of Virginia" Austin, TX 1982

WHITE, WILLIAM

SUMMARY OF EARLY LIFE

William White was born prior to 1730 and was the son of James Taylor and Elizabeth Powe White of Culpeper County, VA. In ca. 1750 he married Sophia Davenport, the daughter of Thomas Davenport. After the French and Indian War, he moved to South Carolina on the Great Pee Dee River near Florence County, SC William White, along with his father and brothers, was active in the Regulator activities that started in South Carolina during the mid 1760's. In one affray with the Regulators, White was captured and seriously wounded. On the eve of the American Revolution the Whites had moved from South Carolina to Burke County, NC on Mulberry Creek and Johns River.

SUMMARY OF PARTISAN ACTIVITY

At the commencement of the Revolution William White, along with his sons, nephews, and brother Reuben White built and maintained a frontier fort on Johns River. The fort was built in defense against the hostile Cherokee Indians, then allied with the British. Known as "White's Fort," it served an important role in the defense of the western perimeter of North Carolina. The fort was abandoned after the war as the Indians were being driven out of the Catawba and Yadkin River valleys.

SUMMARY OF LATER LIFE

William White and Sophia Davenport White had the following offspring:

Mary   m. George Hickman
Phoebe
Sarah
Elizabeth   m. Parmenas Taylor
James Taylor   (see separate sketch)
Ann
Cary or Catherine   m. William DeWitt

Anthony
Thomas
Reuben (see separate sketch)

William White remained active in Burke County civil affairs in the late 1790's and early 1800's. He was a Magistrate and presided over many Court activities. Addressed as "William White, Esquire" he remained one of Burke's most prominent citizens. William White was a surveyor in Burke County and western North Carolina in the 1780's.

William White died in Burke County ca. 1818. His will was presented for probate in the July session of Burke County Court

1818. William Davenport administrator

LAND HOLDINGS AND TRANSACTIONS

1. Craven County, SC 21-438 300 acres south side Jeffery's Creek adjacent to Reuben White, Joshua, Thomas Nesbit and George Miers. 22 July 1771.

2. Burke County NC 640 acres on Sealey's Creek and Mulberry Fork of John's River adjacent to Charles Wakefield. Included the mouth of Mulberry Creek. c.c. Alexander Cole, Thomas Wakefield.
Ent. 11 Jan 1778 Grant #75 Iss. 20 Sept 1779, Book 28 p. 75.

3. Burke County, NC 315 acres on Johns River including the Fork.
Ent. #475 8 Nov 1778 Grant #98 Iss. 20 Sept. 1779 Book 28 p. 98.

4. Burke County, NC 260 acres on Gunpowder Creek adjacent to land of John Huckaby, John Sumpter, Samuel Smith, including the improvements made by Jacob Grider. c.c. Abner Smally, John Fincannon.
Ent.138 18 Nov 1787 Grant #1467 Iss. 4 Jan 1792 Book 75 p.438.

5. Burke County NC 200 acres and 300 acres at head of Watauga River.
Ent. #72 & 74 22 Jul 1790 Grants #1473 & 1474 Iss. 4 Jan 1792 c.c. Richard Callaway, Reuben Whtie Book 75 pp. 440-442.

CENSUS LOCATION

1790 Burke Co., NC 5th Co.
1800 Burke Co., NC
1810 Burke Co., NC

REFERENCES

Burke County, NC Land Grant Records, Morganton Burke Library, Morganton, N.C.
AIS Census Indices, North Carolina
Huggins, Edith, Burke County Records SHP 1987
White, Gifford "James Taylor White of Virginia" Austin, TX 1982

WHITENER, ABRAM

SUMMARY OF EARLY LIFE

Abram Whitener was born c. 1754 in North Carolina and was the son of George Henry and Catherine Mull Whitener. He was a brother to Capt. Henry Whitener and Daniel Whitener, also Revolutionary War soldiers.

SUMMARY OF PARTISAN

On October 7, 1780 Abram Whitner was fighting along side his brother Daniel at the battle of Kings Mountain on October 7, 1780. During this battle, Abram Whitener was mortally wounded.

REFERENCES

McAllister, Anne W., and Sullivan, Kathy Gunter, "Henry Weidner Memorial Booklet", 1988.
Garrou, Hilda Whitener, "The Whitener Family 1717-1971" 1971.

WHITENER, DANIEL

SUMMARY OF EARLY LIFE

Daniel Whitener was born October 14, 1750 either in Pennsylvania or North Carolina, the son of George Henry and Catherine Mull Whitener. The Whiteners were early settlers of what is now Catawba County, NC.

SUMMARY OF PARTISAN ACTIVITY

Daniel Whitener, along with brothers Henry and Abram fought in the epic battle of Kings Mountain on October 7, 1780. Abram was killed during the action. Tradition says that "spying Major Ferguson upon his horse, Daniel Whitener took careful aim and shot the British officer". His bullet was one of the eight that ended his life.

SUMMARY OF LATER LIFE

Daniel Whitener married Mary Elizabeth Wilfong, daughter of Maj. George Wilfong. They had the following children:
Johannes b. 1785 m. (1) Mary Miller, (2) Margaret Dellinger
Elizabeth b. 1786 m. Jacob Corpening
Daniel b. 1788 M. (1) Polly Robinson (2) Ann Hoyle
Mary b. 1790 m. John Setzer II
Henry b. 1791 m. Margaret Sherrill
Catherine b. 1792 m. Zachariah Stacey
Sarah b. 1795 m. David Seitz
Rachel b. 1800 m. (1) Caleb Miller (2) David Killian
George b. 1801 m. Margaret Dellinger
David b. 1805 m. Sarah Stillwell

Daniel Whitener died 8 January 1833 and is buried at the Whitener-Robinson cemetery, Catawba County, N.C.

CENSUS LOCATIONS

1790 Lincoln Co., NC 4th Co.
1800 Lincoln Co., NC
1810 Lincoln Co., NC
1820 Lincoln Co., NC
1830 Lincoln Co., NC

REFERENCES

McAllister, Sullivan, "The Henry Weidner Memorial Booklet" 1988.
Garrou, Hilda Whitener "The Whitener Family 1717-1971", 1971.

WHITENER, HENRY

SUMMARY OF EARLY LIFE

Henry Whitener was born in Anson County (later Rowan and then Catawba County) NC in 1752, the son of George Henry and Catherine Mull Whitener. It appears from early land records that they were living near the confluence of Jacob's Fork and Henry River, now western Catawba County.

SUMMARY OF PARTISAN ACTIVITY

Henry Whitener served as a Capt. in Charles McDowells Burke Regiment. The Revolutionary Army Accounts verify Whitener's military service as Captain of militia.

Whitener participated in the hard fought battle of Ramsours' Mill on June 20, 1780.

Later Whitener commanded his company at the epic battle of Kings Mountain on October 7, 1780. During this action, his younger brother Abram was killed.

In 1782, as a member of the Charles McDowell court martial panel, he described the action at Ramsours' and several of its participants.

SUMMARY OF LATER LIFE

Henry Whitener was married to (1) Anna Sarah Shell (b. 1761-1785 or 1790) and (2) Mary Catherine Shell (c. 1763-1822). Both marriages were in Lincoln County, N.C. Whitener eventually left NC and settled in Missouri.

Children:
Catherine b. 1782 m. Devault Bollinger
Mary b. 1784 m. Henry Meyers
Barbara b. 1784 m. Henry Bollinger
Charity b. 1786 m. Philip Bollinger
Henry b. 1787 m. Elizabeth Bollinger
Jesse b. 1789
Abraham b. 1790 m. Mary Magdoline Bollinger
Daniel b. 1792 m. Mary Clubb
Soloman b. 1794 m. Elizabeth Kinder
John b. 1798 m. Elizabeth Mouser
Benjamin b. 1803 m. (1) Elizabeth Rhodes (2) Pricilla Kelly

Henry Whitener died 1811 in Marquand, MO.

LAND HOLDINGS AND TRANSACTIONS

1. NC Crown Grant "Mecklenburg" County (actually Rowan, due to indefinite boundaries) 200 acres east side of Stoop Creek

WHITENER, HENRY   P.2

joining Whiteners own land and John Mull's in the fork of Henry and Jacob's River. 26 Oct. 1767.
*The early date of this grant probably indicates that these were his father's grant-- George Henry Whitener.
2. Burke County, N.C. 400 acres joining his own line across Jacob's Fork of Catawba "round corner of his old patoned". Ent. 18 Dec. 1778. Warrent issued.

CENSUS LOCATIONS

1790 Lincoln Co., NC 4th Co.
1800 Lincoln Co., NC

WHITSON, BENJAMIN

SUMMARY OF EARLY LIFE

The Whitsons, prior to the Revolution, lived in the Lower Creek area, now Caldwell County, NC.

SUMMARY OF PARTISAN ACTIVITY

Benjamin Whitson was one of the better recognized Loyalists of western North Carolina. Much of the data concerning his activities came from the court martial proceedings of Col. Charles McDowell in 1782.

Benjamin Whitson was a Loyalist leader at the Battle of Ramsour's Mill on June 20, 1780. He was wounded during this battle (testimony by David Falls at Charles McDowell court martial).

Whitson fought as a Loyalist in the Battle of Kings Mountain on October 7, 1780 and was captured there. Later at Bickerstaff's. He was among the 27 men sentenced to hang. (Nine were hanged, the remainder reprieved (including Whitson?) --- testimony of Maj. Joseph McDowell).

According to the testimony of James Blair, Benjamin Whitson along with Horatio Sharp, robbed Blair of several articles including two guns. He stated that Whitson was known over the County as a "plunderer and a villain." In 1781 Whitson was hired as a substitute and served for a short while in the Continental Line. He later deserted.

SUMMARY OF LATER LIFE

Little is known of Whitson's later life. His name was not on the subpoena docket of Burke County in 1782-3. A Benjamin Whitson is listed as being a Deputy Sheriff of Burke County in 1788.

Later many members of the Whitson family moved to McDowell and Buncombe Counties, North Carolina and to Carter County, Tennessee.

REFERENCES

Court Martial papers of Col. Charles McDowell from facsimile copies presented to author by Miss Eunice Ervin. These minutes are also quoted in Huggins, Vol II, page 154.

Court Martial statements were made concerning Benjamin Whitson by James Blair, David Falls, John Russell, and Joseph McDowell, Quaker Meadows.

WILSON, GREENBERRY

SUMMARY OF EARLY LIFE

Greenberry Wilson was born ca. 1755, the son of William and Anna Wilson of Baltimore. He was living in western Burke County on Linville River, during the Revolutionary period. He was a neighbor of Nathan Birchfield.

SUMMARY OF PARTISAN Activity

In 1782, the name of Greenberry Wilson was listed as a suspect Tory and he was to appear in court to show cause as to why his property should not be confiscated. His neighbor Birchfield was also a Loyalist. Wilson was apparently a reasonably wealthy person and frequently appeared as bond for several Loyalists and their family members.

SUMMARY OF LATER LIFE

Wilson married ca. 1778 Cary Emmaline Bradshaw (another source says "Brown"). Children by this union were:
Greenberry, Jr.
Betsy
William B.
Charles B.
Sarah
Goodhue
Nancy

Wilson was active in Burke County affairs from the end of the war until about 1796 or 1797. He began to sell off his land. A notation of 1799 referred to "Greenberry Wilson's old place" After the Revolution he migrated to east Tennessee, Roane County He signed the petition for the creation of Roane County in 1799 In 1803 he was in Bledsoe County settling in the Sequatchie Valley. There may have been a second wife, Temperance. Greenberry Wilson died in 1812, age 57, and was buried in the Wilson cemetery at the home place.

LAND HOLDINGS AND TRANSACTIONS

1. 150 acres Burke County, NC on Linville River and bounded on the lower side by a Granville Grant issued by Griffith Rutherford and sold by John McDowell to Samuel Sherrill. The tract included improvements on both sides of the river. The land lay adjacent to that of Jason Birchfield.
Grant #219, 12 Mar 1780 Book 28 p,. 218.

2. 320 acres Burke County, NC on both sides of Paddy's adjacent to land of Robert Montgomery.
Grant #1508, Iss. Nov. 27, 1792, Book 80 p. 25.

3. 157 acres Burke County, NC on head branch of right hand

fork of Pepper's Branch, on east side of mountain the divides
Catawba dn Toe River valleys..

Grant #1512 Iss. 27 Nov. 1792.

4. 100 acres Burke County, NC on the east side of Linville
River adjacent to his own land.
Grant #1598 Book 80 p.55.

5. 320 acres Burke County, NC on Paddy Creek, adjacent to
his previous survey.
Grant #1752 Iss. 7 July 1794 Book 85 p. 79.

6. Sale of land to Samuel Mackey, October 1795, 300 acres.
Burke County Court records. January session 1796.

7. Sale of land to Thomas Bell, 320 acres, October Session 1796.

8. Bledsoe Co. E. TN Grant #3273 44 acres Nov 17, 1812, BK 4/96

9. Bledso Co. E. TN Grant #1555 150 acres June 12, 1810 BK 2/623

10. Another Grant in same area to Greenberry Wilson, Jr. 7 acres
Dec 22, 1815.

CENSUS LOCATIONS

1790 Burke Co., NC 6th Co.
1799 (tax list) Knox Co. TN
1805 (tax list) Roane Co., TN

REFERENCES

AIS Census Index 1790 Census
Index to Early Tennessee Tax Lists by Bryan and Barbara Sistler,
Evanston, Ill. 1977 p.212
Burke County Court Minutes 1791-1795 and 1795-1798, Edited by
Dan D. Swink, 1986 and 1987, multiple listings.
Huggins, Edith, Burke County Records Vols.I-IV Multiple listings
Morganton-Burke County Library, Verticle Files Greenberry Wilson
records.
Morganton-Burke County Library Land Grant Records.
Phifer, Edward Burke Morganton, NC 1977 Edition p. 390
Tennessee State Archives and Library, Nashville Land Grant
Records.

WISEMAN, WILLIAM

SUMMARY OF EARLY LIFE

William Wiseman was born in London in 1742. As a young man he came to America as a stowaway (along with friends William Penly and William Davis). After being indentured for a period of time, Wiseman and his two friends eventually migrated to western North Carolina, then Rowan County. (He probably resided in the present Burke-Caldwell area near the Davenport family). He was living in western Rowan County at the beginning of the Revolution and was married to Mary Davenport.

SUMMARY OF PARTISAN ACTIVITY

William Wiseman was a cobbler by profession, and in this capacity, he served in the American Revolution. He had an unusual way of measurement of the shoe sizes, using notches. His patriotic service is verified by data in Revolutionary Army Accounts of North Carolina.

SUMMARY OF LATER LIFE

William Wiseman was married first to Mary Davenport and by this union there were eleven children Their names were Thomas, Dorothy, William, Mary, Davenport, Martin, James, John. Celestial, Susannah and Robert. William Wiseman married second a Lydia Bedford. By this union there were seven children. Included were sons Bedford, Alexander and Anthony. William Wiseman was one of the first pioneers to establish a permanent home in the north west North Carolina mountains. From his large family have come millbuilders, carpenters, farmers, writers, preachers, poets, musicians and many others with outstanding talents.

William Wiseman died in 1830 and is buried near Highway 19-E between Ingalls and Spruce Pine, N.C.

LAND HOLDINGS AND TRANSACTIONS

1. Burke County, NC 100 acres on the Clear Creek at "Poplar Hollow", at the fork of Three Mile Creek, a tributary of Toe River and adjacent to land of Alexander Cole.
Ent. 2 May 1793 #400, Grant No. 1353 Iss. 22 Aug 1795 Book 88, p. 44. c.c. William Wiseman, John Wiseman.

2. Burke County, NC 60 acres on water of Toe River and adjacent to his previous survey. The tract included the improvements of Martin Wiseman. Ent. 25 July 1798 #3409 Grant No. 2339 Iss. 21 Dec 1798 Book 100 p. 196.
c.c. Thomas Wiseman, William Wiseman, Jr.

Wiseman, William

CENSUS LOCATIONS

1790 Burke Co., NC 10th Co.
1800 Burke Co., NC
1810 Burke Co., NC
1820 Burke Co., NC

REFERENCES

Pyatte, Martha Personal Conversations. Data presented to Author. (Avery Co., N.C.)
Fink, Emma S. Personal Data, Corssnore, N.C.
Brown, Sam Conversation with Author 1962-1987: Crossnore, N.C.
"Avery County Heritage" Avery County Bicentennial Commission 1976, copy presented to Author by Katherine Shell, Sloop Memorial Hospital 1976.

WOODS, HENRY

Henry Woods was living in Orange County, NC before and during the Revolutionary War. He was age 79 in 1832.

SUMMARY OF PARTISAN ACTIVITY

Henry Woods first entered military service in Orange County in the summer of 1776. He served in a company commanded by Capt. (William) Williams of Ambrose Ramsay's Regiment. Col William Moore of Caswell County was also present. They were to take part in Rutherford's Cherokee Expedition. They marched to Quaker Meadows in Burke County. Here they were ordered back to Hillsborough, since more than enough men were already on their way to Gen Rutherford.

In early 1781, he volunteered to serve a tour under Capt. James Havers of Gen. John Butler's Brigade. They advanced to High Rock Ford on the Haw and then to Guilford Court House. Woods did not participate directly in the battle of March 15, 1781, but instead was assigned to the battle wagons.

In February 1782 he began a tour of duty in Capt. John Taylor's Company of Col. Thomas Taylor's Regiment. Their actions were directed again the Tory activities of the noted Central North Carolina partisan, Col. David Fanning.

Woods also served on several smaller scouting duties.

SUMMARY OF LATER LIFE

Shortly after the Revolution, Woods moved to Burke County, NC. He remained there for the remainder of his life.

Henry Woods married (1) Nancy Butler (1774) and (2) _____Dec. 31, 1793. The following children ware born to Henry Wood and Nancy Butler:

Nancy b. 1775 m. William King
Soloman b. 1777
Isaac b. 1779
Joseph b. 1781
James b. 1783
Henry, Hr. B 1785 m. Catherine McDougal

Henry Woods applied for Revolutionary War Pension in Burke County, NC, October 23, 1832, age 79 years. He was awarded a pension of $30.00 per annum. The records indicate his death by 1844.

LAND HOLDINGS AND TRANSACTIONS

Henry Woods was awarded an NC Land Grant in Burke County for 50 acres on Sandy Run, including the shoals and adjacent to land

belonging to James Ross. c.c. William Woods, Timothy Woods.
Ent. August 17, 1796 No. 2698, Grant # 2208, Book 94, p. 200
Iss. December 2, 1797

CENSUS LOCATIONS

1790 Burke County, NC 13th Company
1800 Burke County, NC
1810
1820 Burke County, NC
1830 Burke County, NC
1840 (Henry Woods listed in Haywood County, but not a pensioner)

REFERENCES

Texas DAR Roster Revolutionary Ancestors (Texas 1976)
Vol IV p. 2340
AIS Census Indices
NC Land Granta Data, Morganton-Burke Library, Morganton, NC
US National Archives; Pension Data; # S7968

WOODS, SAMUEL (Wood)

SUMMARY OF EARLY LIFE

One source gives Samuel Woods birthdate as 1735, Albermarle Co. Virginia, another says 1840. It appears that he is not the Samuel Woods, Jr. Listed in Rowan County Deed and Court records (The son of Samuel and Ann Woods of Coldwater Creek and brother of Andrew Woods.)

During the Revolution he was living in the Muddy Creek area of Burke County.

SUMMARY OF PARTISAN ACTIVITY

Samuel Woods was a Captain of militia in Charles McDowell's Burk regiment. Woods participated in the earlier activities against the Cherokee Indians and against local Loyalists.

In the Kings Mountain Campaign of 1780 Woods was the man of the hour in conducting a delaying action against the invading Briti forces during their penetration into Burke County in September 1780. Woods raised a Company of men, mostly neighbors, and fought a resisting skirmish at Cane Creek on September 12, 1780 During this encounter his neighbor Peter Brank was killed and John Carswell wounded. Other soldiers who fought under Woods' command included George Hodge, Samuel Mackey, William Morrison, Enoch Berry. Other officers with him included James Murphy, James Mackey and Thomas Kennedy. After Cane Creek, Woods accompanied the McDowells into east Tennessee and was with them as they advanced to Kings Mountain. There is some question as whether Woods actually fought in the battle. Several soldiers, in their pension applications list him as their commanding officer. One, however, said that he resigned and that his plac was taken by John McDowell. This was William Morrison, a soldi but also a neighbor of Woods. * Later Woods led his company against the Indians including the Spring 1782 raid of Joseph McDowell. *This may have been the Samuel Woods, Jr. formerly of Rowan Co.

SUMMARY OF LATER LIFE

Samuel Woods remained in Burke County until about 1790 or so. The 1790 census lists him with a full house - five boys and fiv girls. He began selling off his land and shortly afterwards moved to Kentucky, Madison County. This was probably the area that later became Garrard County. Fellow soldiers and neighbor Thomas Kennedy and Robert Brank had moved to the Paint Lick section of Garrard County at about the same time. DAR records say that Woods wife, Margaret, died in Kentucky in 1800 and tha Woods then moved to Tennessee with his son John. (First to Williamson County and then Carroll County ca. 1820.) He died i Carroll County, Tennessee 1825, possibly buried at the old Ferguson cemetery at Livinia. Children of Samuel and Margaret

Woods were as follows:

Martha b. 1770	Jane
Margaret b. 1769	John b. 1774
Samuel b. 1776	David
Daniel	William
Mary	Oliver b. 1783

CENSUS LOCATIONS

1790 Burke County, NC 6th Company

REFERENCES

White, Katherine D. The Kings Mountain Men GPC Baltimore 1970 p. 235.
Draper, L.C. Kings Mountain and its Heroes 1967 Reprint Edition GPC pp. 147-149.
Land Grant Data, Morganton-Burke Library, Morganton, NC
AIS Census indices
Bates-Marsh, Tennessee DAR Records "Roster of Soldiers and Patriots of the American Revolution Buried in Tennessee". 1979.
US National Arichives Pension Declarations of John Dysart, Isaac Grant, Geroge Hodge, Samuel Lusk, Samuel Mackey, Enoch Berry, and William Morrison.
Linn, Jo White, Abstracts of Rowan Deeds 1753-1785 Salisbury 1983
DAR Patriot Index, national Society DAR, Washington, DC 1966 p. 761.
Holcombe, Brent, Marriages of Rowan County, N.C. 1753-1868 Baltimore GPC 1981 p. 435
Woods, Elbert W., letter Author 1982. (Jonesboro, GA)

INDEX

ABSHER,	291
. W.C.	273
. W.O.	15,17,81,137,226
.	243,245,292
ADAMS,CHARLES	11-12,16
. GODFREY	150,224
. POLLY DAVIS	103
AIKEN,ELIZABETH	184
. MARY DEAVER BIFFLE	35
. SAMUEL	35
AINSWORTH,JAMES	257
AKINS,SAM	36
ALBRIGHT,ANNE B.	262
ALEXANDER,ANN	248,290
. ELIAS	196
. JAMES	207,248,256
. JANE PENLAND	252
. JEAN PENLAND	252
. MARY PARKS	244
. POLLY PARKS	244
. REBECCA	43
. ROBERT	67
. RUTH PENLAND	252
. SAMUEL	252
. WILLIAM	207
ALLAIRE,	149,296
. ANTHONY	37,147,271,274
.	282
ALLEN,DANIEL	1
. JOHN	195
. MARGARET	207-208
. RICHARD	102,213
. ROBERT	16
. SARAH	234
. WILLIAM	132
ALLISON,	303
. JAMES	93
. MARY	93
ANDERSON,	45
ANTHONY,PHILIP	32,86
ARMSTRONG,	138,293
. JAMES	92
. JOHN	6,41,89,109,120
.	158,201,204,237
. WILLIAM	60
ARNTS,JOHN	86
ARROWOOD,	3
ARTHURS,	
. CATHERINE NEILL	234
. SARAH A.	234
ARWOOD,JOHN	3
. ZACHARIAH	3
ASBURY,	173
ASHE,JOHN	67,73,267,284
ASHENBRUNNER,ABRAHAM	5
. BARBARA	5
. CATHERINE	5
. ESTHER	5
. HENRY	5
. MARY	5
. PHILIP	5
. SARAH KHYZER	5
. URBAN	5
AVERY,A.C.	253
. WAIGHT	220
AVINGTON,	116
BADDIS,JOHN	116
BAILEY,ALEXANDER	201
. RICHARD	246
. WILLIAM	112,246
BAIN,ANDREW	263
NANCY QUEEN	263
BAKER,	121
. CATHERINE	130
. CHARLES	7
. DAVID	6
. DIMION	6,10
. ELIAS	7
. ELIZABETH	7
. ELIZABETH MONTGOMERY	7
. HENRY	6
. HENRY BARLOW	227
. JAMES	7-8
. JANE	7
. JEHU	9-10
. JOHN	6-7,9-10
. MARGARET	7
. MARY	7
. MOSES	9-10
. NANCY	7
. OSLY	173
. RACHEL	7
. REBECCA	7
. SARAH	7
BALDWIN,ELISHA	11-12,16
. ISAAC	11-12
. JACOB	11-12,15
. JAMES	15
. JOHN	11,14-16
. JOSHUA	11
. WILLIAM	11-12,16
BALLEW,JANE	18
. JOSEPH	112,146
. RICHARD	146
. ROBERT	18,111
. STEPHEN	18
. THOMAS	18
. WILLIAM	16
BALLOU,	18
BALLWE,RICHARD	111

INDEX

BALSER,	285	. JAMES	29
BANNING, ALEX	20	. MARGARET VEGHTE	30
. BENONI	20	. MARY COX	29
. FRAZIER	20	. SARAH COX	29
. HENRY	20	. WILLIAM	29,32,237
. JAMES	20	BELL,	303
BARKLEY, ELENAR CATHEY	21	. CATHERINE	110
. HENRY	21	. COMFORT BRITTAIN	48
. MARY	21	. EDWARD	286
. ROBERT	21	. JAMES	204
. VIOLET	5	. MONTGOMERY	48
BARNETT, HUMPHREY	263	. ROBERT	187
BARR, BETSY	22	. THOMAS	315
. CALEB	22,151	. WILLIAM	200
. DAVID	218	BENFIELD, JOHN	79
. JENNY	22	BENNETT, W.D.	187
. JOSEPH	22	. WILLIAM	120
. MARGARET	22	BENNING, BENONI	20
. SAMUEL	22	BENTON, JOHN	50
. SELOX	22	BERGER, JOHN	246
. SILAS	22	BERRY, AUGUSTON	34
. WILLIAM McCRARY	22	. BARBARA THOMSON	33-34
BARRINGER, MATTHEW	227	. ENOCH	33-34,320-321
. MATTHIAS	227	BEVERLY,	87
BARTON,	39	BICKERSTAFF,	35,55,60,83
. JOHN	81,272	.	110,162,274,313
BATES,	36,53,56,82,279	. JOHN	287
.	321	BIFFLE, JACOB	35
. GEORGE	252	. MARY DEAVER	35
. HUMPHREY	25-26	BIGGERSTAFF,	102,282
. JOHN	116	. AARON	60
. RACHEL MITCHELL	25	. CYNTHIA POLLARD	60
BAXTER, JOHN	67	. JOHN	60,272
BEARD, JONATHON	1	. SAMUEL	60
BEASON,	165	BIRCHFIELD, ELIZABETH	297
BEATTIES,	217	. JASON	314
BEATY,		. JOHN	146
. ELIZABETH SCOTT	272	. NATHAN	314
BEAVER, ELIZABETH	79	. ROBERT	132
BECK, DANIEL	27	BIRD, RICHARD	289
. DAVID	28	BLACK, DAVID	297
. ELIZA	28	BLACKWELL, JOHN	119
. ELIZABETH	27	BLAIR,	168
. JACOB	27-28,218	. ANNE	39
. JOHN	27	. COLBERT	37,39,262,264
. JOSEPH	27,140	. ELIZABETH CLEVELAND	37
. NICHOLAS	27	.	39
BECKNEL,	102	. ELIZABETH POWELL	37,39
BEDFORD, LYDIA	315	. ENOS	37,39
BEEKMAN,	30	. FRANCES HILL	37
. CHRISTOPHER	30-31,44	. GEMMIA SCOTT	272
.	85,118,166,196,209	. GEORGE	224
.	214,237,255	. HANNAH MILLIKEN	37
. CHRISTOPHER W.	29	. JAMES	37-39,262,274
. GERARD	29	.	282,304,313

INDEX

. JANE MURREY	37
. JOHN	37,39
. JOSEPH TERRELL	39
. MARY	37,39
. MARY COLBERT	37
. OLIVER ELSTON	39
. ROBERT E.	40
. ROBERT EOAE	38
. SARAH MORGAN	37,39
BLANTON, JOHN	113
BLOUNT, READING	227
BLUFORD,	263
BOGLE, SUSAN	76
BOIDSTON, JAMES	50
BOLEN, JOHN	12
BOLICK,	285
. CASPER	32
BOLLINGER,	
. BARBARA WHITENER	311
. CATHERINE WHITENER	311
. CHARITY WHITENER	311
. DEVAULT	311
. ELIZABETH	311
. HENRY	311
. MARY M.	311
. PHILIP	311
BOONE, DANIEL	27
. ELEANOR	76
. JONATHAN	76
BORELAND, JOHN	148,195
BOTEAT,	261
BOUCHELLE, SLUYTER	113
. THOMAS	113
BOWMAN,	39
. EDWARD	16
. JOHN	194
. SHERWOOD	117
BOYD,	67
. ALEXANDER SMITH	41
. ELISHA	42
. ELIZABETH	41
. HUGH	42
. JAMES	41
. JOHN	41-42,195
. JOSHUA	41
. MARTHA	41
. MARY ROBERTS	41
. MATILDA	42
. MATTHEW	42
. SPENCER	41
. SUSAN	42
. WILLIAM	42
BOYKIN,	212
BRACKER, WILLIAM	125
BRADDOCK,	183
BRADSHAW,	91,100,105
. ANN	130
. ANNE MONTGOMERY	207
. CARY EMMALINE	314
. FIELD	125
. HELEN L.	5
. ISAIAH	251
. JOEL	125
. WILLIAM	130,207,297
BRANDON, JOSIAH	99,132
BRANK, ELIZABETH	43,252
. JANE	43
. JEAN	43
. PETER	43,166,320
. PRICILLA	43
. RACHEL	43
. RACHEL BRITTAIN	48
. REBECCA ALEXANDER	43
. ROBERT	25,32,43,320
BRASHEAR, JANE SCOTT	272
BRAVARD, JOHN	305
BREVARD,	45
. ABRAHAM	44
. ADAM	44
. ALEXANDER	231,236
. BENJAMIN	44,46
. DAVID FALLS	231
. EPHRAIM	44
. HUGH	29,44-45,194,237
.	267
. JANE McWHORTER	44
. JANE YOUNG	45
. JOEL	231
. JOHN	44,280
. JOSEPH	44
. ROBERT	44
BRIDGES, JOHN	46
BRIDGET, JAMES	47
. WILLIAM	47
BRIGHT,	212
. SAMUEL	257
. SARAH DAVIS	104
BRISTOL, BENEDICT	184
. JESSIE McCALL	184
BRITTAIN, AARON	48
. AMELIA	48
. ARMINTA RUSSELL	48
. BARBARA MULL	217
. BENJAMIN	48,218
. CECIA VANCE	48
. COMFORT	48
. DELILAH	48
. DELILAH STRINGFIELD	48
. ELIZABETH MORROW	48
. GEMIMA	217

INDEX

- HORATIO NELSON 48
- JAMES 48-49,52,132
- JEMIMA 48,52
- JOSEPH 48,52
- KEZIAH 48
- LORENZO DOW 48
- MARK 217
- MARY 48,52
- NANCY 48,52
- PHILIP 48,52
- PHOEBE 48
- RACHEL 48
- RACHEL BRANK 43
- RACHEL CLAYTON 48
- RACHEL SMITH 48
- SAMUEL 48,52
- SHIRLEY 50
- SOPHIA LEWIS 48
- SUSANNAH 48
- WILLIAM 43,48

BROWDER,
- BLANCHE PENLAND 249
. 254,256

BROWN, 132,263
- CARY EMMALINE 314
- CHARITY 57
- ELIZABETH 57
- GEORGE 54,150
- JACOB 59
- JOSEPH 59
- MARY 57
- RICHARD 54,150
- ROBERT 55,99,136,267
- SAM 317
- SAMUEL 57-58
- THOMAS 59

BROWNING,JOHN 280
BRUMLEY, 290
BRUMLEYS, 12
BRYANT,RICHARD 113
BUCHANAN,JOSEPH 127
BUCKNER,
- AMELIA SUMTER 290
BUFORD, 171
- ABRAHAM 64
BULLINGER, 227,304
BULLINGERS, 86
BURCHFIELD, 65
- ABERILLA 66
- BETSY 68
- EBERELIA 66
- ELIZABETH HILL 68
- JOHN 63,68
- KITTY 68
- MARY 68

- MARY PATTERSON 63
- MESHACK 64-67
- NANCY 68
- NATHAN 66
- ROBERT 66-68
- SALLY 68

BURES,ROBERT 155
BURKE,JOHN 112
BURNS,CONRAD 79
- PHILIP 235
- SARAH 177
BUSH,BENJAMIN 16
BUSHELL,SLUYTER 113
- THOMAS 113
BUTLER, 68,123,166
- JOHN 318
- MARGARET QUEEN 263
- MICHAEL 263
- NANCY 318
BUTTS,JOHN 79,218
- SUZANNAH CLINE 79
BYERS, 98
- WILLIAM 114
CALDWELL,SIDNEY 205
CALLAWAY,RICHARD 308
CAMP,JONATHAN 250,258
. 267
CAMPBELL, 162,196
- ARTHUR 278
- RICHARD 150
- WILLIAM 20,141
CAPPS,BARNEY 70
- CORNELIUS 70
- HIRAM 70
- JOHN 70
- LUCINA 70
- NANCY 70
- WILLIAM 70
CARLTON,THOMAS 303
CARPENTER,BARBARA 217
- ELIZABETH 79
CARRETHERS,ROBERT 54
CARRIAH,BETSY 177
CARSON, 114
- JOHN 32,91,96,190,192
. 211
- MARY MOFFETT 192
- RACHEL McDOWELL 190
. 192
CARSWELL,JOHN 320
CARTER,EDWARD 259
CASWELL,WILLIAM 64
CATHEY, 30,64,175,190
. 194,199,233
- ANDREW 72

INDEX

- ANN 72,209
- BOYT H. 72
- DANIEL 72
- ELENAR 21
- ELIZABETH 72
- ELIZABETH PENLAND 250
- GEORGE 67-68,72,108
- 209,219,265
- JACOB 72
- JAMES 72,250
- JOHN 21,72
- MARGARET 72
- MARY 72
- REBECCA 72
- REBECCA HOLEMAN 72
- SARAH 72
- THOMAS 72
- WILLIAM 72,96

CAUSBY, WILLIAM 188
CAVEN, JANE 265
CAWYER,
- SHIRLEY BRITTAIN 50

CERSEY, LEVI 100
CHAMBERS, JAMES 192
- JOHN 96

CHAPMAN, EURITH 73
- GEORGE 74
- JAMES 74
- JOHN 61,73-74,146
- JOSHUA 74
- MARY 74
- NICHOLAS 73-74
- ROBERT 74
- SARAH 74
- SARAH SEALEY 73
- SARAH SEELY 73
- THOMAS E. 74

CHARLES, 190
CHEW, 267
CHRONICLE, 3
CLARK, 52,60,118
- ALEXANDER 305
- ELIJAH 55
- JOHN 103
- MERTIE JUNE 58
- MORDECAI 198
- MURTIE 16
- MURTIE J. 119
- MURTIE JUNE 17
- THOMAS 48
- WANDA L. 298

CLARKE, ALEXANDER 75-77
- CORNELIUS 75
- CORNELIUS W. 76
- ELEANOR BOONE 76
- JEHU 76
- JEREMIAH 75-76
- JOANNA 77
- JOHN 12,76-77
- MARGARET 77
- MARGARET HAYES 77
- MORDECAI 18,70,227,265
- 267,291
- MORNING 76
- NATHAN 76
- SAMUEL 77-78
- SUSAN 76
- SUSAN BOGLE 76
- THOMAS 76

CLAYTON, RACHEL 48
CLELAN, JOHN 178
CLEVELAND, 68,303
- BENJAMIN 39,81,83,87
- 110,241,244,272
- ELIZABETH 37,39
- JOHN 87
- LARKIN 110

CLIFT, GLENN 115
CLINE, BOSTIAN 79
- CATHERINE SHUFORD 79
- CHRISTIAN 79
- CHRISTOPHER 79
- CISCERO 80
- DAVID 79
- EASTER 79
- ELIZABETH BEAVER 79
- ELIZABETH CARPENTER 79
- ELIZABETH DEAL 79
- GEORGE 79
- HENRY 79
- JOHN 79
- LEONARD 79
- MARGARET RAMSOUR 79
- MARY 173
- MARY CONRAD 79
- MICHAEL 99
- POLLY PETERSON 79
- SALLY RADER 79
- SEBASTIAN 79
- SUZANNAH 79
- WILLIAM 79

CLINTON, MARY 234
CLOUD, 289
CLUBB, MARY 311
COCKE, 3,168
COCKRAN, BENJAMIN 20
COFFEE, BENJAMIN 39
COFFER, LEWIS 30
COFFEY, 84
- AMBROSE 84

327

INDEX

- BENJAMIN 11,32,39,81
- 84,136
- JAMES 81
- JESSE 83
- REUBEN 83-84
- THOMAS 81
- COLBERT, MARY 37
- COLE, ALEXANDER 305,308
- 315
- COLES, WILLIAM 46
- COLLETT, 235
- ABRAHAM 217
- COLLIER, JOHN 93
- CONNELLY, JANE BALLEW 18
- JOHN 18
- CONRAD,
- CATROUT SHUFORD 85
- CHRISTIANA
- STOCKINGER 85
- MARY 79
- RUDOLPH 85,107
- CONSTABLE, WILLIAM 60
- COOK, ELERNER 87
- GRACIE 5
- ISAAC 87-88
- JOHN 87
- RICHARD 48
- COOL, WILLIAM 241
- COOPER, JANE 108,112,125
- JOHN 247
- REBECCA 108,125
- REBECCAH 112
- CORNWALLIS, 25,104,136
- 143,150,171,196,203
- 246,289,299
- CORNWELL,
- BARBARA HUFFMAN 152
- WILLIAM 152
- CORPENING, ALBERT 11-12
- 77
- ELIZABETH WHITENER 310
- JACOB 310
- COULTER, MARTIN 217
- COWAN, 45,136,239,303
- COX, DAVY 178
- MARY 29
- MATTHEW 304
- SARAH 29
- CRABTREE, RICHARD 32,211
- CRAGG, WILLIAM 31
- CRAIG, 25,116
- EDWARD 116
- THOMAS 195
- WILLIAM 227
- CRAWFORD, DAVID 76
- SUSAN CLARKE 76
- CREASMAN, 89
- CRESSON, ANDREW 89
- DAVID 89
- ELIJAH 89
- JOHN 89
- JOSIAH 89
- LUCY 89
- NANCY 89
- POLLY 89
- REBECCA 89
- THOMAS 89
- CRIDER, 81
- CRISAWN, 89
- CROSS, HENRY 108
- NANCY 200
- CRUGER, 122
- CRYDER, MARY 184
- CULBERSON, DAVID 57,91
- CULBERTSON, 91
- JOHN 239
- ROBERT 293
- CUMMINGS, ALEXANDER 181
- CUNNINGHAM, 224
- BILL 212
- FRANCIS 196,227,265
- 267
- CURR, PHILIP 31
- CURRIN, PANSY J. 80
- CURTIS, 179
- JONATHAN 32
- JOSEPH 113
- MARY ALLISON 93
- THOMAS 92-93
- CUTHBERTSON, 91
- WILLIAM 91
- DACEAR, JOHN 60
- DAIFER, WILLIAM 60
- DALESON, JOSEPH 253
- DALTON, WILLIAM 95
- DAVENPORT, JAMES 11-12,16
- MARTIN 224,280
- MARY 315
- SOPHIA 305,307
- THOMAS 307
- WILLIAM 308
- DAVIDSON, 14,25,45,99
- 113,132,160,190,199
- 212,233
- BENJAMIN 96
- ELIZABETH 98
- GEORGE 96,98,108
- GEORGE L. 50
- JAMES 50,67,96-98,108
- 138,233

INDEX

- . JANE 98
- . JOHN 59,98-99
- . MARGARET 98
- . MARY SMITH 98
- . MILLIE 242
- . RACHEL 98
- . ROBERT 98
- . SAMUEL 55,67,96,98
- . THOMAS 98
- . WILLIAM 32,58-59,67,96 98,239,247,253
- . WILLIAM L. 136,303
- DAVIS, 103,273,293
- . CLEMENT 100
- . ELIZABETH FLEMMING 100
- . ISAAC 104,272
- . JOHN 103,262
- . NANCY SCOTT 272
- . NATHAN 104
- . POLLY 103
- . REASON 100
- . SAMUEL 104-105
- . SARAH 104
- . SNEAD 102-103
- . WILLIAM 315
- DAWSEY,DIMION 106
- . ENDYMION 106
- . JOHN 227
- . WILLIAM SPENCER 106
- DAWSON,EDWARD 96
- DAYBERRY,ADAM 119
- DEAL,ELIZABETH 79
- . JACOB 107
- . MICHAEL 107
- . PETER 107
- . WILLIAM 107
- DEAVER,MARY 35
- DEITZ,JOHN 218
- DEKALB, 92
- DELAMAR, 259
- . M. 296
- DELLINGER,JOHN 27,284
- . MARGARET 310
- DEMENT,HENRY 108
- . JOHN 108
- . MARY 108
- DENNY,JAMES 88
- WALTER 123
- DENTON,ABRAHAM 210,251
- DERRYBERRY,ADAM 119
- DEWITT,CARY WHITE 307
- . CATHERINE WHITE 307
- . WILLIAM 307
- DIXON,HENRY 89
- DOBSON,ANN 271
- . ANNA MARIE 271
- . FRANCES 276
- . JOHN 194,248,280
- . JOSEPH 27,32,50,66,108 121,123,125,191,257 270-271,276
- DODD,BETSY 4,19-20,129
- DONNAL,ANNA 255
- . ANNIS 255
- DORRAL,ANNA 250
- DORSEY, 106
- DOSSY, 106
- DOTSON,MARTHA 87
- DOTY,AZARIAH 177
- . JOHN 177
- DOUGLAS,WILLIAM 65
- DOUGLASS,ALEXANDER 38
- DOWNEY,JAMES 245
- DOWNMAN, 128
- DOWNS,ZACHARIAH 165
- DRAKEFORD, 169
- DRAPER, 37,45,57,262
- . L.C. 40,43,57,264,271 275,282-283,296,321
- . LYMAN C. 38,58,149,274
- DRESHER,
- . CATHERINE L. MILLER 205
- . DOGFREY 205
- DREW,THOMAS H. 165
- DUGAN,THOMAS 179
- DUNLAP, 55,212,293
- DUNN,JAMES 192
- DURJAM, 109
- DURR,ANDREW 138
- DYER,JOHN 81
- DYSART,JOHN 32,211,321
- EBERHART,DAVID 109,201
- . JACOB 109
- EDINGTON,MICHEAL 6
- EDMISTEN, 14
- . ANNA 190
- EDWARDS,
- . AMELIA BRITTAIN 48
- . ELLIS 48
- . MARY BRITTAIN 48
- . THOMAS 48
- EIGERT,PETER 85
- ELROD, 25,87,269
- . MARY BRITTAIN 48
- ENGLAND, 77
- . MARTHA MONTGOMERY 207
- ENGLISH,NANCY 130
- ERNEST,HENRY 66
- ERVIN,EUNICE 47,54,80,97

INDEX

.	159,193,228,275,283	. JOSHUA	141
.	298,313	FINDLEY,CHARLES	295
ERWIN,	192,293	FINK,EMMA S.	317
. ALEXANDER	14,112,136	FINLEY,	217
.	201,204	FISH,	1
. MARGARET	191	. JOHN	46
. MATILDA SHARPE	191	FISHER,JOHN	285
. W.W.	191	FLEMING,ABRAHAM	112-113
ERWOOD,	3	. BETSY	112
. ROBERT	46	. DAVID	112
ESTES,ANN FULLWOOD	121	. FRANCES	112
. JOHN	121	. JANE	219
. PASCHAL	305	. JOHN	112
ETSKY,	293	. REBECCA	112
EVERHART,	109	. SAMUEL	112
FAIR,	110	. TARLETON	112
. TIM	111	. THOMAS	112
FAIRS,	110	FLEMMING,ELIZABETH	100
FALLS,	45,162,227	FLORD,ABRAHAM	114
. DAVID	267,313	FLOYD,ABRAHAM	114
. GALBRAITH	30-31,231	FORD,	39
.	233,235	. PETER	77,116,302
. GALBREATH	237	. SARAH	116
. GILLY	237	FORE,PETER	77,116,302
FANNING,DAVID	25,57-58	FORESTER,CHARLES	272
.	122,145,179,269,303	. WILL	245
.	318	FORGERY,SAMUEL	98
FARES,EDMUND	130	FORGY,CYNTHIA	229
. SILENCE	76,130	. JAMES	108,229
FARGULER,JAMES	92	. REBECCA	229
FARMER,FANNIE	269	FORSYTHE,JOHN	3
FEARS,AARON	111	FOX,JOHN	27,220,242,245
. CATHERINE BELL	110	FRANKLIN,ANNA	118
. EDMUND	110-111,130	. BENJAMIN	118
. ELIZABETH MAY	110	. DAVID	118-119
. HANNAH	110	. DORSEY W.	118
. JAMES	110	. DORSEY WAYNE	119
. JANE	111	. JEMIMA	118
. LEAH SMITH	111	. JESSE	41,83
. MARGARET	110	. JOHN	118-119,198
. MARY	110	. JONATHAN	118
. REBECCAH	110	. LYDIA	118
. SARAH	110	. MARY	118
. SILENCE	76,110	. MOSES	118-119
. SOPHIA JOSLIN	110	. PHEBA	118
FEBIGER,CHRISTIAN	165	. PHILEMAN	11-12
FERGUSON,	33,64,166,190	. PHILEMON	16
.	295,310	. PHOEBE PARKER	118
. ELIZABETH	177	. RACHEL	118
. PATRICK	43,219,262	. SAMUEL	118
. THOMAS	83	. T. EARL	119
FIELDS,THOMAS	225	FRAZER,	1
FINAZER,	1	FREEMASON,	113
FINCANNON,JOHN	308	FROHOCK,	227
FINCHER,ELIZABETH	141	. JOHN	218

INDEX

FULLBRIGHT, ANDREW 58
FULLERTON,
. JANE HARDIN 176
FULLWOOD, ANN 121
. ELIZABETH 121
. JOHN M. 121
. MARTHA 121
. SAMUEL 121
. SARAH 120
. WILLIAM 120-121
GALBRAITH, 162
GARROU,
. HILDA WHITENER 309-310
GASPERSON, JOHN 122,146
GATES, 92,120,128,199
. 236
. HORATIO 92,186,303
GIBBS, WILLIAM 121
GIBSON,
. ELEANOR PENLAND 252
. NATHAN 252
. RANDY 130
GILLESPIE, LYDIA 184
GINGER,
. CHAUNCEY LUSTER 123
. HENRY 123
. LEWIS 123
GLADNEY, J.B. 174
J.R. 173
GOLPHIN, 200
GOODE, EDWARD 128
GOODMAN, 222
. WILLIAM 286
GOODWIN,
. JANE WAKEFIELD 302
. NEWTON 302
GORDON, 160
GORTNER, JACOB 148
GOWEN, DANIEL 66
GRAGG, JASON 83
GRAHAM, JAMES 46
. WILLIAM 21
GRANT, ISAAC 189,321
GRANVILLE, 112,189
. 216-217,235,297
GRAVES, PATRICIA L. 42
. 133
GRAY, 39
. JOHN 125
. LYDDA 125
. LYDIA 125
. WILLIAM 125,177
GREEN, AARON 126
. ARTHUR 126
. ISABELLA 126

. JAMES 126
. JOHN 126-127
. JOSEPH 126
. T.M. 192
GREENE, 293
. NATHANIEL 9,18,35,100
. 160,187,196,224,229
. 239,265,269,289,291
GREENLEE, JAMES 36
. 252-253,304
. JASON 84
GREER, JOHN 213
GRIDER, JACOB 308
GRIFFIN, JEMIMA 302
GRINDALL, 70
GRINDSTAFF, JACOB 192
. MICHAEL 16,227
GROSS, JOHN 218
GUEST, BENJAMIN 83
. HENRY C. 63
. MARY BLAIR 37
. MOSES 37,83
GUISE, PHILIP 71
GUNTER, KATHY 309
GWIN, REBECCAH FEARS 110
HAFNER, JACOB 285
HALE, NICHOLAS 134
HAMBLIN, 269
HAMBRIGHT, 39
. FREDERICK 267
HAMBY, JAMES 1320
. WILLIAM 32
HAMMOND, LUCINA CAPPS 70
. SAMUEL 126
HAMPTON, 39,187
. ANDREW 267,302
. NED 267
HANEY, CHARLES 128-129
. HANNAH 129
HANON, JAMES 79
HARBINSON, NANCY 227
HARBISON, JAMES 113
HARDEN, 162
. BENJAMIN 3
. JOHN 3,162
HARDGROVE, FRANCIS 87
HARDIN, ELIZABETH 176
. JANE 176
. JOHN 45,166,176,194
. 246,286
. JOSEPH 175
. MARGARET 176
HARGRAVES, HEZEKIAH 122
HARPER, JOHN 112
HARRIS, JAMES 299

INDEX

. JOHN	28	
. NANCY	262	
. RICHARD	227	
. SUSANAH	143	
HARRISON, WILLIAM	30	
HARSHAW, AARON	130	
. ABRAHAM	130	
. ABRAM	130	
. ALLADIN	130	
. ANN BRADSHAW	130	
. ANNIE	130	
. BARBARA WEAVER	130	
. CATHERINE BAKER	130	
. ELIZABETH	130	
. ELIZABETH METCHIM	130	
. ELIZABETH POWELL	262	
. ISAAC	130, 262	
. JACOB	130	
. JOHN	130	
. JOSHUA	130	
. MOSES	130	
. NANCY ENGLISH	130	
. SIDNEY S.	280	
HART, MICHAEL	16	
HARTGRAVES, FRANCIS	303	
HARTGROVE,	83	
HARTLEY,	291	
. LEVI	76	
. MORNING CLARKE	76	
HASSELBARGER, JOHN	85	
HATCHER,	68	
. PATRICIA L.	69	
. PATRICIA L. GRAVES	42	
.	133	
HATHER,	304	
HAUES,	86	
HAUN, W.P.	76	
. WEYNETTE	61	
. WEYNETTE P.	86, 109, 119	
.	215, 286	
HAVERS, JAMES	318	
HAWKINS, JOHN	132, 297	
. JOSEPH	134	
. REBECCA KESTER	132	
. WILLIAM	134	
HAWS, JACOB	234	
HAYDEN, DOUGLAS	3	
HAYES, ELISHA	11	
. GEORGE	136	
. JOHN	12, 136	
. MARGARET	77	
. RANSOM	136	
HEADLEE, CALEB	287	
. DANIEL	287	
. DAVID	287	
. ELISHA JUDGE	287	
. JANE STEELE	287	
. JOSEPH	287	
. MARGARET STEELE	287	
. MARTHA STEELE	287	
. MARY STEELE	287	
. RACHEL STEELE	287	
HEFNER, GEORGE	85	
HEINS, TATE	220	
HEITMAN,	192	
HELDERMAN, CHRISTIAN	138	
. MARY	138	
. NICHOLAS	138	
HEMPHILL, JAMES	167	
HENDERSON,	299	
. CHARLES	291	
. JOHN	297	
HENRY, JANE BRANK	43	
. MARTHA S.	80	
. RACHEL	252	
. ROBERT	43	
. SAMUEL	168	
HENSON, BARTLETT	27	
HERMAN, ELIZABETH	262	
HERNDON, BENJAMIN	224	
HESE,	140	
HICE, BETSY	141	
. CATHERINE		
.	STARRINGER	141
. CONRAD	140-141	
. ELIZABETH	140-141	
. GEORGE	140-141	
. GEORGE W.B.	141-142	
. JACOB	140-141	
. LEONARD	140-141	
. PEGGY	140	
. SALENA A.	141	
. SOPHIA	140	
HICKMAN, GEORGE	307	
. MARY WHITE	307	
HICKS, ARTHUR	111	
. SOLOMON	103	
HIGDON, EVA HUFFMAN	152	
. LEONARD	143, 152	
. SUSANAH HARRIS	143	
HIGHLAND,	77, 205	
. HARRY	122, 145	
. HENRY	63, 122, 145-146	
.	189	
HILDEBRAND,		
. ABBIE SEALS	149	
. CHRISTIAN	147	
. CONRAD	147-148	
. CONRODE	148	
. CUNROD	147	

INDEX

. ELIZABETH	148
. ELIZABETH MULL	147
. GEORGE	148
. HENRY	147-148
. JOHANNAS	148
. KATRINA	148
. MARIA	148
. OLLIE H.	149
HILL, ELIZABETH	68
. FRANCES	37
. WILLIAM	162,164,263
HIPPS, GEORGE	246
HISE,	141
HIXON, INGABOW	154
. REBECCA	154
HOBBS, CALEB	276
HOBKIRK,	239
HODGE,	158
. ELIZABETH M.	295
. GEORGE	192,232,235
.	320-321
HODGES,	273
HOFFMAN,	152-153
HOFMAN, MARGARET	119
HOFMANN, MARGARET	28,80
. MARGARET M.	148,218
HOIL, MARY CHAPMAN	74
HOLCOMB, BRENT	211
HOLCOMBE, BRENT	321
HOLEMAN, REBECCA	72
HOLGATE, JEROME B.	31
HOLLARD, MILDRED	184
HOLMES, ROBERT	60,116,267
.	287
HOLT, PETER	116,241
HOOD, ANDREW	150
. JOHN	22,150
. THOMAS	150
HOOPER, JOHN	259
HORNE,	
. ELIZABETH POTEAT	260
. JOHN	260
. NANCY POTEAT	260
. THOMAS	260
HORSE, PHILIP	227
HOSE,	86
HOUCK, GEORGE	18
. JOHN	18
. NICHOLAS	235
HOUSTON, THOMAS	253
HOUTS, ALICE	288
HOWARD,	148,196
. JOE	148
. JOHN	148
. MARTHA FULLWOOD	121
. WILLIAM	121
HOWE,	122
HOWELL, DAVID	227
HOYLE, ABRAHAM	74
. ANN	310
. MARY CHAPMAN	74
HUCKABY, JOHN	308
HUFFMAN, ABRAM	152
. BARBARA	152
. BARBARA MOSER	152
. BURKHARD	152
. CATHERINE	152
. ELIZABETH	152
. EVA	152
. FRANCES	153
. FRANCES WELLMAN	153
. FREDRICK	152
. GASPER	152
. GENE	153
. GEORGE	152
. JACOB	152
. JOHN	152
. LOTTIE	153
. MARY M.	152
. MICHAEL	152
. SAMUEL	152-153
HUGER,	64,278
. ISAAC	89,186
HUGGINS	74
HUGGINS,	59,109,202,204
.	214,231,272,313
. DITH	80
. E.W.	75,238,245,259
.	281
. EDITH	6,9-10,13,17,43
.	58,61,65-66,78,91,108
.	111,137,163,165,195
.	211,215,261,275,283
.	286,298,305,308,315
. EDITH W.	28,31,47,50
.	76,86,105-107,113,116
.	138,149,159,174,178
.	182,226,232,235,257
.	273,288
. EDITH WARREN	125,131
.	157,161
HUGHES,	245
. ANN	112
. FRANCIS	154
. JOHN	154
. MARGARET	154
HUMPHRIES,	81
HUNT, ELIZABETH	278
. SARAH	177
HUNTER,	138

INDEX

. ANDREW	128	
. EDWARD	164	
. REBECCA	139	
HUNTSMAN, MAUDE	189	
HUSBANDS, ELSA	156	
. HERMAN	156	
. LAOMMI	156	
. ROBERT	156	
. VEAZEY	75-76,156	
. VEAZY	11	
. WILLIAM	156	
HYATT,	158,177	
HYDE,		
. ELIZABETH		
. LEATHERWOOD	177	
INGRAM, GOLDMAN	100	
INMAN, ANNE	158	
. CHARLES	158	
. DANIEL	158	
. ELIZABETH	158	
. EZEKIAL	158	
. HANNAH	158	
. HEZEKIAH	158	
. JERAMIAH	158	
. JOHN	158	
. JOSHUA	196	
. MARGARET	158	
. MARY J. McPETERS	158	
. MARY J. McPHEETERS	158	
. PRUDENCE	158	
. RACHEL	158	
. SARAH	158	
. SHADRACK	158-159	
. SUZANNA	158	
. THOMAS	158	
ISAACS,	186,200,269	
. ELISHA	87,303	
ISBELL, JAMES	290	
. PENDLETON	303	
. THOMAS	87	
. WILLIAM	12	
ISRAEL, MICHAEL	81	
. SOLOMAN	49	
JACK, JAMES	116	
JACKSON, DAVID	12	
. JAMES	160	
. JOSEPH	160	
JAMES,	116	
. JOSEPH R.	275,283	
. JOSEPH ROGER	274	
. JOSEPH ROGERS	162,275	
.	282	
. RAWLINGS	164	
. ROLLINGS	164	
. WILLIAM	12,112-113	
JARETT, SANDRA	264	
JAYNES,	271	
JENKINS, CHARLES	165	
JEWELL, JAMES	166-167	
. JOHN	166	
. WILLIAM	166	
JILLSON,	78,230	
. W.R.	226	
. WILLARD	298	
. WILLARD D.	170	
. WILLARD R.	26,111,176	
.	229	
JOANES, JOHN	181	
JOHNSON,	293	
. JESSE	126	
. JOHN	73,168	
. LUCY	302	
. NANCY	302	
. SAMUEL	87	
. WILLIAM	18,63	
JOHNSTON, ABRAHAM	171	
. ALBERTSON	171	
. ELIZABETH	171	
. JOHN	171	
. LEWIS	171	
. MARY	171	
. MYRA	171	
. NELLY	171	
. ROBERT	169	
. SAMUEL	241	
. SARAH	171	
JONES, ELIZABETH	250	
. JOHN	181,225	
. JONATHAN	267	
. NANCY	250	
. NICHOLAS	54	
. SAMUEL	241	
. SHADRACK	145	
. WILLIAM	18	
JOSLIN, SOPHIA	110	
JULIAN, WILLIAM	114	
JUSTICE, JAMES	50	
KEENER, W.	276	
KELLER, HANNAH	188	
KELLY, JOHN	30	
. PRICILLA	311	
. SALLY BURCHFIELD	68	
KEMP, JONATHAN	212,250	
KENNEDY,	128,212	
. FRANCIS	112	
. JOHN	57	
. THOMAS	25,32,122,132	
.	145,219-220,246,258	
.	260,320	
KERNS, CONRAD	116	

INDEX

KERR, THOMAS	112	. RICHARD N.	153
KESLEY, HENRY	220	LANGFORD,	
KESTER, REBECCA	132	. ELIZABETH REED	270
KEYS, JOHN	87	LANGLEY, HANNAH	303
KHYZER, SARAH	5	LANNOU,	120
KIBLER, MARTIN	18	LAPSLEY, JAMES	189
KILLIAN, ANDREW	173-174	LATTA, WILLIAM	59
. DANIEL	173-174	LATTIMORE, ADAM	285
. DAVID	310	LAUGHRON,	105
. GEORGE	49,173	LAWRANCE, JOHN	7
. JOHN	173	LAWRENCE, JOSEPH	106
. JOSEPH	173	LAWSON,	186
. LYDIA	173	. WILLIAM	259
. MARGARET WATTS	173	LEATHERWOOD, AQUILLA	177
. MARY	173	. BETSY CARRIAH	177
. MARY CLINE	173	. EDWARD	177-178
. NANCY	173	. ELIZABETH	177
. OSLY BAKER	173	. ELIZABETH FERGUSON	177
. RACHEL WHITENER	310	. ELIZABETH WALKER	177
. WILLIAM W.	173	. JAMES	177
. YATES	173	. JOHN	177-178
KINCAID, KATIE	184	. NED	177
KINDER, ELIZABETH	311	. SAMUEL	177
KING,	35	. SARAH BURNS	177
. CHARLES	100	. SARAH HUNT	177
. NANCY WOODS	318	LEDFORD, PETER	179
. WILLIAM	318	. TOWRY	121
KIRKPATRICK, LYDIA	290	LEE, HARRY	289
KISTLER,		. HENRY	289
. MARY ASHENBRUNNER	5	LENEW,	120
KLEIN,	80	LENOIR, WILLIAM	156-157
. BARBARA	217	.	241,244
KNIGHT, JOHN	179	. WILLIAM BALLARD	15
. THOMAS	179	LEWIS, JOEL	286
KNOX, JOHN	130	. MARY MANSFIELD	191
. JOSEPH	46	. MICAJAH	87,91,244
. WILIAM	7	. RICHARD	187
. WILLIAM	21	. SOPHIA	48
KORNS, CONRAD	116	. THOMAS	87
KUYKENDALL, ANDREW	176	. WILLIAM	120,181
. JOHN	176	. WILLIAM T.	181,201
. JOSIAH	176	LICK, JOHN	204
. MARGARET HARDIN	176	LILLINGTON,	207
. MARK	176	LINCOLN, BENJAMIN	22,73
. MARY	175	.	91,166,173,201,204
. MATTHEW	175-176	.	207,267,286,299
. MOSES	176	LINDSAY, JESSE	260
. PEGGY	176	. JINSY POTEAT	260
. PETER	175	LINDSEY, JOHN	100
LACKEY, JOHN	121	LINN, JO WHITE	21,31,58
LAFAYETTE,	104	.	61,113,232,235,298
LAMB, MARTHA JUNE	211	.	321
LAMBERT,	231	LIONS, JOHN	201
LAMBERTH,	235	LITTLE, JAMES	265,267
LANE, JOEL	145	LITTLEJOHN, ABRAHAM	75

INDEX

. JOHN	146
. THOMAS	75
LOCK, JAMES	183
LOCKE,	160
. FRANCIS	29,45,73,186
.	199,267,284
. MATTHEW	3,67
LOCKMAN, ISAAC	138
LOLLEY, BETH	50
LONG, LETTICE SCOTT	272
. MATTHEW	60
LOPP,	35
LOVEING, GABRIEL	245
LOVINGS, GABRIEL	220
LOWE, SAMUEL	93
LOWMAN,	148
. MARGARET	148
. MILDRED	148
. RUBY	148
LUCAS,	128
LURY, NICHOLAS	171
LUSK, SAMUEL	189,321
LUSTER, CHAUNCEY	123
LUTES, GEORGE	85-86
. JACOB	86
LUTZ, GEORGE	85-86
LYONS, ELIJAH	3
LYTLE, ARCHIBALD	22,67,92
.	102
. THOMAS	32,68,265,267
MACKEY, JAMES	201,320
. REBECCA SCOTT	201
. SAMUEL	315,320-321
MACKIE, JAMES	109,286
MACLIN,	227
MALLOY, THOMAS	145
MALMEDY,	160,265
MARCH,	36
. HELEN	146
. HELEN C.	56
. TIMOTHY	146
MARION, FRANCIS	102,120
MARLER,	91,245
MARR,	289
MARSH,	53,279,321
. HELEN	159
MARSHALL, JAMES	203
. JESSE	203
. NANCY	203
MARTIN, ALEXANDER	89
. FRANCIS	204
. HENRY	204
. JOSIAH	28
. WILLIAM	93
MASON, HENRY	92
. MARY FEARS	110
MATLOCK, RICHARD	235
MATTOCKS, JOHN	130
MAY, ELIZABETH	110
MAYS, JOHN	276
MEBANE, ROBERT	48
MERCER, JOANN	80
MERRELL, SAMUEL	87
METCHIM, ELIZABETH	130
MICHAEL, CONRAD	112
MIERS, GEORGE	308
MIFFLIN,	293
MILLER,	81
. CALEB	310
. CATHERINE L.	205
. ELI WASHINGTON	205
. ELISHA PERKINS	205
. GEORGE OSMAN	205
. HORATIO NELSON	205
. JAMES	224
. JOHN WESLEY	205
. MARGARET B.	205
. MARY	310
. MARY PERKINS	205
. RACHEL WHITENER	310
. ROBERT J.	205
. ROBERT JOHNSTONE	205
. SARAH A.	205
. SIDNEY CALDWELL	205
. WILLIAM	220
. WILLIAM SIDNEY	205
MILLIKEN, HANNAH	37
MILLS, AMBROSE	55,65,102
MILTON,	1
. JOHN	1
MITCHELL, RACHEL	25
MOFFETT, GEORGE	191
. JAMES	66
. MARY	191-192
. SARAH McDOWELL	191
MOLL,	216
. PETER	218
MONTGOMERY, ALLEN	207
. ANNE	207
. DAVID	207-208
. DAVID THOMAS	208
. ELIZABETH	7
. HUMPHRY	113
. JANE	207
. JOHN	158-159
. MARGARET ALLEN	207-208
. MARTHA	207
. POLLY	207
. ROBERT	34,314
MOORE,	85,92,118,150,166

INDEX

- . 169,194,207,214,216
- . 237,255
- . ALICE 210,250
- . ANN 210
- . ANN CATHEY 209
- . BENJAMIN 220,302
- . CHARLES AUGUSTUS 210
- . FRANCIS 6,9-10,54,107
- . 173,224
- . JESSE 84
- . JOHN 95,125,278
- . MARGARET 210
- . MARGARET PATTON 209
- . MARGARET PENLAND 210
- . MARY 210,252
- . POLLY 252
- . RACHEL 252
- . ROBERT 54,210
- . SAMUEL 33,210
- . THOMAS 209,251
- . WILLIAM 158,168,196
- . 199,209-210,251,259
- . 318
- MORELAND,WILLIAM 116
- MORGAN, 45
- . DANIEL 14,63,70,145
- . 162,184,187,200,258
- . 269
- . JOHN 264
- . JOSEPH 216,218
- . SARAH 37,39
- MORISON,ELIZA. 215
- MORLER, 91
- MORRIS,JAMES 66,108,125
- . THOMAS 213
- . WILIAM 213
- . WILLIAM 212
- MORRISON,ANDREW 214
- . ELIZABETH 214
- . JAMES 214
- . JANE DAVIDSON 98
- . MARY 214
- . RACHEL 214
- . THOMAS 214
- . WILLIAM 98,189,214
- . 320-321
- MORROW,ELIZABETH 48
- . JAMES 272
- MOSELY,
- . CHRISTIAN
- . WAKEFIELD 302
- . GEORGE 302
- MOSER,BARBARA 152
- MOSS, 6
- . BOBBY G. 6,9-10,54,90
- . 101,103,107,127,151
- . 170,174,223,226,266
- . BOBBY GILMER 115,121
- . 164
- MOSSER,JOHN 152
- . MARY M. HUFFMAN 152
- MOSTELLER, 5
- MOUSER,ELIZABETH 311
- MOYER,JOSEPH 217
- MUHLENBURG,PETER 165
- MULL, 285
- . B. RONDALL 218
- . BARBARA 217
- . BARBARA CARPENTER 217
- . BARBARA KLEIN 217
- . CATHERINE 309-311
- . CATHERINE WEIDNER 217
- . CATHERINE WHITENER 217
- . CHRISTOPHER 216
- . CONRAD 216-217
- . ELIZABETH 147
- . GEMIMA BRITTAIN 217
- . HENRY 217
- . JACOB 217
- . JOHN 148,217,312
- . MABLE 218
- . MARY 148
- . MARY VANHORN 217
- . PETER 27,143,216-218
- . STOFFEL 216
- . SUSANNA 217
- . SUSANNAH 217
- MUMFORD, 213
- MURPHEY, 284
- . WILLIAM 91
- MURPHY,JAMES 219,221,320
- . JANE FLEMING 219
- . JOHN 219
- . MARGARET McDOWELL 219
- MURRAH, 224
- MURRAY, 110,175
- . ABRAHAM 225
- . ALE 225
- . BENJAMIN 222
- . CHARITY 222
- . DAVID 222
- . DORITY 222
- . DOROTHY 222
- . ELIZABETH 222
- . EMANUEL 225
- . EZEKIAL 222
- . JANE 222,225
- . JEREMIAH 225
- . JOHN 110,225
- . JOHN B. 222

INDEX

. JOSEPH	222,225	
. JOSHUA	224-225	
. LUCY	225	
. LUCY SUDDRETH	225	
. MARGARET	225	
. NANCY	222,225	
. PEGGY	222	
. ROBERT	225	
. ROSANNAH	222	
. SALLY	225	
. THOMAS	222	
. WILLIAM	186,199,225	
MURREY,JANE	37	
MUSCANOOK,GEORGE	227	
MUSGRAVE,	158	
MYDDLETON,	150,173	
. C.S.	54	
. CHARLES	224	
. CHARLES S.	6,10	
. CHARLES STARKE	9,107	
.	222	
MYERS,HENRY	311	
. MARY WHITENER	311	
McADAMS,JOHN	22	
McALLISTER,	86,128,310	
. ANNE W.	28,228,285,309	
McBRIDE,WILLIAM	189	
McCAFFERTY,WILLIAM	98	
McCALL,ALEXANDER	184	
. ELIZABETH	184	
. ELIZABETH AIKEN	184	
. HELEN	184	
. HENRY	184	
. HOWARD	185	
. HOWARD H.	40,296	
. JAMES	184	
. JAMES L.	184	
. JANE RECTOR	184	
. JESSIE	184	
. JOHN	184	
. KATIE KINCAID	184	
. LYDIA GILLESPIE	184	
. MARGARET	184	
. MARY CRYDER	184	
. MICHAEL	184	
. MILDRED HOLLARD	184	
. NANCY	184	
. PHOEBE SMITH	184	
. ROBERT	184	
. SAMUEL	184	
. SARAH SHELL	184	
. WILLIAM	184	
McCARSON,DAVID	50	
McCLAIN,JOHN	95	
McCLELLAN,JOHN	178	

McCORD,	150	
McCRARY,MARY JANE	50	
McCULLEN,WILLIAM	6	
McCULLOUGH,JOHN	233-234	
. WILLIAM	114	
McCUSICK,ROBERT	296	
McDANIEL,JAMES	95	
McDANIELS,	187	
. ANN RODGERS	187	
. JAMES	186-187	
. SAMUEL	84	
McDONALD,JAMES	187	
. JOHN	197	
. STEPHEN	187	
McDOUGAL,CATHERINE	318	
McDOWEL,CHARLES	41	
McDOWELL,	45,68,70,81,98	
.	110,132,136,187,196	
.	198,214,219,231,233	
.	248,252,284,290	
. ANNA	190	
. ANNA EDMISTEN	190	
. ANNIE	191	
. ANNIE McDOWELL	191	
. CHARLES	1,14,18,22	
.	29-30,33,39,43,47,54	
.	64,67,72,79-80,85,96	
.	97,132,134,138,145	
.	150,158-160,162,166	
.	168,186,188,190-191	
.	193-194,196-197,199	
.	209,212,216,220,224	
.	228-229,233-234,250	
.	255,258,260,263,265	
.	267,271,274-276,278	
.	282-283,295,297-298	
.	299,311,313,320	
. ELIZABETH	188	
. HANNAH KELLER	188	
. HUGH	145,188,219	
. JAMES	233	
. JAMES MOFFETT	191	
. JOHN	167,188-191,209	
.	220,224,233,235,259	
.	260,314,320	
. JOHN HUGH	192	
. JOSEPH	1,14,33,39	
.	44-45,47,55,63-67,77	
.	95,108,110,125,132	
.	134,145,162,175,186	
.	188-194,196,200,212	
.	219,224,229,239,246	
.	250,258,260,278,302	
.	313,320	
. MARGARET	188,219	

INDEX

- . MARGARET ERWIN 191
- . MARGARET ONEILL 188
- . MARY MANSFIELD
- .   LEWIS 191
- . MARY MOFFETT 191-192
- . RACHEL 190,192
- . SARAH 191
- McELRATH, CHARLES 189
- . ELIZABETH McDOWELL 188
- . JOHN 188
- . MARGARET McDOWELL 188
- . ROBERT 188
- McENTIRE, THOMAS 234
- McFADDIN, THOMAS 120
- McFALLS, ARTHUR 32,97,195
- . 211
- . DAVID McPETERS 192
- . JOHN 55,65
- McFARLAND, JAMES 25,55
- . 132,134,260
- McGIMPSEY, JOHN 84
- . JOSEPH 220
- McGOMERY, R. 91
- McINTOSH, SUSAN CLARKE 76
- McINTYRE, JAMES 181
- . THOMAS 113
- McKEE, JAMES 202
- . THOMAS 248
- McKENNEY, JAMES 119
- McKENZIE, JOHN 102,164
- . 263
- . WILLIAM 164
- McKEY, 220
- McKINNEY, JAMES 119
- . JOHN 127
- . JOSEPH 220
- . PATRICK 220
- McKINZIE, JOSEPH 63
- McKISSOCK, DANIEL 186
- . 194-195,199
- . DAVID 195
- . ELIZABETH 195
- . JAMES 195
- . JANE 195
- . JANE WILSON 194
- . JOHN 194
- . JOSEPH 194
- . MARGARET 194
- . MARY 195
- . WILSON 195
- McLEAN, EPHRAIM 96
- McLIN, 31,237
- McMULLENS, JOHN 248
- McNABB, JAMES 245,247
- McPETERS, 158,235
- . CHARLES 158-159,196
- . 210
- . DAVID 211
- . JOHN 211,235
- . JONATHAN 196-198
- . JOSEPH 196,199-200,211
- . MARY J. 158
- . NANCY CROSS 200
- McPHEETERS, MARY J. 158
- McWHORTER, JANE 44
- NAIL, JOHN 230
- NEALL, JOHN 230
- NEEL, THOMAS 114
- NEIL, CYNTHIA 230
- . JOSEPH 3
- NEILL, ALEXANDER 234
- . ANDREW 97,192,229
- . 231-235
- . ARCH 208
- . ARCHIBALD 234
- . CATHERINE 234
- . CYNTHIA FORGY 229
- . ELIZABETH 229,234
- . GALBRAITH 231,234
- . GILBREATH 229,234
- . GILLY 234
- . HANNAH 234
- . HIRAM 229
- . JAMES 70,229,231
- . 233-234
- . JANE 234
- . JOHN 229,231-232
- . 234-235
- . MARIAH 229
- . MARY 233-235
- . MARY CLINTON 234
- . ROBERT 231,234
- . SAMUEL 231,234
- . SARAH 234
- . SARAH A. ARTHURS 234
- . SARAH ALLEN 234
- . WILLIAM 96,229,231
- . 233-235,246
- NELSON, 95
- . JOHN 67,120
- . WILLIAM 168
- NESBIT, THOMAS 308
- NESBITT, 162
- NICHOLS, 3
- . EVALINE 250
- . JAMES 73
- NICHOLSON, SARAH 219
- NOBLES, WILLIAM 22
- NORTHCUT, SOLOMAN 236
- NORTHERN, SOLOMAN 236

INDEX

NORWOOD,	297
OGLE, JOHN	259
OLIPHANT, ANNE	294
. JOHN	233
OLWAND, JOHN	68
ONEAL,	220
. BETSY BURCHFIELD	68
. PATRICK	32,211
. PETER	303
ONEILL, MARGARET	188
. WALTER	286
OSBORNE,	59
. BENJAMIN	267
. BENNETT	267
. JAMES	207
OVERHILL,	237
OWEN, JESSE	128
OWENS, EDMOND	290
. ELIZABETH SUMTER	290
. GEORGE	30
OXFORD, JOHN	57
OZGATHORPE, RICHARD	260
.	261
PACE, JEREMIAH	48
. KEZIAH BRITTAIN	48
PAINTER, JACOB	237,239
. JOHN	237,239-240
. JOSEPH	237
PAISLEY, JOHN	303
PARKER, JOHN	291
. PHOEBE	118
PARKS,	242,271
. ALFRED	242
. BENJAMIN	242,244,280
. CARLTON	242
. CATHERINE	242
. CATHERINE REED	242
. CURTIS	242
. ELIZABETH	242,244,252
. FLORA WAKEFIELD	302
. GABRIEL	244
. GEORGE	241-242,244
. HANNAH	242
. HENRY	241
. JAMES	242
. JOHN	242
. JOHN S.	244
. LINESFIELD	280
. MARTIN	244
. MARY	244,271
. MEREDITH	242
. MILLIE	242
. MILLIE DAVIDSON	242
. NANCY	242
. PLEASANT	242
. POLLY	242,244
. RANSOME	244
. REBECCA	242
. ROBERT	302
. SAMUEL	241-242,244-245
. SARAH	242
. WILLIAM	244
PATEETE,	260
PATHER,	293
PATTEN,	246
PATTERSON, LEONARD	148
. MARY	63
PATTON, CHARITY	209
. ELIJAH	96
. GEORGE	30
. JOHN	270
. MARGARET	209
. ROBERT	1,64,66,108,125
.	196,199,219,278
. SAMUEL	181
. THOMAS	235,246
. WILLIAM	1,9-10,181
PEARSON,	
. ELIZABETH HICE	140
. HENRY	75
PENLAND,	154
. ABRAHAM	250
. ALEXANDER	248,255
. ALICE MOORE	210,250
. ANN ALEXANDER	248
. ANNA DONNAL	255
. ANNA DORRAL	250
. ANNIS DONNAL	255
. BLANCHE	249,254,256
. CHARLES DAVIDSON	250
. CHRIS	248
. ELEANOR	252
. ELIZABETH	250
. ELIZABETH BRANK	43,252
. ELIZABETH JONES	250
. ELIZABETH PARKS	244
.	252
. EVALINE NICHOLS	250
. GEORGE	27,248,252-253
.	255
. GEORGE NEWTON	250
. HARRY	252
. HENRY	252
. JAMES	255
. JANE	248,252
. JEAN	252
. JOHN	192,210,250,252
.	255
. JOHN HARVEY	250
. LEAH	252

INDEX

. MARGARET 210
. MARY MOORE 210,252
. MARY SMITH 250
. NANCY JONES 250
. NANCY STEPHENS 250
. PETER 252,255
. POLLY MOORE 252
. PRICILLA 252
. RACHEL 248
. RACHEL HENRY 252
. RACHEL MOORE 252
. ROBERT 43,210,248,250
. 252-254,256
. RUTH 252
. WILLIAM 248,250,252
. 255-256
PENLEY,WILLIAM 259
PENLY,JOHN 251
. WILLIAM 315
PENN, 289
PENNLY,JOHN 251
PENYAN,JOHN 253
PEPPER, 315
. CATHERINE 257
. ROBERT 257
PERKINS, 145
. ELISHA 57
. JOHN 57-58,205-206
. MARY 205
. PETER 289
PETER,JOHANNIS 218
PETERSON,POLLY 79
PHELPS,JOHN 18
PHIFER, 269
. EDWARD 113,117,157,159
. 191,211,315
. EDWARD W. 106,192,202
. 249,256
. JOHN 141
. MARTIN 141
PHILBECK, 76
. MILES 119,215,245,254
. MILES S. 142
PIERCE, 106,228,236
PIERCY,BLAKE 258-259
. ELIZABETH 259
. EPHRAIM 258
. MARY 258
. SEBON 258
. STEPHEN 27
. WILBOURN 258
. WILLIAM 258
. WILLIS 258
PIERSON, 156
PINLAND, 253

PITTMAN, 4
. BETSY D. 144,146,151
. 178,182,184,189,292
. BETSY DODD 19-20,129
. 245
. BETSY S. 140
PITTS,PHILIP 217
. SUSANNA MULL 217
POKE,JOHN 9-10
POLK,DANIEL 12
. JOHN 9-10
. THOMAS 207
POLLARD,CYNTHIA 60
PORTERFIELD, 303
. CHARLES 165
POTEAT,EDWARD 189
. 260-261
. ELIZABETH 260
. JAMES 260
. JINSY 260
. MARTHA 260
. NANCY 260
. PHOEBE BRITTAIN 48
. SAMUEL D. 260
. SARAH 260
. WILLIAM 260
POTEET, 260
POTTER, 148
POWE,ELIZABETH 307
POWELL, 103,130
. AMBROSE 38,264
. ANNE B. ALBRIGHT 262
. BENJAMIN 262
. CATHERINE 262
. ELIAS 38,84,262,264
. ELIZABETH 37,39,262
. ELIZABETH HERMAN 262
. GEORGE 262
. JAMES 262
. JOHN 262,290
. LUCINDA ROWE 262
. MARY 262
. MARY SMITH 262
. NANCY HARRIS 262
. PHILIP 262
. ROBERT 264
PRICE, 55
PRICHARD,ALFRED 280
. ELIZABETH 280
. JAMES 111-112,280-281
. JAMES C. 280
. LUCINDA 280
. MARY 280
. PHEBA 280
. SARAH 280

INDEX

. SUSAN	280
. THOMAS	280
PRITCHARD, JAMES	280
PROVINCE, JOHN	145
PRUETT, A.B.	139
PRUITT,	227
. A.B.	195, 228, 285
PUETT, HANNAH PARKS	242
. JOSEPH	205
. SARAH A. MILLER	205
. WILLIAM	242
PYATT, JOSEPH	289
PYATTE, MARTHA	317
QUAM, LAVINA SUMTER	290
QUEEN, ELIOTT	263
. ELIZABETH	263
. JAMES	263
. JOHN	263
. MARGARET	263
. NANCY	263
. THOMAS	263
RABURN, JOHN	212
RADER, SALLY	79
RAINBOULT, ADAM	61
RAMSAY,	239
. AMBROSE	318
RAMSEY,	290
. AMBROSE	92
. SIMON	290
RAMSOUR,	21, 31, 39, 41, 45
.	64, 83, 136, 162, 175, 186
.	197, 199, 217, 219, 229
.	231, 233, 237, 242, 246
.	278, 313
. MARGARET	79
RANDALL, JUDITH	290
RANDOLPH,	273
RANKIN, HUGH F.	232
RECTOR, JANE	184
REED, CATHERINE	242
. ELIZABETH	270
. JANE CAVEN	265
. RICHARD	68, 265, 267
. ROBERT	192, 265, 267-268
.	270
REID,	269
. RICHARD	265, 289
REPATOE, DAVID	130
. ELIZABETH HARSHAW	130
REVIS, THOMAS	100
REYNOLDS, GEORGE S.	97, 99
RHODES, ELIZABETH	311
RICHARDSON,	39, 120
. AMOS	164, 269
. FANNIE FARMER	269

. JAMES	67, 199, 220
. RICHARD	169
RICHEY, WILLIAM	235
RICKEY, WILLIAM	235
RIDDLE, ELERNER COOK	87
RIDER, F.	37
ROBERTS, BRACTON	304
. MARY	41
. MARY BURCHFIELD	68
ROBERTSON,	106
. SAMUEL	138
ROBINSON, JAMES	237
. JOHN	239, 304
. POLLY	310
ROCHEL, JOHN	52
RODDY, JAMES	264
RODGERS, ANN	187
. ROBERT	178
ROGERS,	162
. JESSIE	27
. JOSEPH	162
ROPER,	
. CATHERINE HUFFMAN	152
. ELIJAH	152
ROSE, BENJAMIN	141
ROSS, JAMES	319
. THOMAS	114
ROTHSTEIN,	259
. E.	296
ROUSE, J.K.	183, 206
ROWE, LUCINDA	262
RUDOLPH, ANDREW	7, 280
. JOHN	280
RUGELEY,	92, 128, 171, 303
RUSSELL, ARMINTA	48
. JOHN	33, 313
. LETTICE	272
. WILLIAM	89
RUST, PETER	25
RUTHERFORD,	45, 67, 143
.	154, 168, 183, 186, 207
.	219, 237, 244, 284, 303
. ANN MOORE	210
. GRIFFITH	3, 22, 25, 29-30
.	44, 72-73, 85, 92, 134
.	141, 166, 169, 188, 190
.	194, 196, 199, 209, 214
.	216, 234, 255, 267, 299
.	314
. HENRY	145
. JOHN	113
SALINGS, JOHN	239
SALISBURY,	45
SAMUELS,	168
SANCHEZ, SAAVEDRA	165

342

INDEX

SAULMAN, JOHN	252
. LEAH PENLAND	252
SAUNDERS,	162
SAVAGE, BENJAMIN	128
SCOTT,	60
. ANNA MARIE DOBSON	271
. ELIZABETH	272
. GEMMIA	272
. J.W.	141
. JANE	272
. JOHN	271
. JOSEPH	201, 271
. LETTICE	272
. LETTICE RUSSELL	272
. MARTIN	272
. MARY	272
. MARY PARKS	271
. NANCY	271-272
. REBECCA	201
. RICHARD	150, 272
. ROBERT	259
. SAMUEL B.	272
. THOMAS	256, 271-273
SEAGLE,	138
SEALEY,	74, 308
. SARAH	73
SEALS, ABBIE	149
SEAWELL, BENJAMIN	171
SEELY, GEORGE	73
. SARAH	73
SEIGEL, SAMUEL	5
SEITZ, DAVID	310
. SARAH WHITENER	310
SELLARS, JOHN	84
SETZER, JOHN	310
. MARY WHITENER	310
SEVIER,	134, 168
. JOHN	65, 67, 83, 154, 276
.	278
SHARP, HORATIO	313
. JOHN	156
. MATTHEW	116
. WILLIAM	116
SHARPE,	39, 162
. HORATIO	274, 282
. JEREMIAH	274, 282
. JOHN	274
. MATILDA	191
. MATTHEW	274, 282
. RACE	282
. ROBERT	104
SHAW,	289
SHELBY,	162
. ISAAC	35, 83
SHELL,	85
. ANNA SARAH	311
. CASPER	217
. HENRY	86
. JOHN	184, 218
. KATHERINE	317
. MARGARET McCALL	184
. MARY CATHERINE	311
. SARAH	184
SHEPHERD, ABRAHAM	7
SHEPPARD, JAMES	41, 245
SHERRILL, ELIZABETH	276
. ELIZABETH HUNT	278
. ELIZABETH THOMPSON	276
. FRANCES DOBSON	276
. GEORGE	276, 278
. GEORGE D.	279
. JOHN	276
. JOSEPH	276
. MARGARET	310
. NANCY	279
. PENINA	279
. SAMUEL	279, 314
. URIAH	276, 279
. UTE	276
. WILLIAM L.	174
SHOKY,	269
SHOOK, ANDREW	32, 86
. JACOB	32
SHUFFLER, PHILLIP	27
SHUFORD, CATHERINE	79
. CATROUT	85
. DANIEL	5
. JACOB	138
SIDWELL,	59
SIGMAN, JOHN	85
SIGMON, CATHERINE	284
. ELIZABETH	284
. EM.	285
. GEORGE	284-285
. HENRY	284
. JOHN	284
. PEGGY	284
. POLLY	284
. SALLY	284
SIMANTON, WILLIAM	235
SIMMONS, RICHARD	299
SIMPSON, JOHN	248
. SAMUEL	186, 199
SISLER, BARBARA	195
. BYRON	195
SISTLER, BARABRA	36
. BARBARA	34, 78, 159, 315
. BRYON	34, 36
. BYRON	78, 159, 167, 315
SLAVEN, WILLIAM	31

INDEX

SLOAN, WILLIAM	227
SMALLWOOD,	18,92
SMALLY, ABNER	308
SMIRE, JOHN	227
SMITH, ADAM	16
. B.	85
. CHARLES	305
. DANIEL 14,55,91,98,132	
	212,217-218,267
. DAVY	245
. DORA W. 26,115,168,170	
.	226
. EDWARD	217
. HANNAH FEARS	110
. JARED	100
. JOHN	74
. JOSHUA	302
. KITTY BURCHFIELD	68
. LEAH	111
. MARGARET LOWMAN	148
. MARY	98,250,262
. NATHAN	220
. PEGGY WAKEFIELD	302
. PHOEBE	184
. RACHEL	48
. ROBERT	299
. SAMUEL	308
. THOMAS	289
. WILLIAM	146
SMYORS, JOHN	227
SNODDY, WILLIAM	196
SORRELS, JOHN	286
SOTHARD,	290
SPAINHOUR, PETER	77
SPAINHOWER,	284
SPARKS, SOLOMON	241
SPEAGLE,	
. BARBARA ASHENBRUNNER	5
. CATHERINE	
. ASHENBRUNNER	5
. MILDRED LOWMAN	148
. NICHOLAS	173
SPEARS, JOHN	218
SPRINGFIELD, EZEKIAL	112
STACEY,	
. CATHERINE WHITENER	310
. ZACHARIAH	310
STANSBERRY, WILLIAM	220
STARK, JAMES	100
STARKE, CHARLES	173
STARNES,	140
. JOSEPH	235
STARR, EASTER CLINE	79
STARRINGER, CATHERINE	141
STEELE, ANDREW	54,287
. JANE	287
. MARGARET	287
. MARTHA	287
. MARY	287
. RACHEL	287
. SAMUEL	61,79,287
. WILLIAM	67
STEPHENS, NANCY	250
STEPP, ANBER	39
. THOMAS	39
STEPPE,	84
STEVENS, EDWARD	128
STEVILIE, J.H.	91
STILL,	269
STILLWELL, SARAH	310
STOCKINGER, CHRISTIANA	85
STRANGE, ABRAHAM	84
STRICKLAND, EUNICE	295
STRINGFIELD, DELILAH	48
. EZEKIAL	246-247
. JAMES	48-50,247
STROTHER, JOHN	259
STROUD, JESSE	128
STROUPE, ETHEL	178
STUART, JACOB	48
. NANCY BRITTAIN	48
STUMP,	118
. CHRISTOPHER	145
SUDDERTH, ABRAHAM	11
. JOHN	304
SUDDRETH, JOHN	205
. LUCY	225
. MARGARET	225
. MARGARET B. MILLER	205
. WILLIAM	225
SULLIVAN,	86,293,310
. DANIEL	289
. KATHY G.	28,228,285
. KATHY GUNTER	309
SUMMER,	267
SUMMERS, LEWIS PRESTON	20
SUMNER, JETHRO	171,204
.	286
SUMPTER,	39
. JOHN	308
. WILLIAM	116
SUMTER,	198
. AMELIA	290
. ANN ALEXANDER	290
. CHARLOTTE TEMPLE	290
. ELIZABETH	290
. FIELDING	290
. JAMES	290
. JANE	290
. JOHN	290

INDEX

. JUDITH	290	THURMAN,		102
. JUDITH RANDALL	290	TILLEY,		
. LAVINA	290	. CATHERINE POWELL		262
. LIVINGSTON	290	. STEPHEN		262
. LYDIA KIRKPATRICK	290	TILMAN, MARY		295
. SALLY	290	TINNIN, HUGH		92
. SARAH A. MILLER	205	TIPPONG, CONRAD		86,227
. THOMAS	6,9,102,150,162	TIPPS, CONRAD		32,86
.	173,263,290	. JACOB		32,86
. WILLIAM	12,290	TIPS, CONRAD		227
SWANSON, WILLIAM	291-292	TIPTON,		65
SWINK, D.D.	53,106	. JONATHAN		67,278
. DAN	78,298	TOPKINS, ROBERT M.		197
. DAN D.	34,124,137,178	TORRENCE,		14
.	195,235,243,245,256	TRABUE,		231
.	259,296,315	. JAMES D.		232,235
. DANIEL D.	50,111,113	TRABUR, JAMES D.		230
.	121,129,135,182,202	TRIMBLE, WILLIAM		67
. DAVID D.	28	TROSPER, ELIJAH		297-298
. LOTTIE HUFFMAN	153	. JAMES		297
TARLETON,	64,100,186,199	. JOHN		297
.	278	. LEONARD		297
TARTER, JOHN	12	. NICHOLAS		297-298
TATE, ANNE OLIPHANT	294	. PETER		297
. DAVID	220	. ROBERT		297
. JOHN	293-294	. SALLEY		297
TAYLOR,	222	. WILLIAM		297
. ELIZABETH WHITE	307	TURNBULL, JOHN		237
. JOHN	138,318	TURNER,		76
. LEE	284	. AGNES		299
. LEROY	32,186,199,284	. GRACE	119,142,215,245	
. PARMENAS	307	.		254
. THOMAS	318	. ROBERT		299
TEMPLE, CHARLOTTE	290	TUTT, BANJAMIN		210
TEMPLETON,	33	. MARGARET MOORE		210
THACKSTON, JAMES	92,109	TUTTLE, ANDREW HALL		184
.	201,286	. ELIZABETH McCALL		184
THOMAS, ELIZABETH	50	UMPHREY, DAVID		41
. I.W.	75-76,78,264	URSURY, WILLIAM		12
THOMPSON,	296	VANCE, CECIA		48
. ALEXANDER	295	. DAVID		43,98,231
. ELIZABETH	276	. PRICILLA BRANK		43
. ELIZABETH M. HODGE	295	VANDAVER, JANE FEARS		111
. ESTHER	295	VANHORN, MARY		217
. EUNICE STRICKLAND	295	VEGHTE, MARGARET		30
. ISAAC	32	VOCHKO, ETHEL STROUPE		178
. JAMES	295	VOLKEL, LOWELL	26,115,163	
. JOHN	295	.		170,226
. MARY TILMAN	295	WADE, THOMAS		143
. ROBERT	57,295	WADKINS, THOMAS		244
. RUTH	295	WAGGENER, THOMAS		118
. SARAH	295	WAGGERLY, JOHN		220
. THOMAS	126	WAGONER, CONRAD		218
. WILLIAM	295	WAKEFIELD, CHARLES		11-12
THOMSON, BARBARA	33-34	.	16,76,239,302,308	

345

INDEX

. CHRISTIAN 302
. FLORA 302
. HAMILTON 302
. HENRY 160,255-256
. HENRY NELSON 302
. JANE 302
. JEMIMA GRIFFIN 302
. JOSEPH 302
. LUCY JOHNSON 302
. LUCY M. 302
. MARTHA 302
. MARY GEORGE 302
. NANCY 302
. NANCY JOHNSON 302
. PEGGY 302
. PRICILLA PENLAND 252
. THOMAS 11-12,16
. 301-302,308
WALKER, 169,260
. ELIJAH 261
. ELIZABETH 177
. ELIZABETH HUFFMAN 152
. GEORGE 25,32,148,169
. 212
. JAMES REUBEN 32,177
. JESSE 52
. POLLY CRESSON 89
. THOMAS 152
. WEST 261
. WILLIAM 89
WALLIS,MARGARET BAKER 7
WALTON, 49,103
. JESSE 67
. JOSEPH MOORE 219,221
. TLMAN 251
WARD, 7
. CHARLES 239
WASHINGTON, 293
. GEORGE 52,104,123,205
. 231
. WILLIAM 63-64,70,269
. 289
WATKINS,JOHN 189
WATSON,DAVID 267
. JOHN 25
WATTS,MARGARET 173
WAUGH, 168
WAYNE, 293
. ANTHONY 263
WEAVER,BARBARA 130
WEBSTER, 64,186,199,278
. JOHN 234
WEIDNER,CATHERINE 217
WELCH,NICHOLAS 5
WELLMAN,FRANCES 153

WELLS,ZACHARIAH 15
WESLEY,JOHN 184
WEST,ALEXANDER 303-304
. BETHIAH 303
. ELIZABETH 303
. HANNAH LANGLEY 303
. ISAAC 304
. LEONARD 225
. MARGARET 303
. MARY 303
. MARY SCOTT 272
. RICHARD 79,86
. THOMAS 303-304
WESTMORELAND,
. POLLY MONTGOMERY 207
WETHERS,JESSE 67
WHEELER,JOHN H. 31,50
. 149,218,256
. THOMAS 138
WHISNANT, 227
WHITAKER, 212
WHITARN,
. NANCY BURCHFIELD 68
WHITE, 190
. ANN 307
. ANTHONY 307
. BENJAMIN 75
. CARY 307
. CATHERINE 307
. ELIZABETH 307
. ELIZABETH POWE 307
. EMMETT R. 43,195,228
. GIFFORD 305,308
. JAMES 299,305
. JAMES TAYLOR 75,305
. 307-308
. JO 21,31,58,61,298,321
. JOHN 305
. JOSEPH 9-10,41,44,122
. 158,166,220,258
. KATHERINE D. 321
. KATHERINE K

346

www.ingramcontent.com/pod-product-compliance
Lightning Source LLC
Chambersburg PA
CBHW020638300426
44112CB00007B/162